ATLAS OF GLOBAL DEVELOPMENT
third edition

Collins

THE WORLD BANK
Washington, D.C.

Design © HarperCollins Publishers

Published for the World Bank by Collins Geo.
An imprint of HarperCollins Publishers
Westerhill Road
Bishopbriggs
Glasgow G64 2QT

www.collinsbartholomew.com

First Published 2007
Second edition 2009
Third edition 2011

The findings, interpretations, and conclusions expressed herein are those of the author(s)
and do not necessarily reflect the views of the Executive Directors of the International Bank
for Reconstruction and Development / The World Bank or the governments they represent.
The World Bank does not guarantee the accuracy of the data included in this work.
The boundaries, colors, denominations, and other information shown on any map in this
work do not imply any judgement on the part of The World Bank concerning the legal status
of any territory or the endorsement or acceptance of such boundaries.

ISBN: 978-0-8213-8583-8
E-ISBN: 978-0-8213-8664-4
DOI: 10.1596/978-0-8213-8583-8

Printed in China by South China Printing Co Ltd.

Contents

4   **Acknowledgments**

5   **Foreword**

6   **Guide to the online atlas**

8   **Classification of economies**

10   **The Millennium Development Goals**

14   **Rich and poor**
Measuring income | Growth and opportunity | How poor is poor?

28   **People**
Population growth and transition

34   **Education**
Children at work | Education opens doors
Gender and development—the role of infrastructure

48   **Health**
Children under 5—struggling to survive
Improving the health of mothers
Communicable diseases

62   **Economy**
Structure of the world's economy | Governance
Infrastructure for development | Investment for growth
The integrating world | People on the move
Aid for development | External debt

100   **Environment**
The urban environment
Feeding a growing world | A thirsty planet gets thirstier
Protecting the environment | Energy security and climate change | Where is the wealth of nations?

128   **Statistics**
Key indicators of development
Ranking of economies by GNI per capita
Definitions, sources, notes, and abbreviations

143   **Index**

Acknowledgments

The text and data for the third edition of the *Atlas of Global Development* were prepared by the Development Economics Data Group of the World Bank under the management of Shaida Badiee. The team consisted of Mehdi Akhlaghi, Uranbileg Batjargal, Lopamudra Chakraborti, David Cieslikowski, Mayhar Eshragh-Tabary, Richard Fix, Masako Hiraga, Buyant Khaltarkhuu, Soong Sup Lee, Ibrahim Levent, Sulekha Patek, Beatriz Prieto-Oramas, William Prince, Evis Rucaj, and Giovanni Ruta. Eric Swanson was the general editor. Jeff Lecksell made valuable contributions. Aziz Gökdemir, Stephen McGroarty, Santiago Pombo, Stuart Tucker, and Shana Wagger from the World Bank's Office of the Publisher managed the development and dissemination of the book and its online companion.

The Publishing, Design, Editorial, Creative Services, and Database teams at Collins Geo, HarperCollins Publishers, provided overall design direction, editorial control, mapping, and typesetting.

Foreword

Human and economic development are closely linked to geography. Throughout history natural resources, landscapes, climate, and natural routes have shaped the development of political and economic institutions, nation-states, and markets. People, in turn, have reshaped their economic and social geography, through communication and transport infrastructure, trade and migration, innovation, and conflicts and cooperation. And their activities increasingly influence the global climate, through deforestation, urbanization, water use, and the release of greenhouse gases.

Location is an important predictor of a person's welfare, with one's prospects in life being decided in good measure by one's place of birth. But the diversity of outcomes across countries is great and cannot be explained by one or even a few factors. Landlocked states, for example, have a harder time participating in the global markets, and their development is often retarded, but Botswana has consistently grown faster than the rest of Sub-Saharan Africa. Small, island economies and those in tropical regions face other obstacles to development, but Mauritius has overcome those challenges and prospered. Although people's welfare and prospects depend on the location and size of their economies, economic success also depends on the dynamism and openness of their political and economic institutions, the degree of social and political cohesion, and the effectiveness of their education and health services.

The mission of the World Bank Group is to assist countries to overcome poverty and establish a sustainable path for their development. Providing reliable information about the state of the world and its people is an important part of that mission. Recognizing the formidable challenges and great successes that have been achieved should strengthen our resolve to work together to fight poverty and increase human welfare. To that end the World Bank has published an atlas for over 40 years. This edition of the *Atlas of Global Development* draws on a global database compiled from the work of the World Bank, other international agencies, and national statistical offices of member countries. Now, as part of the World Bank's Open Data Initiative, this database is available to every reader of the Atlas for free and without restriction. I encourage you to go to our data website at data.worldbank.org to explore the wealth of information available. There is also an electronic companion to the Atlas, available at data.worldbank.org/atlas-global, which provides additional tools for mapping and charting the data and comparing country outcomes. By sharing our data, tools, and research findings, we hope to enlist many more people and their ideas from around the globe in creating a better world for all.

Justin Yifu Lin
Chief Economist and Senior Vice President
Development Economics
The World Bank

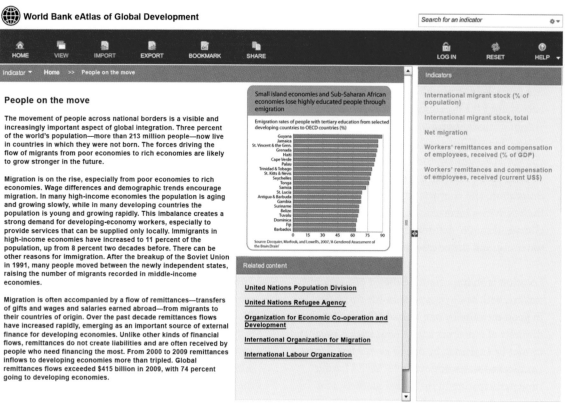

Figure 1

USER'S GUIDE TO THE WORLD BANK eATLAS OF GLOBAL DEVELOPMENT

Easy navigation from the home page (accessible via data.worldbank.org/atlas-global)

- Use the **right-hand panel** to select a main topic and see related indicators for mapping. (When you make a selection, a description appears, and the panel refreshes with the indicators [figure 1])

- Use the **search box** (top right) to search for any word in an indicator title or description (e.g., "malnutrition").

- Use **indicator** (top left, gray toolbar) to drill quickly from topic to indicator.

- However you start, selecting a specific indicator launches a world map that shows the latest available data per country, with many other visualizations and options.

Mapping basics (figure 2)

Once you have selected your indicator, the mapping application launches.

- The **world map** shows your indicator with the latest available data for each country. Mouse over the map to see country names, details, and indicator data.

- The **indicator name** (above the map, gray toolbar) is linked to the definition and source information.

- The **ranking table** (bottom right-hand panel), which shows indicator data, toggles from table to chart.

- A **time series chart** (across the bottom) is created; clicking on any country adds data to the chart.

- **View** (top left, red toolbar) lets you launch a second map alongside the first, providing a *Comparative View*.

Changing and viewing countries (figure 2)

- View and zoom to countries:
  - Click any country on the map or in the **ranking table** to zoom, or
  - Use **countries** (above the map, gray toolbar) to select a country, or
  - Use **locations** (above the map, gray toolbar) to select a country.

- Restore the full view by clicking the map area or by using the inset map at the top.

- Each time you zoom to a country, it is
  - Added to the **time series chart** (bottom).
  - Given more context (top right-hand panel)
  - Highlighted in the **ranking table** (bottom right-hand panel)

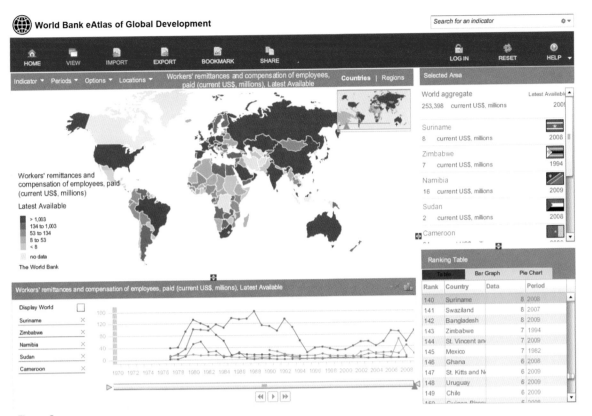

Figure 2

Changing years, colors, intervals, and more (figure 2)

- Use **periods** (above the map, gray toolbar) to select different years and "latest available" data.
- Use **options** (above the map, gray toolbar) to change colors, intervals, and analysis methods.
- Use **locations** (above the map, gray toolbar) to select a country.

Comparing maps and data

- Use **view** (top left, red toolbar) to select *Comparative View* and see two maps.
- Use **indicators, periods, options,** and **locations** (above each map, gray toolbar) to select what you want to compare, including any combination of indicators and years.
- Select the tabs below each map to see the **ranking table**, the **time series chart**, and more.
- Use **view** (top left, red toolbar) to select *Standard View* and return to one map with all the features.

Using the time series chart (figure 2)

- When you select a country (up to five), related time series data appear on the **chart** (bottom); country name and data are shown when you mouse over.

- Use the **play** button below the chart to dynamically map the time series for your indicator. As the map changes for each year, the **ranking table** and other information refresh.

Exporting, importing, bookmarking, and more with login (figure 2)

- Create a login (top right, red toolbar) to use the following features:
  - Use **export** (top left, red toolbar) to export your selections as various image or data files.
  - Use **import** (top left, red toolbar) to bring your own data into the eAtlas for mapping and graphing.
  - Use **bookmark** and **share** (top left, red toolbar) to retrieve and share your maps and graphs.

Classification of economies

Low- and middle-income economies

- East Asia & Pacific
- Europe & Central Asia
- Latin America & Caribbean
- Middle East & North Africa
- South Asia
- Sub-Saharan Africa

High-income economies

- OECD
- Other

no data

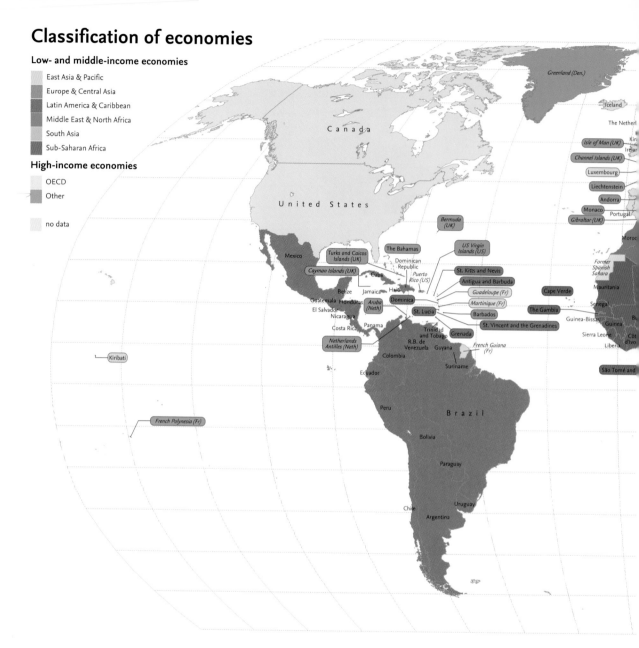

The World Bank classifies economies as low-income, middle-income (subdivided into lower-middle and upper-middle), or high-income based on gross national income (GNI) per capita. Low- and middle-income economies are sometimes referred to as *developing economies*. This is not intended to imply that all economies in the group are experiencing similar development or that other economies have reached a preferred or final stage of development.

The regions used in this atlas are based on the regions defined by the World Bank for

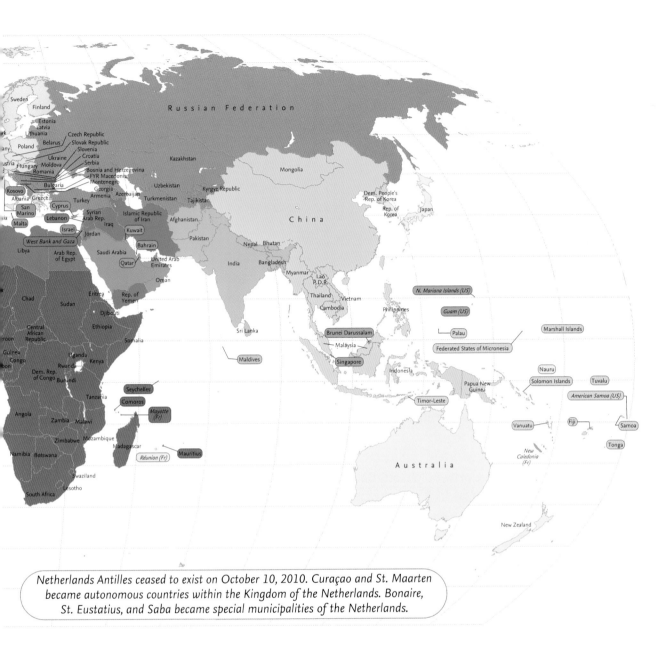

Sweden
Finland
Estonia
Latvia
Lithuania
Czech Republic
Belarus
Slovak Republic
Poland
Slovenia
Ukraine
Croatia
Hungary Moldova
Serbia
Romania
Bosnia and Herzegovina
Montenegro
Bulgaria
FYR Macedonia
Georgia
Kosovo
Armenia Azerbaijan
Albania Greece
Turkey
San
Cyprus
Marino
Syrian
Lebanon
Arab Rep.
Malta
Israel
Iraq
Jordan
West Bank and Gaza
Libya
Arab Rep.
of Egypt
Saudi Arabia
Qatar

Russian Federation

Kazakhstan

Mongolia

Uzbekistan
Kyrgyz Republic
Turkmenistan
Tajikistan
Islamic Republic
of Iran
Afghanistan
Kuwait
Pakistan
Bahrain
United Arab
Emirates
Oman

China

Dem. People's
Rep. of Korea
Rep. of
Korea
Japan

Chad
Sudan
Eritrea
Rep. of
Yemen
Djibouti
Central
African
Ethiopia
Republic
Somalia
Guinea
Uganda
Congo
Rwanda
Kenya
Dem. Rep.
of Congo
Burundi
Tanzania
Seychelles
Comoros
Angola
Mayotte
(Fr)
Zambia Malawi
Zimbabwe
Mozambique
Madagascar
Mauritius
Namibia Botswana
Réunion (Fr)
Swaziland
South Africa
Lesotho

India
Bangladesh
Nepal Bhutan
Myanmar
Lao
P.D.R.
Thailand
Vietnam
Cambodia
Philippines
Sri Lanka
Brunei Darussalam
Maldives
Malaysia
Singapore
Indonesia

N. Mariana Islands (US)
Guam (US)
Palau
Marshall Islands
Federated States of Micronesia
Nauru
Solomon Islands
Tuvalu
American Samoa (US)
Papua New
Guinea
Timor-Leste
Vanuatu
Fiji
Samoa
New
Caledonia
(Fr)
Tonga

Australia

New Zealand

Netherlands Antilles ceased to exist on October 10, 2010. Curaçao and St. Maarten
became autonomous countries within the Kingdom of the Netherlands. Bonaire,
St. Eustatius, and Saba became special municipalities of the Netherlands.

alytical and operational purposes. These
gions may differ from common geographic
age or from the regions defined by other
ganizations. Regional groupings and the
gregate measures for regions include only
w- and middle-income economies.

Data are shown for economies as they were
constituted in 2009. Additional information
about the data is provided in *World Development
Indicators 2010* or on the World Bank website
(data.worldbank.org).

In 2000 the Millennium Declaration, ratified by the 189 member states of the United Nations, committed rich and developing countries to work in partnership to achieve a set of critical development outcomes. Those commitments are embodied in the eight Millennium Development Goals (MDGs) for 2015, supported by 18 quantified targets and 60 indicators measuring progress since 1990. Progress has been uneven and many countries will not reach the targets set for 2015, but others have met or exceeded the targets, improving the lives of hundreds of millions of people.

Goal 1: Eradicate extreme poverty and hunger

Defined as average daily consumption of $1.25 or less, extreme poverty means living on the edge of subsistence. In 1990 more than 1.8 billion people lived on less than $1.25 a day. Since then, the poverty rate in developing countries has fallen from 42 percent to 25 percent in 2005—largely due to progress in China and India. Even in Sub-Saharan Africa, which stagnated in most of the 1990s, poverty rates have started to fall. By 2015 the global rate for extreme poverty is expected to be 15 percent and the number of people living in poverty will fall to 900 million.

Goal 2: Achieve universal primary education

More than 20 years ago the world community committed itself to providing at least a primary school education to every child. Ensuring that all children receive a good-quality education is the foundation of sustainable development and poverty alleviation. In 2007 the primary school completion rate reached 87 percent for developing countries: 92 percent for middle-income countries but just 67 percent for low-income ones. That means that some 70 million children worldwide were not enrolled in primary school—and about half will receive no formal education.

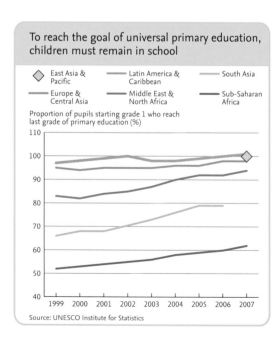

All regions but Sub-Saharan Africa are on track to reach the poverty reduction target

Legend: East Asia & Pacific; Latin America & Caribbean; South Asia; Europe & Central Asia; Middle East & North Africa; Sub-Saharan Africa

People living on less than $1.25 a day (%)

Source: World Bank calculations

To reach the goal of universal primary education, children must remain in school

Legend: East Asia & Pacific; Latin America & Caribbean; South Asia; Europe & Central Asia; Middle East & North Africa; Sub-Saharan Africa

Proportion of pupils starting grade 1 who reach last grade of primary education (%)

Source: UNESCO Institute for Statistics

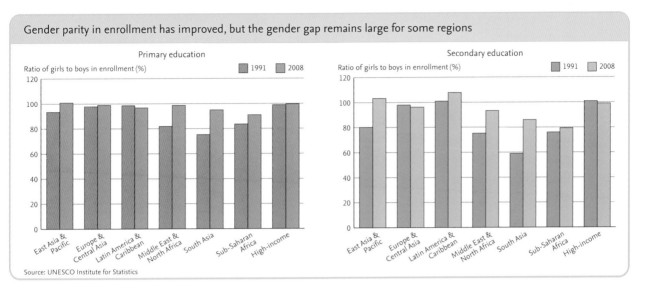

Gender parity in enrollment has improved, but the gender gap remains large for some regions

Primary education

Ratio of girls to boys in enrollment (%)

■ 1991 ■ 2008

East Asia & Pacific · Europe & Central Asia · Latin America & Caribbean · Middle East & North Africa · South Asia · Sub-Saharan Africa · High-income

Secondary education

Ratio of girls to boys in enrollment (%)

■ 1991 ■ 2008

East Asia & Pacific · Europe & Central Asia · Latin America & Caribbean · Middle East & North Africa · South Asia · Sub-Saharan Africa · High-income

Source: UNESCO Institute for Statistics

Goal 3: Promote gender equality and empower women

Promoting gender equality and empowering women are important in their own right and because they foster progress toward other MDG targets, such as those for reducing poverty, hunger, and disease and improving access to education. When women make decisions, household resources tend to be shared more equitably. And educated women are better able to care for children and more likely to send their children to school.

Education opportunities for girls have expanded since 1990. Enrollment patterns in upper-middle-income countries now resemble those in high-income countries, and those in lower-middle-income countries are nearing equity. But gender gaps remain large in low-income countries, especially at the primary and secondary levels.

Goal 4: Reduce child mortality

Deaths of children under age 5 have been declining since 1990. In 2006, for the first time, the number of children who died before their fifth birthday fell below 10 million. Child mortality in developing countries dropped more than 25 percent between 1990 and 2008, from 101 per 1,000 live births to 73. Though this progress is impressive, it will be insufficient to meet the fourth MDG of reducing under-5 child mortality by two-thirds.

Success in reducing infant and child mortality is a general indicator of progress on human development outcomes under the MDGs, reflecting falling poverty

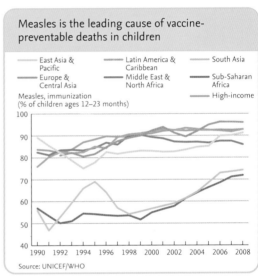

Measles is the leading cause of vaccine-preventable deaths in children

East Asia & Pacific · Europe & Central Asia · Latin America & Caribbean · Middle East & North Africa · South Asia · Sub-Saharan Africa · High-income

Measles, immunization
(% of children ages 12–23 months)

Source: UNICEF/WHO

rates, improved nutrition, increasing female literacy, disease prevention, access to medicine and health facilities, and safe water and sanitation. Immunizations for measles—a leading cause of vaccine-preventable deaths among children—continue to expand worldwide. Coverage in all regions now exceeds 70 percent, markedly improving child survival rates.

For more information about the Millennium Development Goals, see the World Bank eAtlas of the MDGs data.worldbank.org/mdg-atlas.

Goal 5: Improve maternal health

Every year hundreds of thousands of women die from complications related to pregnancy or childbirth. Some 99 percent of these deaths occur in developing countries. And for every woman who dies, about 20 suffer injuries, infections, or diseases. In developing countries pregnancy-related complications are among the leading causes of death and disability for women between 15 and 49.

Prenatal care and the presence of skilled health workers at delivery are critical to reducing maternal mortality. In developing countries the share of births attended by skilled health staff rose from about half in 1990 to two-thirds in 2008 and the proportion of pregnant women receiving prenatal care is rising. Countries in Europe and Central Asia have made the most progress in ensuring safe deliveries. Most have achieved universal coverage, and the rest are on track to achieve it by 2015.

Goal 6: Combat HIV/AIDS, malaria, and other diseases

For many reasons—including poverty, climate, bad policies, and inadequate services—people in developing countries are highly susceptible to life-threatening diseases. Some of these, such as malaria and tuberculosis, have

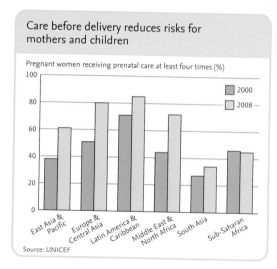

Care before delivery reduces risks for mothers and children

Pregnant women receiving prenatal care at least four times (%)

Source: UNICEF

been eliminated or largely contained in high-income countries, yet continue to kill millions a year in developing countries, and HIV/AIDS remains a global pandemic.

Worldwide, 33.4 million people were living with HIV/AIDS in 2008. Sub-Saharan Africa contains just over one-tenth of the world's population but is home to two-thirds of people living with HIV/AIDS, with women far more likely to be infected than men. In 2008 there were 2.7 million new HIV infections worldwide—a 17 percent decline over eight years—and 2 million AIDS-related deaths.

The World Health Organization estimates that in 2008 there were 250 million cases of malaria, leading to nearly 1 million deaths. Though malaria is endemic in most tropical and subtropical regions, 90 percent of malaria deaths occur in Sub-Saharan Africa—and most are among children under 5.

The number of new tuberculosis cases peaked globally in 2004 and is leveling off, but prevalence is still high in Sub-Saharan Africa, and some South Asian countries appear to have returned to 1990 levels. In 2008 there were 11 million cases of tuberculosis globally—down from 14 million in 2007.

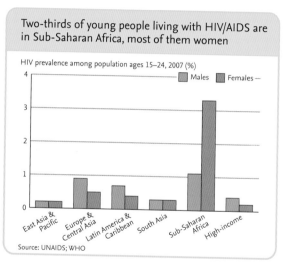

Two-thirds of young people living with HIV/AIDS are in Sub-Saharan Africa, most of them women

HIV prevalence among population ages 15–24, 2007 (%)

Source: UNAIDS; WHO

Goal 7: Ensure environmental sustainability

The 1992 Earth Summit adopted comprehensive global, national, and local responses for every area where humans affect the environment. This agenda was incorporated into the Millennium Declaration along with commitments to reduce greenhouse gas emissions, protect biodiversity, and prevent desertification.

Also included among the MDGs targets are commitments to reduce the number of people lacking access to improved water and sanitation facilities. An improved water source meets basic standards for access to a protected water supply, but water from improved sources—such as public taps or hand pumps—may not meet standards set by the World Health Organization and may require considerable fetching and carrying. In 1990 more than 1 billion people in developing countries lacked access to such a minimal convenience. In 2008, 884 million people—37 percent of whom live in Sub-Saharan Africa—still lacked access to improved sources for drinking-water, but most regions made progress.

Around the world, 2.6 billion people lack access to toilets, latrines, and other forms of improved sanitation, and more than 40 percent of these people practice open defecation. In developing countries the share of people with access to improved sanitation rose from 43 percent in 1990 to 54 percent in 2008. To halve the proportion of people without basic sanitation by 2015, more than 1.3 billion people would have to gain access to an improved facility—so the global target will be missed.

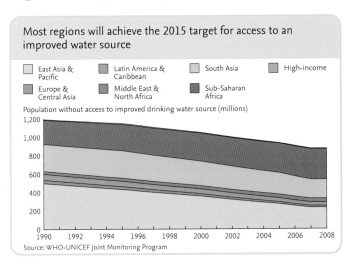

Most regions will achieve the 2015 target for access to an improved water source

Source: WHO-UNICEF Joint Monitoring Program

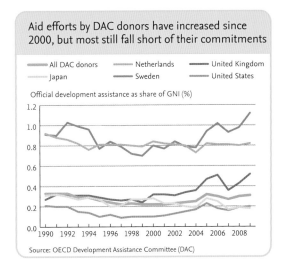

Aid efforts by DAC donors have increased since 2000, but most still fall short of their commitments

Source: OECD Development Assistance Committee (DAC)

Goal 8: Develop a global partnership for development

Prospects for sustaining the current economic recovery will be enhanced if advanced and developing countries continue to cooperate in implementing policies aimed at increasing growth, protecting the poor and vulnerable, maintaining infrastructure investment, and sustaining private sector growth.

Private investment and remittances from migrants have become increasingly important sources of financing for developing countries. However, official development assistance—grants and loans made at low interest rates—remains an important source of support for development programs in the poorest countries. In 2005 the leaders of the richest industrial countries made specific commitments to increase aid to Africa. Aid received by all developing countries has increased substantially in real terms—from $73 billion in 2000 to $129 billion in 2008. Aid to Africa increased to $40 billion in 2008, but it has fallen far short of the commitments made in 2005.

Standards of living vary substantially across the globe. Comparing income or consumption or poverty levels among countries requires a common unit of measurement. Exchange rates reflect the relative value of currencies as traded in the market. Purchasing power parities (PPPs) take into account differences in price levels. Both have important roles in measuring the size of economies.

What is a developing country? Because development encompasses many factors—economic, environmental, cultural, educational, and institutional—no single measure gives a complete picture. However, the total earnings of the residents of an economy, measured by its gross national income (GNI), is a good measure of its capacity to provide for the wellbeing of its people. The World Bank classifies countries according to their average income, or GNI per capita, converted to U.S. dollars using three-year average market exchange rates (commonly called the *World Bank Atlas method*). Countries with average incomes of less than $12,196 in 2009 are classified as low- and middle-income (often referred to as *developing economies*). Countries with average incomes of $12,196 or more in 2009 are classified as high-income or developed economies. In 2009, the 1 billion people in high-income economies had an average income of $38,139 a person; the 4.8 billion residents in middle-income economies had average incomes of $3,385; and the 1 billion people in low-income economies earned only $504, with some as low as $150.

To measure differences in welfare, comparisons of income among economies should take into account differences in

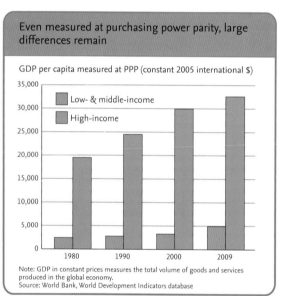

Even measured at purchasing power parity, large differences remain

GDP per capita measured at PPP (constant 2005 international $)

Note: GDP in constant prices measures the total volume of goods and services produced in the global economy.
Source: World Bank, World Development Indicators database

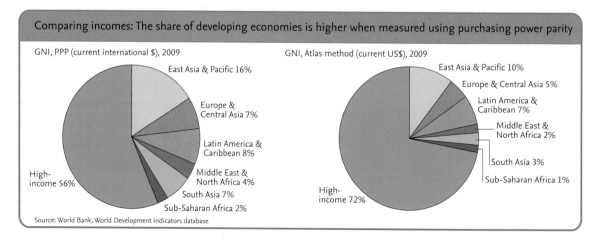

Comparing incomes: The share of developing economies is higher when measured using purchasing power parity

GNI, PPP (current international $), 2009

- East Asia & Pacific 16%
- Europe & Central Asia 7%
- Latin America & Caribbean 8%
- Middle East & North Africa 4%
- South Asia 7%
- Sub-Saharan Africa 2%
- High-income 56%

GNI, Atlas method (current US$), 2009

- East Asia & Pacific 10%
- Europe & Central Asia 5%
- Latin America & Caribbean 7%
- Middle East & North Africa 2%
- South Asia 3%
- Sub-Saharan Africa 1%
- High-income 72%

Source: World Bank, World Development Indicators database

domestic price levels. This is done using PPPs. Using PPPs instead of market exchange rates, the standard of living among countries can be compared in real terms, as if the people purchased goods and services at the same prices. Measured using PPPs, developing economies receive 44 percent of world income. But when measured using the Atlas method they receive only 28 percent. The difference is due to the lower cost of services and nontraded goods in developing economies, a fact that travelers frequently observe.

As the most comprehensive measure of living standards, GNI per capita is closely related to other—nonmonetary—measures of the quality of life, such as life expectancy at birth, the mortality rate of children, and enrollment rates in school. Low incomes are both a cause and effect of low levels of health, education, and other human development outcomes. Poor people have a hard time obtaining good healthcare and education, while poor health and poor education leave them less able to improve their incomes.

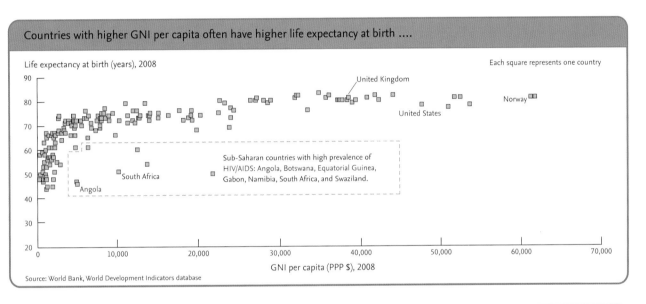

Countries with higher GNI per capita often have higher life expectancy at birth ....

Life expectancy at birth (years), 2008

Each square represents one country

Sub-Saharan countries with high prevalence of HIV/AIDS: Angola, Botswana, Equatorial Guinea, Gabon, Namibia, South Africa, and Swaziland.

GNI per capita (PPP $), 2008

Source: World Bank, World Development Indicators database

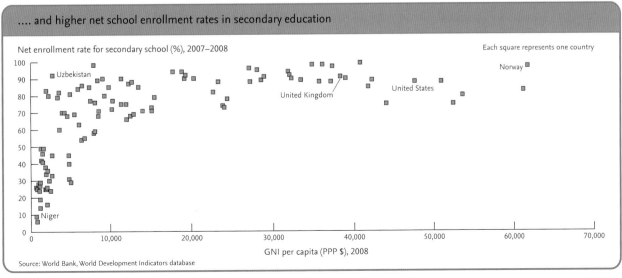

.... and higher net school enrollment rates in secondary education

Net enrollment rate for secondary school (%), 2007–2008

Each square represents one country

GNI per capita (PPP $), 2008

Source: World Bank, World Development Indicators database

Income

GNI per capita, World Bank Atlas method, 2009

- Low-income countries ($995 or less)
- Lower-middle-income countries ($996–$3,945)
- Upper-middle-income countries ($3,946–$12,195)
- High-income countries ($12,196 or more)
- no data

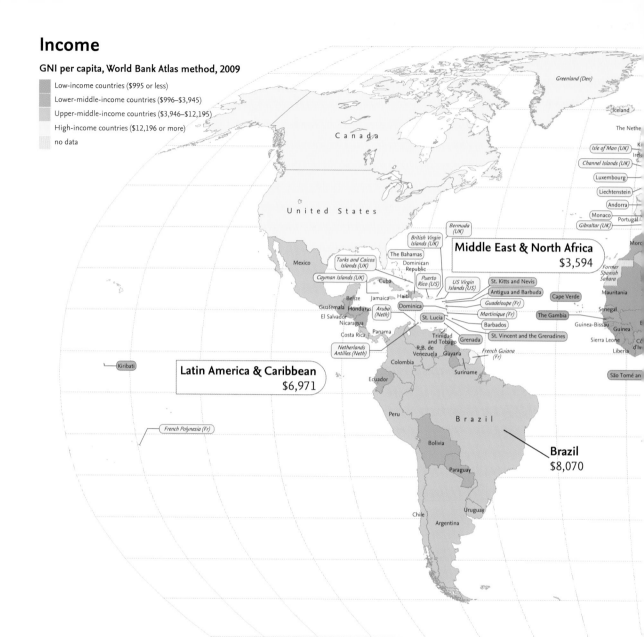

Greenland (Den)

Iceland

The Nethe

Canada

Isle of Man (UK)
Irela
Channel Islands (UK)
Luxembourg
Liechtenstein
Andorra
Monaco
Portugal
Gibraltar (UK)

United States

Bermuda (UK)

British Virgin Islands (UK)

Middle East & North Africa
$3,594

Morc

Mexico

Turks and Caicos Islands (UK)
The Bahamas
Dominican Republic

Former Spanish Sahara

Cayman Islands (UK)
Cuba

Puerto Rico (US)
US Virgin Islands (US)
St. Kitts and Nevis
Antigua and Barbuda
Cape Verde
Mauritania

Belize
Jamaica
Haiti
Guadeloupe (Fr)
Senegal

Guatemala Honduras
Aruba (Neth)
Dominica
Martinique (Fr)
The Gambia
Guinea-Bissau
Guinea

El Salvador
Nicaragua
St. Lucia
Barbados
Sierra Leone
Cô
d'Iv

Costa Rica
Panama
St. Vincent and the Grenadines
Liberia

Trinidad and Tobago
Grenada

Netherlands Antilles (Neth)
R.B. de Venezuela
French Guiana (Fr)
São Tomé an

Kiribati

Colombia
Guyana

Latin America & Caribbean
$6,971

Suriname

Ecuador

Peru

Brazil

French Polynesia (Fr)

Brazil
$8,070

Bolivia

Paraguay

Chile

Uruguay

Argentina

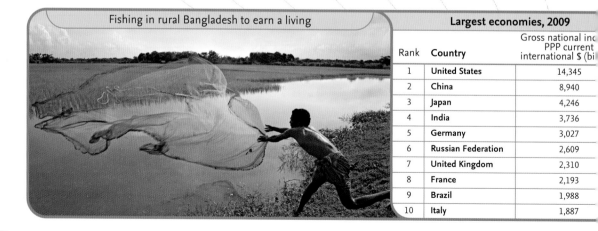

Fishing in rural Bangladesh to earn a living

Largest economies, 2009

Rank	Country	Gross national inc PPP current international $ (bi
1	United States	14,345
2	China	8,940
3	Japan	4,246
4	India	3,736
5	Germany	3,027
6	Russian Federation	2,609
7	United Kingdom	2,310
8	France	2,193
9	Brazil	1,988
10	Italy	1,887

Russian Federation
$9,370

Europe & Central Asia
$6,793

Russian Federation

Sweden
Finland
Estonia
Latvia
Lithuania
Czech Republic
Poland
Belarus
Slovak Republic
Slovenia
Ukraine
Croatia
Hungary Moldova
Serbia
Romania
Bosnia and Herzegovina
FYR Macedonia
Bulgaria
Montenegro
Georgia
Kosovo
Armenia Azerbaijan
Albania Greece
San Marino
Cyprus
Turkey
Malta
Lebanon
Syrian Arab Rep.
Israel
Jordan
West Bank and Gaza
Libya
Arab Rep. of Egypt
Qatar

Kazakhstan

Mongolia

Uzbekistan
Kyrgyz Republic
Turkmenistan
Tajikistan
Islamic Republic of Iran
Afghanistan

Dem. People's Rep. of Korea
Rep. of Korea
Japan

China

China
$3,620

Chad
Sudan
Rep. of Yemen
Djibouti
Ethiopia
Central African Republic
Somalia

Saudi Arabia
Oman
United Arab Emirates
Bahrain
Kuwait
Iraq

Pakistan
Nepal Bhutan
India Bangladesh
Myanmar
Lao P.D.R.
Thailand
Cambodia
Vietnam
Philippines

India
$1,170

Sri Lanka

N. Mariana Islands (US)

Guam (US)

East Asia & Pacific
$3,163

Brunei Darussalam
Malaysia
Singapore
Maldives

Palau

Marshall Islands

Federated States of Micronesia

Guinea
Congo
Uganda
Rwanda Kenya
Dem. Rep. of Congo Burundi
Tanzania

Seychelles
Comoros
Mayotte (Fr)

Indonesia

Papua New Guinea

Nauru
Solomon Islands
Tuvalu

American Samoa (US)

South Asia
$1,079

Angola
Zambia Malawi
Zimbabwe Mozambique
Madagascar
Namibia Botswana
Réunion (Fr) Mauritius

Vanuatu
Fiji
Samoa

Tonga

Swaziland
South Africa Lesotho

New Caledonia (Fr)

Australia

Sub-Saharan Africa
$1,096

New Zealand

Facts	Internet links	
Of the 40 economies classified as low-income in 2009, 29 are in Sub-Saharan Africa, 8 are in Asia, 2 are in Europe, and 1 is in Latin America and the Caribbean.	► World Development Indicators database	**data.worldbank.org/indicator**
Most economies in Latin America and the Caribbean, Middle East and North Africa, and Europe and Central Asia are middle-income economies.	► Organisation for Economic Co-operation and Development Statistics Portal	**www.oecd.org/statistics**
Variations of income within each region can be large. For example, in 2009 Botswana's GNI per capita surpassed $6,260, while GNI per capita in neighboring Mozambique was only $440.	► International Monetary Fund Dissemination Standards Bulletin Board	**dsbb.imf.org**
Average GNI per capita in the low- and middle-income countries was $2,956 in 2009, while in high-income economies it was $38,139.	► United Nations Statistics Division, National Accounts Main Aggregates database	**unstats.un.org/unsd/snaama**
As of 2009, 26 economies had moved from developing to high-income status, 13 of them in the last three years.	► International Comparison Program	**www.worldbank.org/data/icp**

Economic growth reduces poverty and, among fast-growing developing countries, is closing the income gap with high-income economies. But growth must be sustained over the long term and the gains from economic growth must be shared to make lasting improvements in the wellbeing of all people. The recent financial crisis has interrupted that process.

Sustained growth is essential to reduce poverty, but few developing countries— especially low-income countries—have seen strong and steady growth in the past. Only one out of five low-income countries has increased per capita income by 3.0 percent a year or more since 1980. For many countries in Sub-Saharan Africa the 1990s brought little or no growth. Growth accelerated in the following decade, however; since 2000 more than half of all developing countries achieved an average growth of per capita income of 3.2 percent a year or more. In Sub-Saharan Africa 13 countries grew faster than 3.2 percent a year and more than half grew by 2.1 percent or more, despite formidable development challenges such as conflict and epidemic disease.

The financial crisis, which began in 2007 and spread from high-income to low- and middle-income economies in 2008, became in 2009 the most severe global recession in 50 years. Gross domestic product (GDP) fell by 3.3 percent in high-income economies and grew by only 1.6 percent in developing countries. The crisis was transmitted from high-income countries to developing countries as exports, private capital flows,

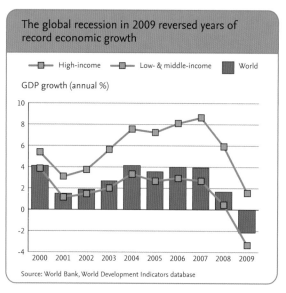

The global recession in 2009 reversed years of record economic growth

GDP growth (annual %)

Source: World Bank, World Development Indicators database

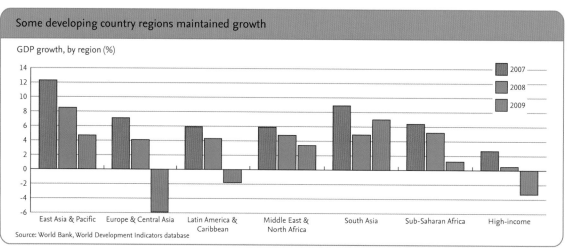

Some developing country regions maintained growth

GDP growth, by region (%)

Source: World Bank, World Development Indicators database

commodity prices, and workers' remittances all declined. Many developing countries entered the crisis in better shape than in previous recessions, but for countries with large portions of their populations clustered around the poverty line, even brief periods of economic slowdown can have severe effects. As a result of the current crisis, 89 million more people are expected to end up living in extreme poverty by end-2010. In the poorest developing countries, health and education outcomes move with the economic cycle; they deteriorate during economic crisis and take a long time to recover. World Bank research estimates that the current downturn could have resulted in 30,000 to 50,000 additional infant deaths in Sub-Saharan Africa in 2009.

Different parts of the world were hit differently by the crisis. Among developing regions, Europe and Central Asia fared the worst as GDP fell by 5.9 percent. Latin America and the Caribbean economies contracted by 1.8 percent. Mexico, which relies heavily on the U.S. market for its exports, saw output fall by 6.5 percent, the sharpest decline among major Latin America and the Caribbean countries. China, with 8.7 percent rate of growth, managed to continue growing at nearly the same rate as before, while India did even better with a growth rate of 7.7 percent in 2009 compared with 5.1 in 2008. Growth in the Middle East and North Africa dropped to 3.4 percent because of oil price declines and lower exports to Europe. Sub-Saharan Africa barely grew as

exporters were hurt by dropping commodity prices. The region also suffered from falling remittances, lower tourism revenues, and declines in private capital flows. Sub-Saharan Africa is particularly vulnerable to the severest consequences of the crisis because it includes 29 of the 40 poorest countries in the world.

Although higher growth rates help reduce global poverty, rising income inequality weakens the poverty reduction impact of economic growth. Even in fast-growing economies, poor people may not share fully in the benefits of growth. A country with high initial inequality will need to grow faster than a country with more equal income distribution to achieve the same poverty reduction. If inequality increases, poverty reduction will be slower. Since the mid-1990s, income inequality, as measured by the Gini coefficient, has increased in slightly more than half of developing countries with available data.

To achieve broad-based economic growth, all people must have equal opportunity to participate. There are many ways to increase the opportunities for poor people. Access to education, health services, and water and sanitation systems increases productivity. Improvements to transportation and communication systems help improve access to markets. Secure tenure to property increases incentives for new investment. Finally, protection through the rule of law reduces risks and uncertainties that undermine growth.

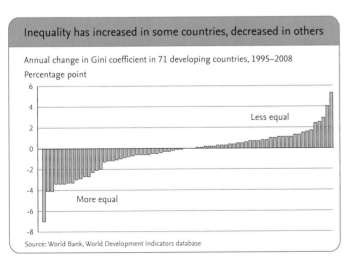

Inequality has increased in some countries, decreased in others

Annual change in Gini coefficient in 71 developing countries, 1995–2008
Percentage point

Less equal

More equal

Source: World Bank, World Development Indicators database

Economic growth

average annual growth of GDP per capita, 2000–2009

- less than 0.0%
- 0.0–1.9%
- 2.0–3.9%
- 4.0–5.9%
- 6.0% or more
- no data

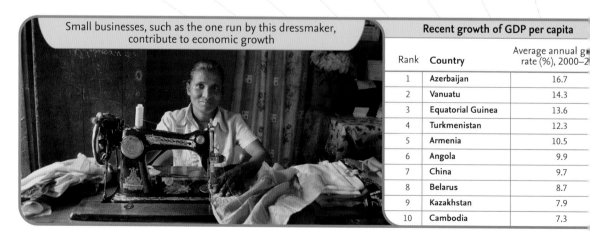

Small businesses, such as the one run by this dressmaker, contribute to economic growth

Recent growth of GDP per capita

Rank	Country	Average annual growth rate (%), 2000–2009
1	Azerbaijan	16.7
2	Vanuatu	14.3
3	Equatorial Guinea	13.6
4	Turkmenistan	12.3
5	Armenia	10.5
6	Angola	9.9
7	China	9.7
8	Belarus	8.7
9	Kazakhstan	7.9
10	Cambodia	7.3

Facts	Internet links	
The last 17 years saw a surge of growth, especially among countries that opened their economies to trade and investment, maintained sound monetary and fiscal policies, and strengthened the rule of law.	▶ World Development Indicators database	data.worldbank.org/indicator
In contrast to record economic growth from 2000 to 2007, the global economy fell by 2 percent in 2009 as a result of the 2008 financial crisis.	▶ World Bank Prospects for Development	www.worldbank.org/prospects
Among 10 developing countries with the highest GDP per capita growth in 2000–2009, 2 are from low-income economies and 1 is from Sub-Saharan Africa.	▶ IMF World Economic Outlook	www.imf.org/weo
GDP per capita growth varied substantially across the regions. Whereas GDP per capita more than tripled in East Asia and Pacific between 1990 and 2008, it was still less than the GDP per capita in Latin America and the Caribbean, Europe and Central Asia, and the Middle East and North Africa.	▶ OECD statistics	www.oecd.org/statistics
	▶ The Commission on Growth and Development	www.growthcommission.org

Inequality

share of income going to the poorest quintile, 1992–2008, most recent year available

- less than 4.0%
- 4.0–5.9%
- 6.0–6.9%
- 7.0–7.9%
- 8.0% or more
- no data

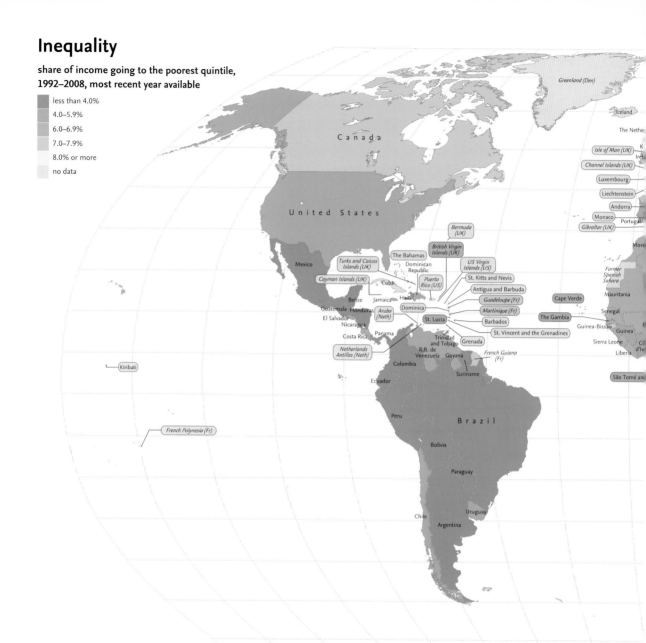

Ten countries with high inequality ratios

One commonly used measure of income inequality is the inequality ratio, calculated as the ratio of income or consumption shares of the richest 20 percent to the poorest 20 percent of the population. A ratio of 10 means that the top 20 percent of the population earns (or spends) 10 times as much as the bottom 20 percent of the population. Generally the higher this ratio, the more unequal the income distribution. Countries with high inequality ratios are mostly in Latin America and Africa. The highest inequality ratio among Asian countries is 12.

Country, population over 1 million	Year	Income or consumption shares	Ineq r
Namibia	1993	income	
Angola	2000	consumption	
Colombia	2006	income	
Haiti	2001	income	
Honduras	2006	income	
Panama	2006	income	
Bolivia	2007	consumption	
Botswana	1994	consumption	
South Africa	2000	consumption	
Brazil	2007	income	

Facts	Internet links	
Income inequalities between high-income countries and developing countries have improved compared with a decade ago. Still, in 2009 an average high-income country's gross national income per capita measured in purchasing power parity terms was 30 times that of an average low-income country and 6 times that of an average middle-income country.	▶ World Bank *World Development Report 2006*	**www.worldbank.org/wdr2006**
Inequality within countries has significantly increased in many parts of the world, including Colombia, Côte d'Ivoire, Honduras, FYR Macedonia, and Peru.	▶ United Nations Development Programme *Human Development Report*	**hdr.undp.org**
Inequality ratios have improved significantly in some countries, including Bolivia, Central African Republic, Lesotho, Nicaragua, and Paraguay.	▶ World Bank World Development Indicators database	**data.worldbank.org/indicator**
Inequality in access to schooling has fallen as school participation rates have risen in most countries.	▶ World Bank Poverty Reduction and Equity	**www.worldbank.org/poverty**

Poverty and deprivation remain, but there has been progress. The proportion of people in developing countries living in extreme poverty has fallen from about 42 percent in 1990 to slightly more than 25 percent in 2005, with about 1.4 billion people living on less than $1.25 a day. With rapid economic growth in many developing countries, poverty rates have continued to fall, but progress has been slowed by the recent economic and financial crisis.

Women sorting through freshly picked grains during harvest in Uzbekistan

The number of people living in extreme poverty has been falling since the 1980s, perhaps for the first time in human history. A poverty line set at $1.25 a day in 2005 purchasing power (revised from the previous $1.08 a day in 1993 prices) is used as the working definition of extreme poverty. Based on this, the number of people living in extreme poverty fell from 1.9 billion in 1981 to 1.8 billion in 1990 and to about 1.4 billion in 2005. This is an important

success, but greater effort will be required to further reduce poverty.

For hundreds of millions of people, poverty is a consequence of circumstances beyond their control. Poor health and lack of education deprive people of productive employment. People living in poverty are often unable to obtain sufficient nourishment to meet their daily needs, costing billions of dollars in lost productivity and increasing their susceptibility to disease. As many as 1 billion people, or 14 percent of the world's population, were undernourished in 2008. But poverty is also a cause of ill health and lack of education. Poor people lack financial resources and are

data.worldbank.org/atlas-global/poor
See pp. 6–7 for more information

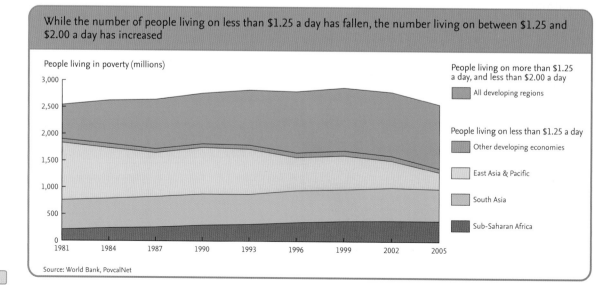

While the number of people living on less than $1.25 a day has fallen, the number living on between $1.25 and $2.00 a day has increased

People living in poverty (millions)

People living on more than $1.25 a day, and less than $2.00 a day
- All developing regions

People living on less than $1.25 a day
- Other developing economies
- East Asia & Pacific
- South Asia
- Sub-Saharan Africa

Source: World Bank, PovcalNet

further disadvantaged by lack of knowledge about how to access basic social services. Compounded by weak social institutions, lack of adequate infrastructure, and environmental resources that have been depleted or spoiled, they may become caught in poverty traps. A multidimensional development strategy, coupled with good governance, is required to escape.

The significant reduction in extreme poverty over the past quarter century disguises large regional differences. The greatest decline occurred in East Asia and the Pacific, led by China, where the poverty rate fell from 78 percent in 1981 to 17 percent in 2005 and the number of people living on less than $1.25 a day dropped more than 750 million. Over the same period, the poverty rate in South Asia fell from 59 percent to 41 percent. In contrast, the poverty rate has fallen only slightly in Sub-Saharan Africa rising from 53 percent in 1981 to 59 percent in 1999, then dropping to 51 percent in 2005, while the number of people living in poverty nearly doubled. The Millennium Development Goals (MDGs) call for 1990 poverty rates to be cut in half by 2015. At present many countries are falling short of that goal.

The average daily income of those living on less than $1.25 a day increased slightly in most regions during the 1990s. A marked exception is Sub-Saharan Africa, where average income of the poor did not increase—remaining at a meager $0.73 a day—pointing to the severity and depth of poverty in this region. The number of people living on less than $1.25 a day is expected to fall to less than 1 billion by 2015, but the number living on between $1.25 and $2.00 a day will remain constant at about 1.1 billion for the next decade. These are still very poor people whose prospects will improve only through continued growth.

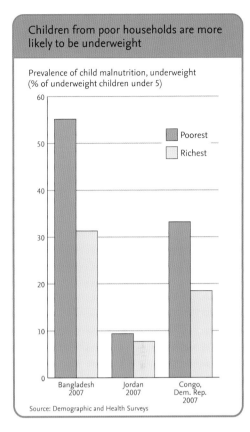

Children from poor households are more likely to be underweight

Prevalence of child malnutrition, underweight (% of underweight children under 5)

Poorest
Richest

Bangladesh 2007 | Jordan 2007 | Congo, Dem. Rep. 2007

Source: Demographic and Health Surveys

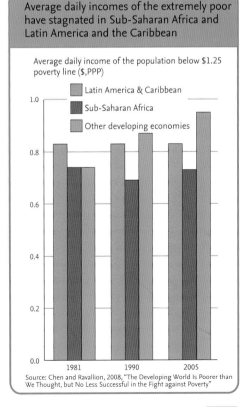

Average daily incomes of the extremely poor have stagnated in Sub-Saharan Africa and Latin America and the Caribbean

Average daily income of the population below $1.25 poverty line ($,PPP)

Latin America & Caribbean
Sub-Saharan Africa
Other developing economies

1981 | 1990 | 2005

Source: Chen and Ravallion, 2008, "The Developing World Is Poorer than We Thought, but No Less Successful in the Fight against Poverty"

Poverty

share of population living on less than $1.25 a day, 2005

- 50.0% or more
- 25.0–49.9%
- 10.0–24.9%
- 2.0–9.9%
- less than 2.0%
- no data

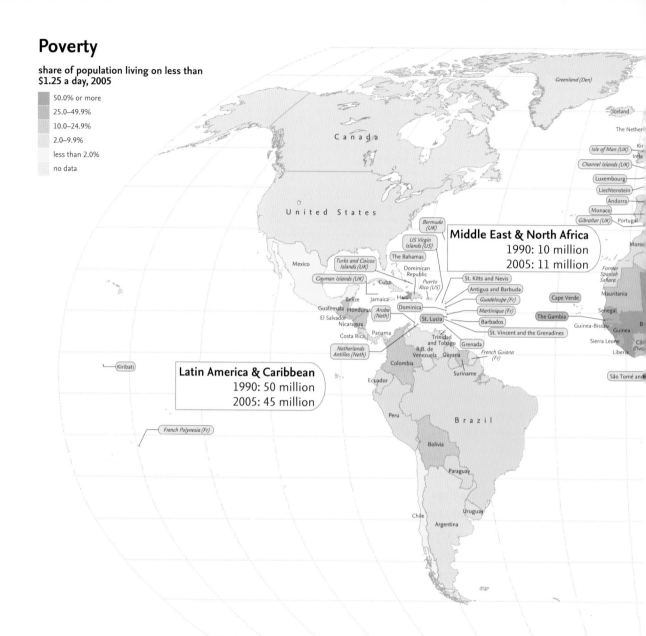

Middle East & North Africa
1990: 10 million
2005: 11 million

Latin America & Caribbean
1990: 50 million
2005: 45 million

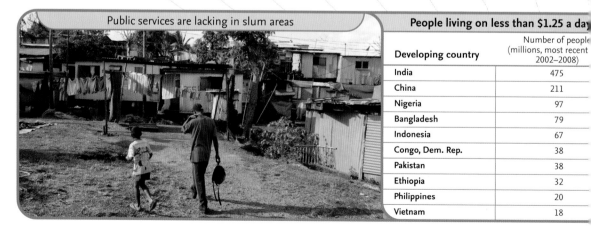

Public services are lacking in slum areas

People living on less than $1.25 a day

Developing country	Number of people (millions, most recent 2002–2008)
India	475
China	211
Nigeria	97
Bangladesh	79
Indonesia	67
Congo, Dem. Rep.	38
Pakistan	38
Ethiopia	32
Philippines	20
Vietnam	18

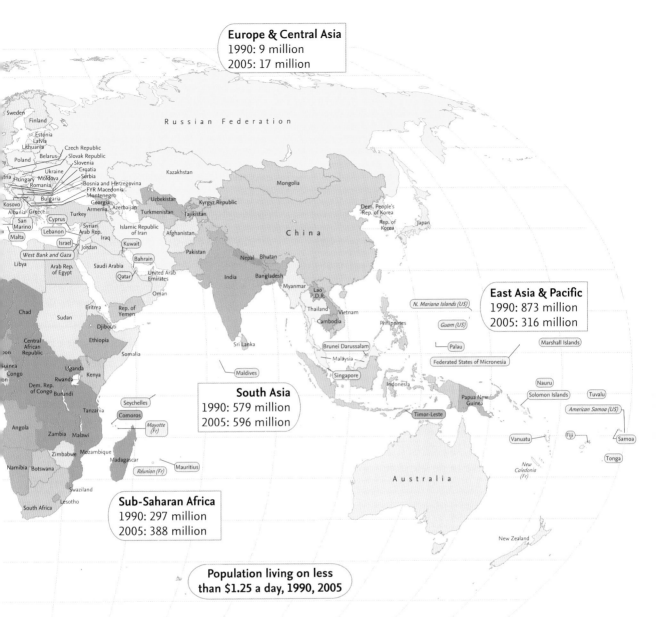

Europe & Central Asia
1990: 9 million
2005: 17 million

East Asia & Pacific
1990: 873 million
2005: 316 million

South Asia
1990: 579 million
2005: 596 million

Sub-Saharan Africa
1990: 297 million
2005: 388 million

Population living on less than $1.25 a day, 1990, 2005

Facts	Internet links	
Africa has more countries with high poverty rates than any other developing region, but Asia has the most people living in extreme poverty.	▶ World Bank PovcalNet Online Poverty Analysis Tool	iresearch.worldbank.org/PovcalNet
In China the number of people living in extreme poverty fell from 635 million in 1981 to 208 million in 2005.	▶ World Bank: Country poverty assessment	www-wds.worldbank.org (go to By Doc Type in left hand bar and select Poverty Assessment from Economic and Sector Work)
Although extreme poverty occurs mostly in rural areas, urban slums also have high poverty rates.	▶ United Nations Millennium Project	www.unmillenniumproject.org
If economic growth rates in developing countries are sustained, the poverty target of the Millennium Development Goal of halving poverty by 2015 is likely to be achieved at the global level.	▶ Oxford Poverty and Human Development Initiative	www.ophi.org.uk

We live in a world of unprecedented demographic change, which will shape the lives of our children and grandchildren. We also live in a world of unprecedented demographic diversity, resulting from different changes in the key determinants of population growth and structure: fertility, mortality, and migration. This diversity presents countries with different opportunities and challenges.

The 20th century witnessed extraordinary growth of world population—from 1.6 billion in 1900 to 6.1 billion in 2000, reaching 6.7 billion in 2008. Eighty-four percent of the world's people live in developing countries. East and South Asia, with half the world's population in 1960, added 2 billion people over 50 years. Sub-Saharan Africa, whose population more than tripled in the same time period, from 230 million to 820 million, had the highest population growth rate.

In developing countries, life expectancy at birth increased steadily, from 47 years in 1960 to 67 years in 2008. Fertility rates declined, but at 2.7 births per woman, they remain well above those in high-income countries, fueling population growth as births exceed deaths. Fertility rates are particularly high in Sub-Saharan Africa at five births per woman in 2008.

In high-income countries life expectancy has reached 80 years, 11 years longer than in 1960. The increase in life expectancy has coincided with income growth. With a fertility rate of 1.8 births per woman— well below replacement level—the average age of the population will rise, and population size may fall in the absence of immigration. A majority of international migrants are from developing countries, and these migrants make up a significant part of population growth in industrial countries. However, the total number of migrants is too small to have much impact on population growth in most developing countries.

The world's population is expected to grow to 7.2 billion in 2015 and 8.0 billion

data.worldbank.org/atlas-global/population
See pp. 6–7 for more information

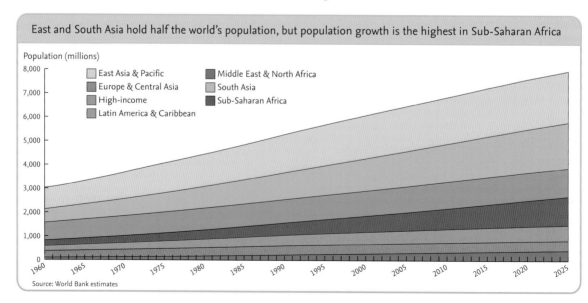

East and South Asia hold half the world's population, but population growth is the highest in Sub-Saharan Africa

Population (millions)

East Asia & Pacific
Europe & Central Asia
High-income
Latin America & Caribbean
Middle East & North Africa
South Asia
Sub-Saharan Africa

Source: World Bank estimates

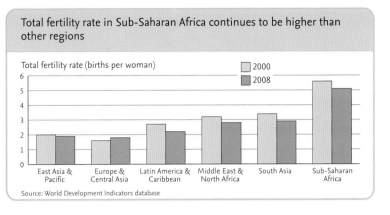

Total fertility rate in Sub-Saharan Africa continues to be higher than other regions

Total fertility rate (births per woman)

☐ 2000
☐ 2008

East Asia & Pacific — Europe & Central Asia — Latin America & Caribbean — Middle East & North Africa — South Asia — Sub-Saharan Africa

Source: World Development Indicators database

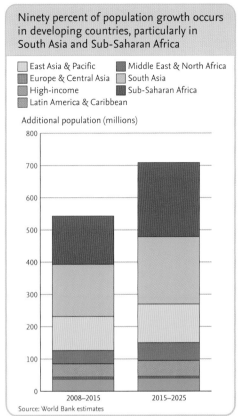

Ninety percent of population growth occurs in developing countries, particularly in South Asia and Sub-Saharan Africa

☐ East Asia & Pacific
☐ Europe & Central Asia
☐ High-income
☐ Latin America & Caribbean
■ Middle East & North Africa
☐ South Asia
■ Sub-Saharan Africa

Additional population (millions)

Source: World Bank estimates

in 2025, with 90 percent of the growth in developing countries. Urbanization will intensify. About 90 percent of the additional population will be in urban areas. A third of people in urban areas will live in slums that lack basic social services such as clean water and sanitation and decent housing. In Sub-Saharan Africa, about 60 percent of urban dwellers will be in slums.

The average age of the population will increase as fertility slows down and people live longer. About 20 percent of the population will be 65 years and older in high-income countries in 2025. The population will age at a higher rate in developing countries, although the share of elderly will remain lower than in high-income countries. In 2025, 9 percent of the population in developing countries will be 65 and older, a 45 percent increase since 2008.

Future population growth, mainly concentrated in urban areas, poses challenges for many countries. Those which cannot meet the needs of their current populations will be hard pressed to provide more schools, healthcare, employment opportunities, and infrastructure for growing populations. Although cities offer more favorable settings to deliver services because of their advantages of scale and proximity, the challenge is how to take advantage of their possibilities. Aging populations bring their own burden of chronic and non-communicable diseases such as heart disease and stroke, cancer, and diabetes. Such diseases currently account for 60 percent of all deaths, and they are rapidly increasing in developing countries, putting additional pressure on health budgets.

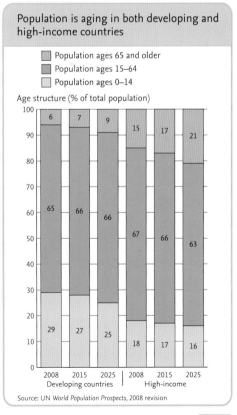

Population is aging in both developing and high-income countries

☐ Population ages 65 and older
☐ Population ages 15–64
☐ Population ages 0–14

Age structure (% of total population)

Developing countries: 2008, 2015, 2025 | High-income: 2008, 2015, 2025

Source: UN *World Population Prospects*, 2008 revision

Population growth

annual average growth rate, 2000–2009

- 3.0% or more
- 2.0–2.9%
- 1.0–1.9%
- 0.0–0.9%
- less than 0.0%
- no data

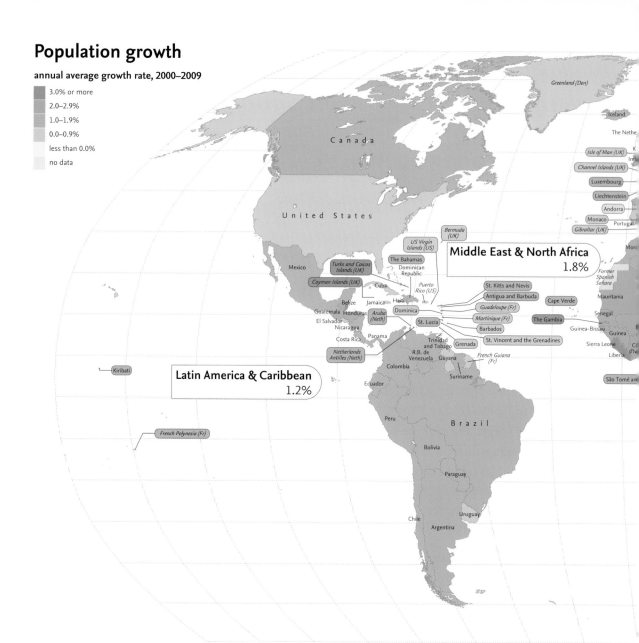

Greenland (Den)

Iceland

The Nethe

Isle of Man (UK)

Irela

Channel Islands (UK)

Luxembourg

Liechtenstein

Andorra

Monaco   Portugal

Gibraltar (UK)

Canada

United States

Mexico

Bermuda (UK)

US Virgin Islands (US)

Middle East & North Africa
1.8%

Mor

Former Spanish Sahara

Turks and Caicos Islands (UK)

The Bahamas

Dominican Republic

Cayman Islands (UK)

Cuba

Puerto Rico (US)

Mauritania

St. Kitts and Nevis

Antigua and Barbuda

Cape Verde

Belize

Jamaica

Haiti

Guadeloupe (Fr)

Senegal

Guatemala Honduras   Aruba (Neth)

Dominica

Martinique (Fr)

The Gambia

El Salvador

Nicaragua

St. Lucia

Barbados

Guinea-Bissau   Guinea

Costa Rica

Panama

Trinidad and Tobago

Grenada

St. Vincent and the Grenadines

Sierra Leone

Co

Netherlands Antilles (Neth)

R.B. de Venezuela

Guyana

French Guiana (Fr)

Liberia   d'Iv

Kiribati

Latin America & Caribbean
1.2%

Colombia

Ecuador

Suriname

São Tomé an

Peru

Brazil

French Polynesia (Fr)

Bolivia

Paraguay

Chile

Uruguay

Argentina

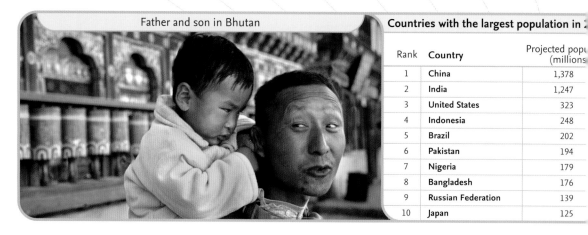

Father and son in Bhutan

Countries with the largest population in 2

Rank	Country	Projected popu (millions
1	China	1,378
2	India	1,247
3	United States	323
4	Indonesia	248
5	Brazil	202
6	Pakistan	194
7	Nigeria	179
8	Bangladesh	176
9	Russian Federation	139
10	Japan	125

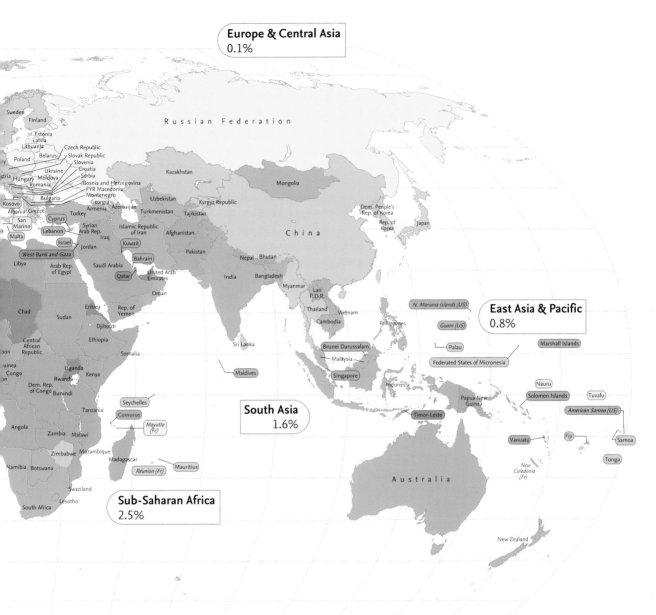

Europe & Central Asia
0.1%

East Asia & Pacific
0.8%

South Asia
1.6%

Sub-Saharan Africa
2.5%

Facts		Internet links	
took human history up to the early 1800s to reach 1 billion people; oday the world gains 1 billion people every 12 to 14 years.		▶ UN Population Information Network	www.un.org/popin
he world's population is expected to reach 9 billion by 2050, with rtually all population growth occurring in developing countries.		▶ UN Population Fund	www.unfpa.org
ub-Saharan Africa will experience the largest proportional increase population, from 13 percent of the world's population today to 0 percent by 2050, while East Asia and Pacific's share, which stands t 30 percent today, is expected to fall to 24 percent by 2050.		▶ Demographic and Health Surveys	www.measuredhs.com
		▶ World Bank HNPStats	data.worldbank.org/data-catalog/health-nutrition-and-population-statistics
7 percent of population growth between 2008 and 2025 will occur in rban areas, the vast majority of them in developing countries.		▶ Population Reference Bureau	www.prb.org
		▶ U.S. Census Bureau	www.census.gov

Life expectancy

life expectancy at birth, 2008

- less than 50 years
- 50–59 years
- 60–69 years
- 70–74 years
- 75 years or more
- no data

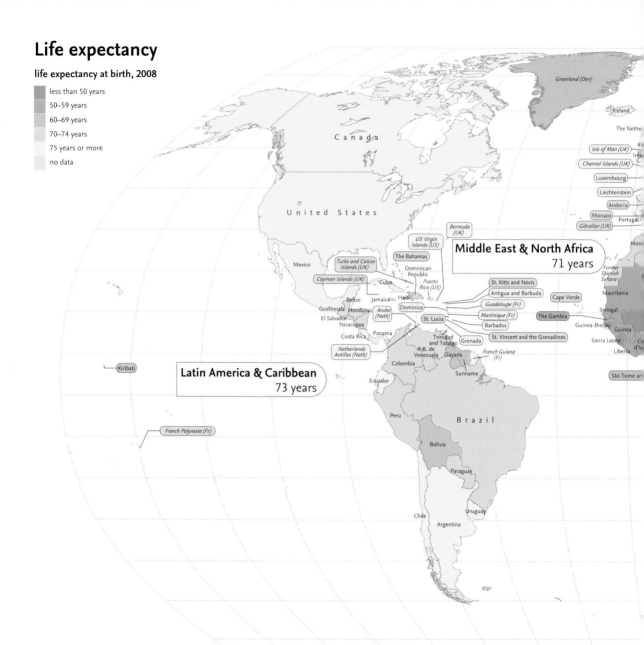

Middle East & North Africa
71 years

Latin America & Caribbean
73 years

A child in Sub-Saharan Africa can only expect to reach, on average, the age of 52

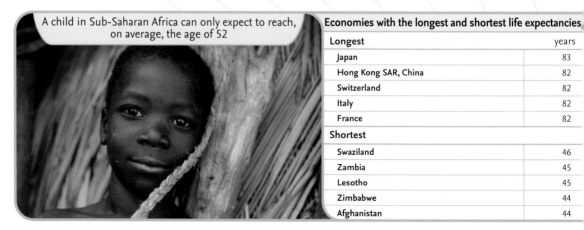

Economies with the longest and shortest life expectancies

Longest	years
Japan	83
Hong Kong SAR, China	82
Switzerland	82
Italy	82
France	82
Shortest	
Swaziland	46
Zambia	45
Lesotho	45
Zimbabwe	44
Afghanistan	44

Europe & Central Asia
69 years

East Asia & Pacific
72 years

South Asia
64 years

Sub-Saharan Africa
52 years

Facts	Internet links	
Life expectancy at birth has reached 80 years in high-income countries, 11 years longer compared with 1960. South Asia and Sub-Saharan Africa have always had the shortest life expectancy. South Asia and Sub-Saharan Africa started at about the same level of life expectancy in 1960, at 43 years and 41 years respectively, but today there is a 12-year gap between South Asia (64 years) and Sub-Saharan Africa (52 years).	▶ UN Population Information Network	**www.un.org/popin**
	▶ UN Population Fund	**www.unfpa.org**
Life expectancy for Zimbabwe and Swaziland is over 15 years shorter today than in 1990, the result of the HIV/AIDS epidemic.	▶ Demographic and Health Surveys	**www.measuredhs.com**
Male life expectancy in Europe and Central Asia was shortened from 65 years to 61 years between 1988 and 1994. Life expectancy started to recover and was back to 65 years in 2008.	▶ World Bank HNPStats	**data.worldbank.org/data-catalog/health-nutrition-and-population-statistics**
	▶ Population Reference Bureau	**www.prb.org**
In 8 countries, 5 of them in Europe and Central Asia, female life expectancy is longer by over 10 years.	▶ U.S. Census Bureau	**www.census.gov**

Across the developing world 215 million children work as child laborers. Some perform simple tasks within the family; others endure long hours in harsh and damaging conditions. Children's work interferes with their education and can affect normal physical and mental development, reducing their prospects for leading healthy and productive lives.

The number of working children ages 5–17 has fallen by 30 million since 2000, down from 11 percent of the world's children to 7 percent. But in Sub-Saharan Africa, where the incidence of child labor is the highest at 25 percent, the number of child laborers increased to 65 million in 2008. Sixty percent of child laborers are found in agriculture, and about 70 percent work for their own families without pay. The number of children in hazardous work has declined by 30 percent since 2000, but there are still 115 million children, more than half of all working children, engaged in hazardous occupations. Exposure to workplace hazards at an early age has consequences for children's immediate safety and long-term health.

A substantial proportion of working children manage to attend school, at least some of the time. But children cannot benefit from their time in the classroom if they are tired or stressed by work or made ill by hazardous conditions at work. And many drop out early to devote more time to work. In the little time available to them, children balancing school and work are unable to fully enjoy their rights to

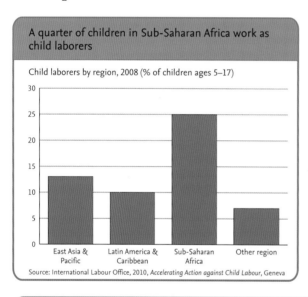

A quarter of children in Sub-Saharan Africa work as child laborers

Child laborers by region, 2008 (% of children ages 5–17)

Source: International Labour Office, 2010, *Accelerating Action against Child Labour*, Geneva

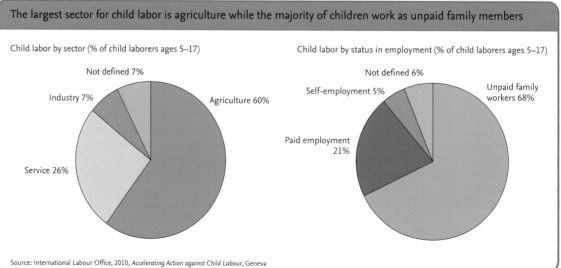

The largest sector for child labor is agriculture while the majority of children work as unpaid family members

Child labor by sector (% of child laborers ages 5–17)

Not defined 7%
Industry 7%
Agriculture 60%
Service 26%

Child labor by status in employment (% of child laborers ages 5–17)

Not defined 6%
Self-employment 5%
Unpaid family workers 68%
Paid employment 21%

Source: International Labour Office, 2010, *Accelerating Action against Child Labour*, Geneva

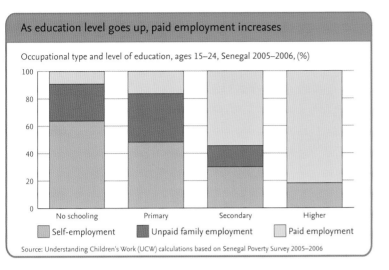

As education level goes up, paid employment increases

Occupational type and level of education, ages 15–24, Senegal 2005–2006, (%)

Legend: Self-employment | Unpaid family employment | Paid employment

Categories: No schooling | Primary | Secondary | Higher

Source: Understanding Children's Work (UCW) calculations based on Senegal Poverty Survey 2005–2006

leisure and rest. Girls are particularly disadvantaged because they often undertake household chores after work.

The effects of child labor extend into adulthood. Lacking adequate education, young people are likely to wind up in low-paid, insecure work, or to be unemployed. They are more likely to be self-employed or in unpaid family work rather than paid employment. They also suffer from lower productivity, stigma, and lower job aspirations.

Child labor is not only a serious violation of the rights of children, it has broader consequences for national development. For too long, child labor has been seen as an isolated issue. Because it cuts across many development issues, including schooling, healthcare, labor market conditions, labor standards and legislation, and social protection, child labor requires action by governments, employers, labor organizations, schools, and by families themselves.

Child carrying bricks in El Salvador

Brazil has rapidly reduced children's employment and raised school attendance

Children's employment rate by age (%), Brazil

Legend: 1992 | 1999 | 2008

Age (years)

Children's school attendance by age (%), Brazil

Legend: 1992 | 1999 | 2008

Age (years)

Source: UCW calculations based on Brazilian Pesquisa Nacional por Amostra de Domicilios (PNAD) surveys, 1992, 1999, and 2008

Child laborers are often exposed to hazardous conditions

Number of children exposed to specific work hazards, thousands, Mali 2005

Categories (top to bottom): Work underground | Insufficient lighting | Radiation | Noisy environment | Exposure to chemicals | Dangerous tools | Excessive hours | Extreme temperatures | Dust, fumes, gas

Axis: 0, 150, 300, 450, 600, 750, 900

Source: UCW calculations based on l'Enquet nationale sur le travail des enfants au Mali 2005

Children at work

economically active children as a share of children
ages 7–14, 1994–2007, most recent year available

- 40% or more
- 25–39%
- 15–24%
- 5–14%
- less than 5%
- no data

Greenland (Den)

Iceland

The Nethe

Isle of Man (UK)

Channel Islands (UK)

Luxembourg

Liechtenstein

Andorra

Monaco   Portugal

Gibraltar (UK)

Canada

United States

Mexico

Bermuda (UK)

British Virgin Islands (UK)

The Bahamas

Dominican Republic

Turks and Caicos Islands (UK)

Cayman Islands (UK)   Cuba

Puerto Rico (US)

US Virgin Islands (US)

St. Kitts and Nevis

Antigua and Barbuda

Guadeloupe (Fr)

Martinique (Fr)

Barbados

St. Lucia

Dominica

Cape Verde

Former Spanish Sahara

Mauritania

Belize

Jamaica

Haiti

Guatemala   Honduras

El Salvador

Nicaragua

Costa Rica

Panama

Aruba (Neth)

Netherlands Antilles (Neth)

Trinidad and Tobago

Grenada

St. Vincent and the Grenadines

R.B. de Venezuela   Guyana

French Guiana (Fr)

Colombia

Suriname

Ecuador

The Gambia   Senegal

Guinea-Bissau   Guinea

Sierra Leone   C

d'I

Liberia

São Tomé an

Kiribati

Latin America & Caribbean
10%

Peru

Brazil

French Polynesia (Fr)

Bolivia

Paraguay

Chile

Uruguay

Argentina

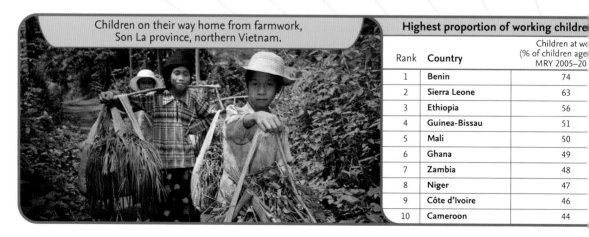

Children on their way home from farmwork,
Son La province, northern Vietnam.

Highest proportion of working childre

Rank	Country	Children at wo (% of children age MRY 2005–20
1	Benin	74
2	Sierra Leone	63
3	Ethiopia	56
4	Guinea-Bissau	51
5	Mali	50
6	Ghana	49
7	Zambia	48
8	Niger	47
9	Côte d'Ivoire	46
10	Cameroon	44

East Asia & Pacific
13%

Sub-Saharan Africa
25%

Facts	Internet links	
In Sub-Saharan Africa, 25 percent of the children work, compared with 10 percent in Latin America and the Caribbean.	▶ Understanding Children's Work Project	www.ucw-project.org
Slightly more boys are engaged in child labor than girls in all regions. But there are wide variations among countries. In Bangladesh, Burkina Faso, and Guatemala, the gender difference is more than 10 percentage points.	▶ UNICEF Childinfo— Child Labor	www.childinfo.org/labour.html
More than half the child laborers work less than 24 hours per week.		
In Mongolia, Zambia, and Uganda, more than 90 percent of children work in the agricultural sector. By contrast, in Mexico and R.B. Venezuela about half the children work in the service sector, and less than 40 percent in the agriculture sector.	▶ International Labour Organization— Child Labor	www.ilo.org/global/Themes/ Child_Labour/lang--en/ index.htm

Since 1990, the world has promised that by 2015 all children would be able to complete a full course of primary education. School enrollment rates are rising, but many children still do not enroll, attend, or complete primary schooling. A good quality education is the foundation of sustainable development and poverty alleviation. Education accelerates improvement in other areas as well.

Progress has been made toward universal primary education since 1990. In 2008, 88 percent of school-age children in the world were enrolled in primary schools. Primary completion rates—the proportion of children completing the last year of primary school—directly measure progress toward this goal. Three regions—East Asia and the Pacific, Europe and Central Asia, and Latin America and the Caribbean—are close to enrolling all their primary-school-age children. But South Asia and Sub-Saharan Africa, with primary completion rates of just 80 and 60 percent, respectively, are in danger of falling short. There are inequalities across and within countries. Children in poor families and those living in rural areas are less likely to enroll and attend school and more likely to drop out earlier. There are many reasons children drop out or never attend school. Schools may be inaccessible or inadequate; teachers may be absent or indifferent, especially in rural areas; parents may not be able to afford school-related costs; or there may be demands for children's labor and their income. Worldwide, some 70 million primary school-age children remained out of school in 2008. About 70 percent of these were in South Asia and Sub-Saharan Africa.

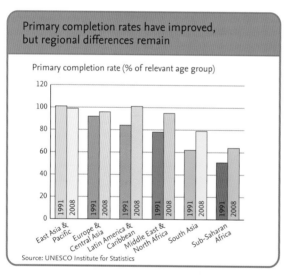

Primary completion rates have improved, but regional differences remain

Primary completion rate (% of relevant age group)

Source: UNESCO Institute for Statistics

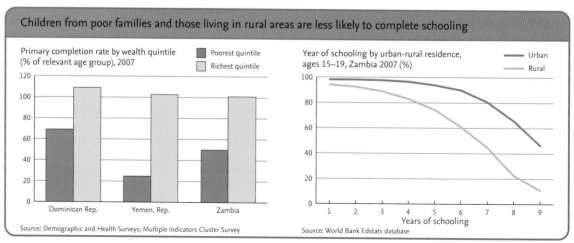

Children from poor families and those living in rural areas are less likely to complete schooling

Primary completion rate by wealth quintile (% of relevant age group), 2007

Poorest quintile
Richest quintile

Source: Demographic and Health Surveys; Multiple Indicators Cluster Survey

Year of schooling by urban-rural residence, ages 15–19, Zambia 2007 (%)

Urban
Rural

Years of schooling

Source: World Bank Edstats database

data.worldbank.org/atlas-global/education
See pp. 6–7 for more information

Community school in Macaci, a suburb of Abidjan—Centre d'Action Communautaire, Côte d'Ivoire

Enrollment is an important measure of school participation, but it does not always indicate successful education. Many students who are enrolled on the first day of school do not actually attend during some or part of the year, or unenrolled children might attend schools during the school year. Hence there is an increased focus on measuring and monitoring school attendance. But attendance alone does not guarantee that children receive quality education, and despite an obvious interest in what education achieves, it is not easy to systematically monitor learning outcomes and achievement. But it is important to go beyond enrollment to understand whether children actually attend and stay in schools, and learn what they are taught.

Beyond primary schooling

To compete in today's knowledge-driven economy and shifting global markets, countries need a flexible, skilled work force, able to create and apply knowledge. This is usually achieved through strong secondary and tertiary education systems. While all regions have made progress in expanding secondary and tertiary enrollments between 1991 and 2008, there are disparities. Europe and Central Asia and Latin America and the Caribbean have enrollment rates of about 90 percent in secondary education. In Sub-Saharan Africa, where primary enrollment is lower than all other regions, the secondary enrollment ratio is even lower, about 35 percent. Only Europe and Central Asia has tertiary enrollment reaching 50 percent.

Enrollment does not always mean attendance

	Primary school net enrollment ratio MRY 2003–2008		Primary school net attendance ratio MRY 2003–2008	
	male	female	male	female
East Asia & Pacific *	98	97	88	88
Europe & Central Asia	92	90	94	92
Latin America & Caribbean	95	95	92	93
Middle East & North Africa	92	88	85	81
South Asia	87	82	83	79
Sub-Saharan Africa	76	70	65	63

* Excludes China

Source: UNICEF, 2010, *State of the World's Children*

Achievements in secondary and tertiary enrollment vary among regions

Gross enrollment ratio, 2008 (% of relevant age group)

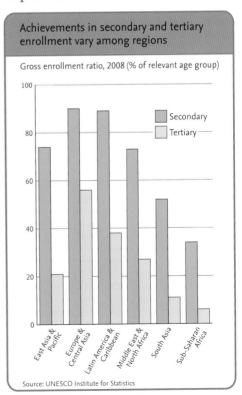

Source: UNESCO Institute for Statistics

Education for all

primary completion rate, 2005–2009, most recent year available

- less than 50%
- 50–69%
- 70–84%
- 85–94%
- 95% or more
- no data

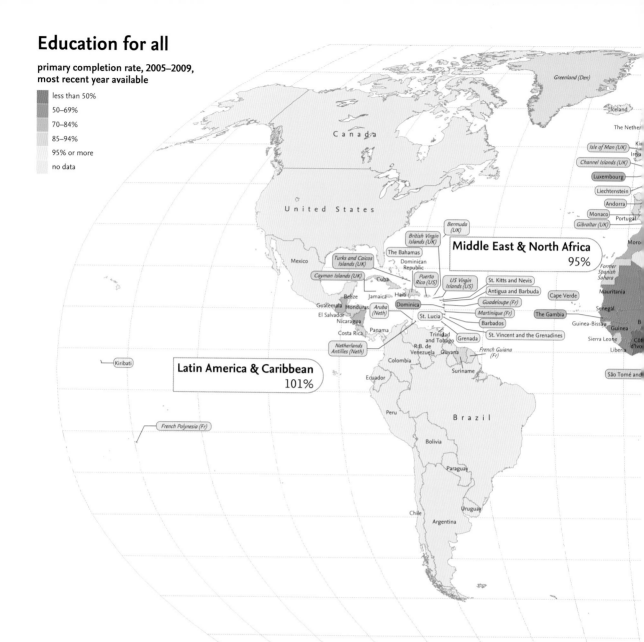

Middle East & North Africa
95%

Latin America & Caribbean
101%

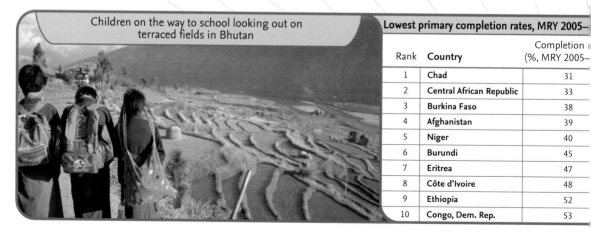

Children on the way to school looking out on terraced fields in Bhutan

Lowest primary completion rates, MRY 2005–

Rank	Country	Completion (%, MRY 2005–
1	Chad	31
2	Central African Republic	33
3	Burkina Faso	38
4	Afghanistan	39
5	Niger	40
6	Burundi	45
7	Eritrea	47
8	Côte d'Ivoire	48
9	Ethiopia	52
10	Congo, Dem. Rep.	53

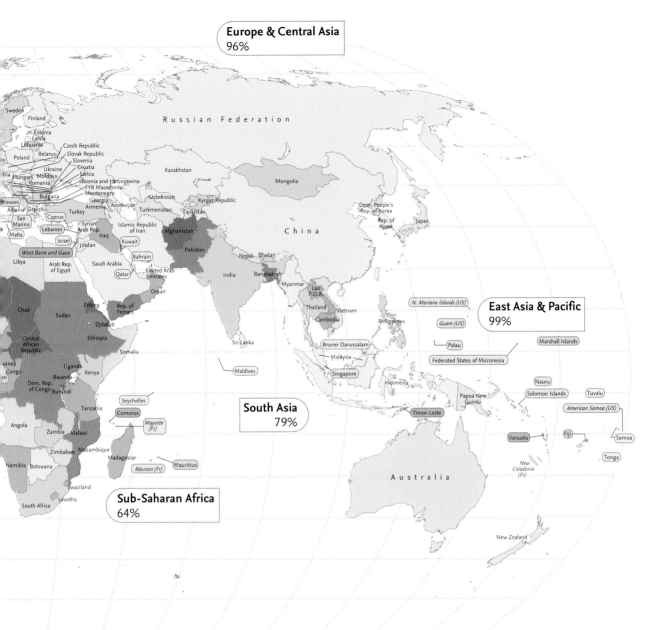

Europe & Central Asia
96%

East Asia & Pacific
99%

South Asia
79%

Sub-Saharan Africa
64%

Facts	Internet links	
here are 70 million children of primary school age who are out of chool. About 50 percent of them are in Sub-Saharan Africa.	► UNESCO	www.unesco.org
	► UNESCO Institute for Statistics	www.uis.unesco.org
atin America and the Caribbean has one of the highest primary et enrollment rates at 94 percent, but also one of the highest ercentage of repeaters at 10 percent—the same level as that of ub-Saharan Africa, which has the lowest net enrollment ratio.	► World Bank Edstats	data.worldbank.org/data-catalog/ed-stats
	► Demographic and Health Surveys	www.measuredhs.com
n the Middle East and North Africa, South Asia, and Sub-Saharan frica, the adult literacy gap between men and women is more han 20 percentage points. The gap is much smaller among young eople ages 15–24, reflecting the recent improvement in education articipation.	► UNICEF Childinfo—Education	www.childinfo.org/education.html
	► UN MDG Indicators	unstats.un.org/unsd/mdg

Empowering women through education and labor market opportunities leads to faster and more equitable development. Women allocate more time than men to household chores such as fetching water and collecting fuel wood, often at the expense of their health and more productive work. Roads, water systems, and other types of infrastructure can reduce the conflict between women's productive and reproductive roles and thus increase their economic empowerment.

Transport and Reproductive Health

Access to appropriate healthcare can have a tremendous impact on maternal mortality rates. Three-quarters of the current maternal deaths could be averted if the full range of services and interventions were provided to all women. These include antenatal care and a skilled attendant during delivery, preferably in a health facility, combined with ready access to other levels of care. When childbirth-related complications occur, there is a need for timely and safe transport of the mother to a healthcare center with the necessary drugs, equipment, and other supplies for effective management of the problem.

Transport plays a critical role in access to services and in the overall effectiveness of the referral process for maternal health. In effect, transport and road infrastructure act as a key link between potential accessibility and actual utilization of health and obstetric services. Transport services are particularly important in sparsely populated rural areas of most developing countries, where health facilities that provide maternal services tend to be widely dispersed. In many countries, women living in rural and remote areas have less easy access to health services than women living close to urban centers. And these distances are aggravated if the quality and efficiency of road infrastructure is poor. The majority of women in Mali and Haiti, for example, live in communities accessible only by seasonal roads, which can become impassable during the rainy season.

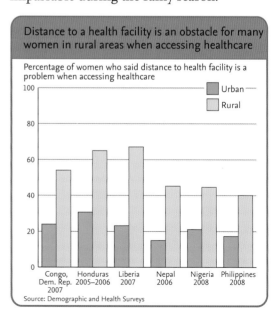

Women in urban areas are more likely to deliver at a health facility than women in rural areas

Births at health facility (% of total)

- Urban
- Rural

Bangladesh 2007 · Kenya 2008–2009 · Philippines 2008

Source: Demographic and Health Surveys

Distance to a health facility is an obstacle for many women in rural areas when accessing healthcare

Percentage of women who said distance to health facility is a problem when accessing healthcare

- Urban
- Rural

Congo, Dem. Rep. 2007 · Honduras 2005–2006 · Liberia 2007 · Nepal 2006 · Nigeria 2008 · Philippines 2008

Source: Demographic and Health Surveys

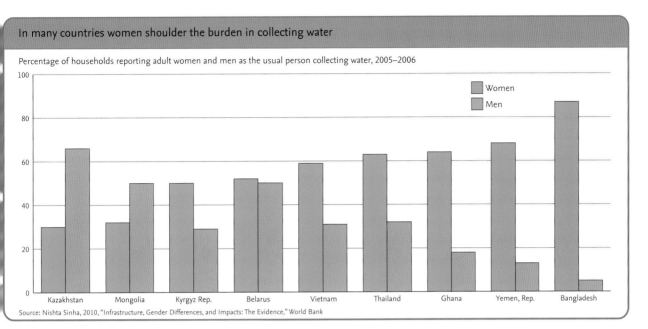

In many countries women shoulder the burden in collecting water

Percentage of households reporting adult women and men as the usual person collecting water, 2005–2006

Source: Nishta Sinha, 2010, "Infrastructure, Gender Differences, and Impacts: The Evidence," World Bank

Water

The availability of safe and adequate quantities of drinking water nearby reduces the physical burden of carrying water and lowers the risk of waterborne infections. In 1990, almost 1 billion people in developing countries lacked convenient access to a safe water source.

Among developing-country households that have to collect water from a source outside their home, the task of fetching water is mostly carried out by women and girls. Recent surveys show that in Bangladesh, Burkina Faso, Malawi, and Nepal, for example, women are the primary water carriers in 85 percent of the households. In most parts of the world women spend more time than men on water collection activities and work longer hours than men. The savings in time and drudgery of collecting water are not only important on their own merit but are also instrumental in increasing women's participation in economic and socially beneficial activities.

While there is considerable evidence of time savings from improved infrastructure in poor households, the "tradeoff" between income-earning activities and household chores may mean increased health risks for women, or using girls' labor to substitute for mothers. Girls' schooling is often jeopardized by mothers using them to collect water and fuel wood. In addition, providing improved and safe water facilities does not necessarily lead to changes in women's practices; for the benefits to be realized, additional institutional support, such as access to credit, to markets for income generating activities, or to education, may be required.

In most parts of the world women spend more time than men on water collection activities

	Time spent on fetching water (minutes per day)	
	Women	Men
Benin (1998)	45	12
South Africa (2000)	8	3
Madagascar (2001)	27	9
Ghana (1998–1999)	41	33
India (2000)	43	30

Source: Nishta Sinha, 2010, "Infrastructure, Gender Differences, and Impacts: The Evidence," World Bank

Gender equity

ratio of girls to boys in primary and secondary
education, 2005–2009, most recent year available

- less than 80%
- 80–89%
- 90–97%
- 98–100%
- 101% or more
- no data

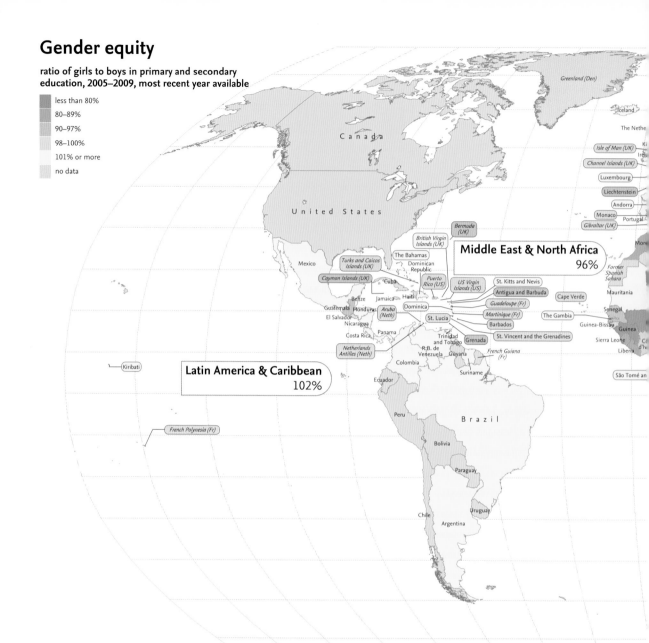

Greenland (Den)

Iceland

The Nethe

Canada

Isle of Man (UK)

Channel Islands (UK)

Luxembourg

Liechtenstein

Andorra

Monaco   Portugal

Gibraltar (UK)

United States

More

Middle East & North Africa
96%

Bermuda
(UK)

British Virgin
Islands (UK)

The Bahamas

Dominican
Republic

Mexico

Former
Spanish
Sahara

Turks and Caicos
Islands (UK)

Cayman Islands (UK)

Puerto
Rico (US)

US Virgin
Islands (US)

St. Kitts and Nevis

Cape Verde

Mauritania

Cuba

Antigua and Barbuda

Belize   Jamaica   Haiti

Guadeloupe (Fr)

Senegal

Guatemala Honduras   Aruba
(Neth)

Dominica

Martinique (Fr)

The Gambia

El Salvador

St. Lucia

Barbados

Guinea-Bissau   Guinea

Nicaragua

Costa Rica   Panama

Trinidad
and Tobago   Grenada

St. Vincent and the Grenadines

Sierra Leone

C
d'Iv

Netherlands
Antilles (Neth)

R.B. de
Venezuela   Guyana

French Guiana
(Fr)

Liberia

Kiribati

Latin America & Caribbean
102%

Colombia

Suriname

São Tomé an

Ecuador

Peru

B r a z i l

French Polynesia (Fr)

Bolivia

Paraguay

Chile

Uruguay

Argentina

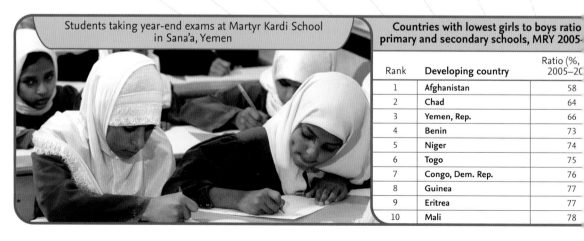

Students taking year-end exams at Martyr Kardi School in Sana'a, Yemen

Countries with lowest girls to boys ratio primary and secondary schools, MRY 2005–

Rank	Developing country	Ratio (%, 2005–20
1	Afghanistan	58
2	Chad	64
3	Yemen, Rep.	66
4	Benin	73
5	Niger	74
6	Togo	75
7	Congo, Dem. Rep.	76
8	Guinea	77
9	Eritrea	77
10	Mali	78

Europe & Central Asia
97%

East Asia & Pacific
102%

South Asia
91%

Sub-Saharan Africa
88%

Facts	Internet links	
In 2008, 64 percent of 800 million people who were illiterate were women—a share that has remained unchanged since 1990.	► World Bank Genderstats	**www.worldbank.org/genderstats**
In 2008, there were 96 girls for every 100 boys enrolled in primary school in developing countries compared with 87 girls per 100 boys in 1991. Despite this progress, schools are still out of reach for many girls. In Afghanistan and Somalia, less than 70 girls per 100 boys were in primary school.	► UNESCO Institute for Statistics	**www.uis.unesco.org**
	► UNICEF Childinfo— Education	**www.childinfo.org/education.html**
In Sub-Saharan Africa, where secondary enrollment rates are the lowest, the median ratio of girl's to boy's enrollment rates is 81 percent.	► UN Development Fund for Women	**www.unifem.org**
Women's political participation remains low in both developed and developing countries. Only 19 percent of parliament seats were occupied by women globally in 2009.	► Inter-Parliamentary Union	**www.ipu.org**

Women in employment

share of women in total employment, 2008

- less than 25%
- 25–34%
- 35–39%
- 40–44%
- 45% or more
- no data

Middle East & North Africa
25%

Latin America & Caribbean
40%

Maputo-Fapel, paper mill and paper recycling factory;
women working in the recycling section

Economies with lowest share of female employment

Rank	Economy	Share of wo (%, 200
1	Qatar	10
2	United Arab Emirates	14
3	Saudi Arabia	15
4	Iraq	17
5	Jordan	17
6	Oman	18
7	Pakistan	19
8	West Bank and Gaza	19
9	Syrian Arab Republic	19
10	Afghanistan	22

Europe & Central Asia
44%

East Asia & Pacific
45%

South Asia
29%

Sub-Saharan Africa
42%

Facts	Internet links	
Women are more likely than men to be vulnerable workers—that is, less likely to have social protection and safety nets to guard against economic shocks. In developing countries, 65 percent of women were in vulnerable jobs compared with 57 percent for men.	► World Bank Genderstats	www.worldbank.org/genderstats
Only 26 percent of women in the Middle East and North Africa were in the labor force—the lowest among all the regions. More than half of the employed women in this region were vulnerable workers.	► UN Development Fund for Women	www.unifem.org
	► Inter-Parliamentary Union	www.ipu.org
Women's share in nonagricultural paid employment has risen slowly since 1990. It remains below 20 percent in the Middle East and North Africa and in South Asia.	► OECD Wikigender	www.wikigender.org

In 2008, 9 million children died before their fifth birthday. Of these, the vast majority died from causes that are preventable through a combination of good care, nutrition, and simple medical treatment. Child mortality is closely linked to poverty, and poor children are twice as likely to die before their fifth birthday compared with children from rich families.

Child mortality has improved in every region since 1970, when one in six children died before the age of 5. By 2008, this rate had fallen to 1 in 14 children. Latin America and the Caribbean and the Middle East and North Africa made the greatest progress: child mortality in 2008 was less than one-fifth the level of 1970. Much of the decline in these two regions in recent years was fueled by improvements among the poorest segments of the population. Improved healthcare and public health measures such as immunization, use of insecticide-treated bednets for malaria prevention, prevention of mother-child HIV transmission, and increased access to

antiretroviral drugs, safe drinking water, and sanitation have all contributed to this decline.

Child mortality is increasingly concentrated in Sub-Saharan Africa and South Asia, where under-5 mortality rates are 144 and 76 per 1,000, respectively. In high-income countries the mortality rate is less than one-tenth that. Half of all child deaths occurred in only five countries—India, Nigeria, Democratic Republic of the Congo, Pakistan, and China. India and Nigeria together account for nearly one-third of the total number of under-5 deaths worldwide. Under-5 mortality is higher among children living in rural areas and in poorer households. These children are less likely to have access to good-quality healthcare or to avail themselves of these services.

Good childcare practices, such as early and exclusive breastfeeding, and low-cost treatment and interventions, such as antibiotics for respiratory infections, oral rehydration for diarrhea, immunization, and the use of treated bednets and appropriate drugs in malarial regions, can prevent many unnecessary deaths. However, only 16 percent of children sleep under treated bednets in Sub-Saharan Africa, where 90 percent of malaria deaths occur.

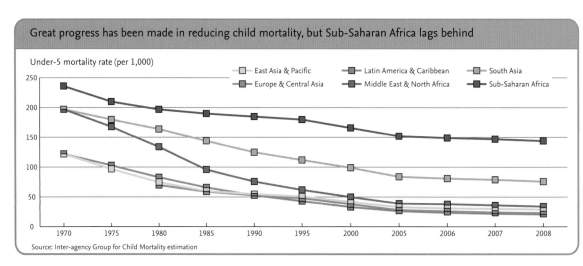

Great progress has been made in reducing child mortality, but Sub-Saharan Africa lags behind

Under-5 mortality rate (per 1,000)

Source: Inter-agency Group for Child Mortality estimation

Children of a slum-dwelling family have a high risk of dying before the age of 5

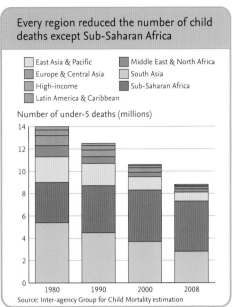

Every region reduced the number of child deaths except Sub-Saharan Africa

- East Asia & Pacific
- Europe & Central Asia
- High-income
- Latin America & Caribbean
- Middle East & North Africa
- South Asia
- Sub-Saharan Africa

Number of under-5 deaths (millions)

Source: Inter-agency Group for Child Mortality estimation

About 40 percent of children with respiratory infections are not taken to health providers and 20 percent of children in developing countries lack immunization against measles. Improved public services, such as safe water and sanitation and education, especially for girls and mothers, can help save children's lives. Greater effort is needed to make sure the services reach poor families and people in rural areas because they suffer the most and are the hardest to reach.

Nutrition and child mortality

Malnutrition is implicated in one-third of all child deaths worldwide. Malnutrition weakens children's immune systems and reduces resistance to diseases. The process often begins at birth, when poorly nourished mothers give birth to underweight babies. Improper feeding and childcare practices contribute to worsen malnutrition. In South Asia and Sub-Saharan Africa, over 40 percent of children under 5 are stunted, or too short for their age, as a result of chronic malnutrition. Breast milk alone is the ideal nourishment for infants for the first six months, providing all of the nutrients as well as antibodies that help to prevent disease. However, exclusive breastfeeding is often stopped in favor of commercial breast milk substitutes or early introduction of solid or soft foods. Less than 40 percent of infants under six months in developing countries enjoy the benefit of exclusive breastfeeding.

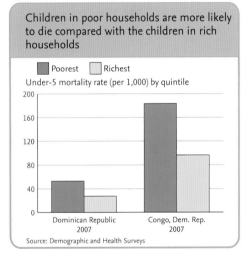

Children in poor households are more likely to die compared with the children in rich households

- Poorest
- Richest

Under-5 mortality rate (per 1,000) by quintile

Source: Demographic and Health Surveys

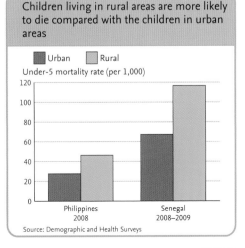

Children living in rural areas are more likely to die compared with the children in urban areas

- Urban
- Rural

Under-5 mortality rate (per 1,000)

Source: Demographic and Health Surveys

Child mortality

under-5 mortality rate per 1,000, 2008

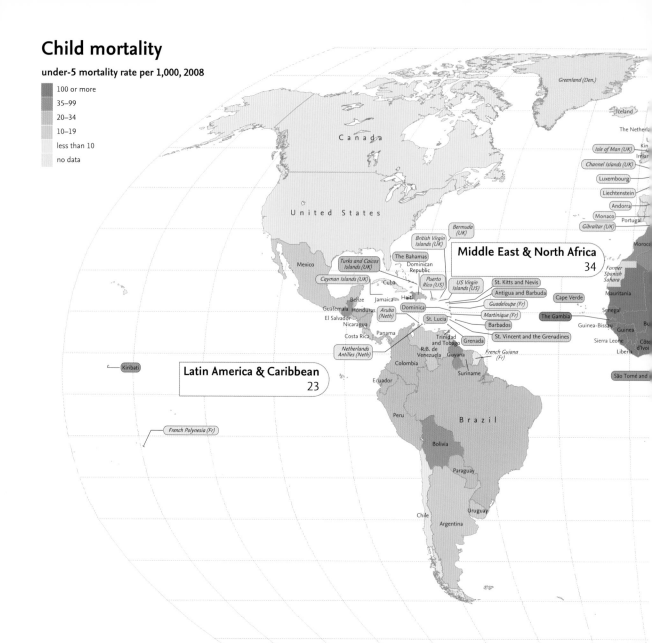

- 100 or more
- 35–99
- 20–34
- 10–19
- less than 10
- no data

Greenland (Den.)

Iceland

The Netherla

Canada

Isle of Man (UK)
Channel Islands (UK)
Luxembourg
Liechtenstein
Andorra
Monaco — Portugal
Gibraltar (UK)

United States

Moroc

Former
Spanish
Sahara

Mauritania

Middle East & North Africa
34

Bermuda (UK)

British Virgin
Islands (UK)

The Bahamas
Dominican
Republic

Mexico

Turks and Caicos
Islands (UK)

Cayman Islands (UK)

Cuba

Puerto
Rico (US)

US Virgin
Islands (US)

St. Kitts and Nevis
Antigua and Barbuda

Cape Verde

Jamaica

Haiti

Dominica

Guadeloupe (Fr)

Senegal

Belize
Guatemala
El Salvador

Honduras
Nicaragua

Aruba
(Neth)

Martinique (Fr)

The Gambia

Guinea-Bissau Guinea

Costa Rica

Panama

Barbados

St. Lucia

St. Vincent and the Grenadines

Sierra Leone

Bu

Côte
d'Ivoi

Netherlands
Antilles (Neth)

Trinidad
and Tobago
R.B. de
Venezuela

Grenada

Liberia

Colombia

Guyana

French Guiana
(Fr)

Kiribati

Latin America & Caribbean
23

Ecuador

Suriname

São Tomé and

Peru

B r a z i l

French Polynesia (Fr)

Bolivia

Chile

Paraguay

Argentina

Uruguay

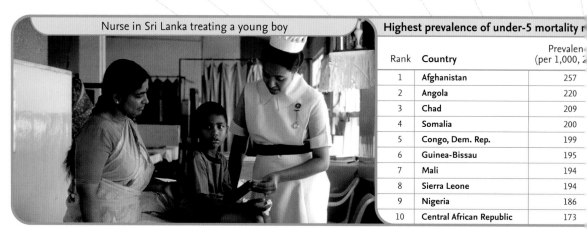

Nurse in Sri Lanka treating a young boy

Highest prevalence of under-5 mortality r

Rank	Country	Prevalen (per 1,000, 2
1	Afghanistan	257
2	Angola	220
3	Chad	209
4	Somalia	200
5	Congo, Dem. Rep.	199
6	Guinea-Bissau	195
7	Mali	194
8	Sierra Leone	194
9	Nigeria	186
10	Central African Republic	173

Europe & Central Asia
22

East Asia & Pacific
29

South Asia
76

Sub-Saharan Africa
144

Facts	Internet links	
.8 million children a year die before their fifth birthday, more than 0 percent of them during their first four weeks of life. At least vo-thirds of all child deaths are preventable.	▶ UNICEF Childinfo— Child Mortality	www.childinfo.org/ mortality.html
ubstantial progress has been made toward reducing child mortality. n 2008, 10,000 fewer children under age 5 died every day compared rith 1990, and the rate of decline in under-5 mortality increased etween 2000 and 2008.	▶ World Health Organization— Child and Adolescent Health and Development	www.who.int/child_adolescent_ health/data/child/en
	▶ World Bank HNPstats	data.worldbank.org/data-catalog/health-nutrition-and-population-statistics
our diseases—pneumonia, diarrhea, malaria, and AIDS—accounted or 43 percent of all deaths in children under 5 worldwide in 2008.	▶ Demographic and Health Surveys	www.measuredhs.com
	▶ UN MDG	unstats.un.org/unsd/mdg
hild deaths have decreased since 1990 in all regions except Sub-Saharan frica, where they increased from 4.2 million to 4.5 million by 2008.	▶ Inter-agency Group for Child Mortality Estimation	www.who.int/child_adolescent_ health/data/child/en

Malnourished children

proportion of children under 5
who are underweight, 2000–2008,
most recent year available

- 30% or more
- 20–29%
- 10–19%
- 5–9%
- less than 5%
- no data

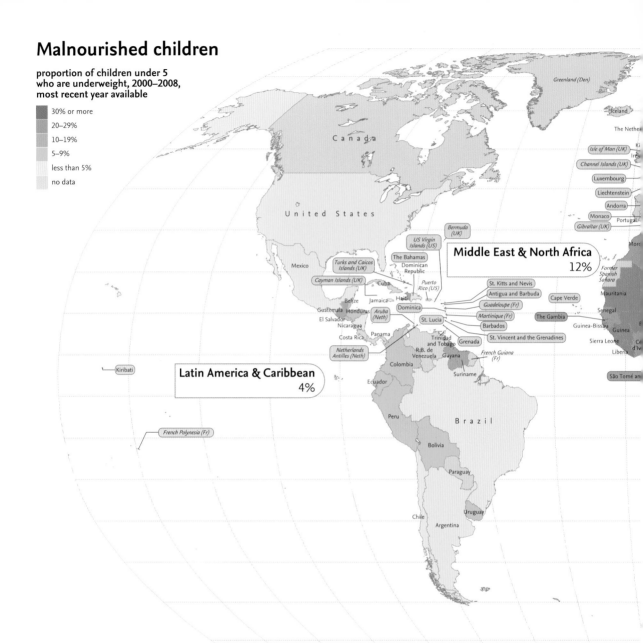

Middle East & North Africa
12%

Latin America & Caribbean
4%

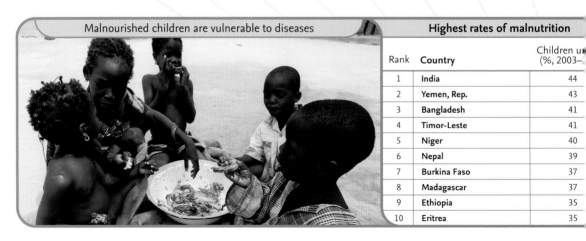

Malnourished children are vulnerable to diseases

Highest rates of malnutrition

Rank	Country	Children u█ (%, 2003–█)
1	India	44
2	Yemen, Rep.	43
3	Bangladesh	41
4	Timor-Leste	41
5	Niger	40
6	Nepal	39
7	Burkina Faso	37
8	Madagascar	37
9	Ethiopia	35
10	Eritrea	35

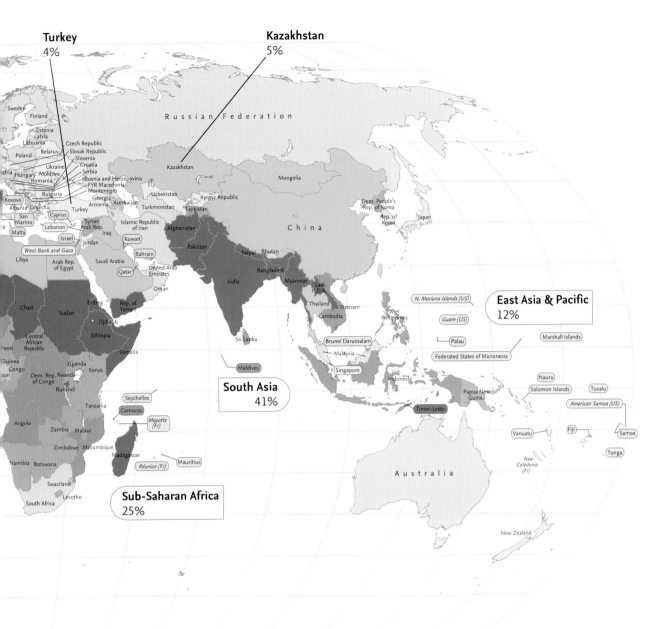

Turkey
4%

Kazakhstan
5%

Sweden
Finland
Estonia
Latvia
Lithuania
Czech Republic
Slovak Republic
Slovenia
Poland
Belarus
Croatia
Ukraine
Moldova
Hungary
Romania
Bosnia and Herzegovina
FYR Macedonia
Montenegro
Georgia
Serbia
Bulgaria
Kosovo
Greece
Albania
Armenia
Azerbaijan
Cyprus
Turkey
San Marino
Syrian Arab Rep.
Lebanon
Malta
Israel
Jordan
Iraq
West Bank and Gaza
Kuwait
Bahrain
Libya
Arab Rep. of Egypt
Saudi Arabia
Qatar
United Arab Emirates
Oman

Russian Federation

Kazakhstan

Mongolia

Uzbekistan
Kyrgyz Republic
Turkmenistan
Tajikistan
Islamic Republic of Iran
Afghanistan
Pakistan

China

Dem. People's Rep. of Korea
Rep. of Korea
Japan

Nepal
Bhutan
India
Bangladesh
Myanmar
Lao P.D.R.
Thailand
Vietnam
Cambodia
Sri Lanka

East Asia & Pacific
12%

N. Mariana Islands (US)
Guam (US)
Palau
Marshall Islands
Federated States of Micronesia

Maldives

Brunei Darussalam
Malaysia
Singapore
Philippines

South Asia
41%

Indonesia

Nauru
Solomon Islands
Tuvalu

Papua New Guinea

American Samoa (US)

Chad
Sudan
Eritrea
Rep. of Yemen
Djibouti
Ethiopia
Somalia
Central African Republic
Uganda
Kenya
Congo
Guinea
Dem. Rep. of Congo
Rwanda
Burundi
Tanzania

Seychelles
Comoros
Mayotte (Fr)

Timor-Leste

Vanuatu
Fiji
Samoa
Tonga

New Caledonia (Fr)

Angola
Zambia
Malawi
Zimbabwe
Mozambique
Namibia
Botswana
Madagascar
Réunion (Fr)
Mauritius

Australia

Swaziland
South Africa
Lesotho

Sub-Saharan Africa
25%

New Zealand

Facts	Internet links	
Malnutrition is an underlying cause for one-third of all child deaths worldwide.	► WHO Global Database on Child Growth and Nutrition	**www.who.int/nutgrowthdb/en**
One-quarter of children under 5 (about 130 million) in developing countries are underweight. Ten percent of them are severely underweight.	► UNICEF Childinfo—Undernutrition	**www.childinfo.org/ undernutrition.html**
South Asia has the highest prevalence of underweight children, with more than 40 percent of children under 5 underweight. In contrast, Latin America and the Caribbean has the lowest prevalence of underweight children at 4 percent.	► UNICEF Health Statistics	**www.unicef.org/health/index_ statistics.html**
Children in rural areas are nearly twice as likely to be underweight as those in urban areas, and poor children are more than twice as likely to be underweight as rich children.	► FAO Food Security Statistics	**www.fao.org/faostat/ foodsecurity**

Having a baby is a happy event. But for many mothers, it is also life-threatening. More than 350,000 women die each year from pregnancy-related causes, although most of them are avoidable with access to healthcare and prompt medical procedures. Ninety-nine percent of all maternal deaths occur in developing countries, the majority in poor countries in Sub-Saharan Africa and South Asia.

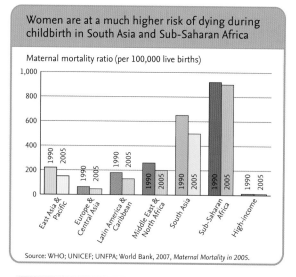

Women are at a much higher risk of dying during childbirth in South Asia and Sub-Saharan Africa

Maternal mortality ratio (per 100,000 live births)

Source: WHO; UNICEF; UNFPA; World Bank, 2007, *Maternal Mortality in 2005.*

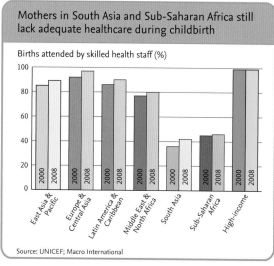

Mothers in South Asia and Sub-Saharan Africa still lack adequate healthcare during childbirth

Births attended by skilled health staff (%)

Source: UNICEF; Macro International

data.worldbank.org/atlas-global/mothers
See pp. 6–7 for more information

The risk of maternal death is often seeded early in a poor childhood. When malnourished girls become mothers, they are more vulnerable to complications or death during delivery. These mothers often do not have adequate access to healthcare before, during, and after pregnancy, resulting in untreated complications and higher risk of death. Three-quarters of all maternal deaths occur during and immediately after delivery. Care by skilled health staff is crucial for handling normal deliveries safely, recognizing the onset of complications, and referring the mother for emergency care as needed. Less than half of births were attended by skilled health staff in South Asia and Sub-Saharan Africa, compared to 99 percent in high-income countries.

Prenatal care during pregnancy presents important opportunities to provide pregnant women with interventions that may be vital to their health and wellbeing and that of their infants. Eighty-two percent of pregnant women had at least one prenatal visit in developing countries. But in any country poor women are much less likely to receive care by skilled health staff.

A mother's death is not just a human tragedy but also an economic and social catastrophe for the family. Her children lose an opportunity of mother's nurture and too often the chance of education, leading the family even further into poverty. Maternal deaths are both caused by poverty and a cause of it.

Compounding the risks of poor reproductive healthcare are poorly timed and inadequately spaced births, which expose women to frequent pregnancies in short intervals. Although cheap and easy methods of preventing unwanted pregnancies are available, every year more than 100 million couples, or 17 percent of married women, wanting to avoid pregnancy do not use contraception. As a result, 40 percent of pregnancies are unintended, and a quarter of pregnant women seek abortions; over a third of these abortions are performed by untrained providers and 70,000 women die every year because of them. Contraceptive use among women in developing countries has risen, from less than 10 percent in 1960 to 61 percent in 2008. But there is much variation. In Sub-Saharan Africa, only about 23 percent of women plan their pregnancies.

Teenage pregnancies are high risk for both mother and child. They are more likely to result in premature delivery, low birthweight, delivery complications, and death. About 14 million girls ages 15–19 give birth each year, accounting for more than 10 percent of all births. In addition to the risk of death during pregnancy and childbirth, which is twice as high as for older pregnant women, adolescent mothers often give up opportunities for education and future employment and earnings.

In the long run, promoting girls' and women's education and offering them opportunities for success are just as important in reducing birth rates as promoting contraception and family planning. Education and greater gender equity

become a form of social contraception for women. A woman's education provides knowledge and skills to improve the nutritional and health status of the family and build job skills that allow her to join the workforce and marry later in life, and gives her the power to say how many children she wants and when. These are enduring qualities she will hand down to her daughters as well.

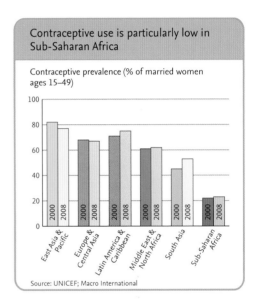

Contraceptive use is particularly low in Sub-Saharan Africa

Contraceptive prevalence (% of married women ages 15–49)

Source: UNICEF; Macro International

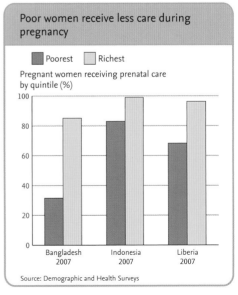

Poor women receive less care during pregnancy

Pregnant women receiving prenatal care by quintile (%)

Source: Demographic and Health Surveys

Adolescent fertility rate is decreasing everywhere, but with large variation among regions

Adolescent fertility rate (births per 1,000 women ages 15–19)

Source: UN *World Population Prospects*, 2008

Total fertility rate

births per woman, 2008

- 5.0 or more
- 3.5–4.9
- 2.2–3.4
- 1.5–2.1
- less than 1.5
- no data

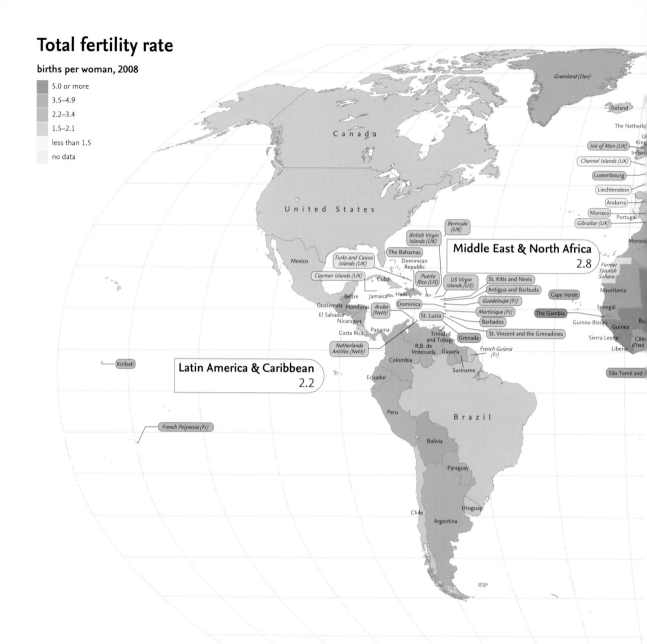

Greenland (Den)

Iceland

The Netherl...

Canada

Isle of Man (UK)

Channel Islands (UK)

United States

Luxembourg

Liechtenstein

Andorra

Monaco Portugal

Gibraltar (UK)

Moroc...

Bermuda (UK)

British Virgin Islands (UK)

Middle East & North Africa
2.8

Former Spanish Sahara

The Bahamas

Mexico

Turks and Caicos Islands (UK)

Dominican Republic

Mauritania

Cayman Islands (UK)

Cuba

Puerto Rico (US)

US Virgin Islands (US)

St. Kitts and Nevis

Cape Verde

Senegal

Haiti

Antigua and Barbuda

Belize

Jamaica

Dominica

Guadeloupe (Fr)

The Gambia

Guatemala

Honduras

Aruba (Neth)

Martinique (Fr)

Guinea-Bissau Guinea

El Salvador

St. Lucia

Barbados

Nicaragua

Sierra Leone Côte d'Ivoi...

Costa Rica

Panama

Trinidad and Tobago

Grenada

St. Vincent and the Grenadines

Liberia

Netherlands Antilles (Neth)

R.B. de Venezuela

Guyana

French Guiana (Fr)

Kiribati

Colombia

Latin America & Caribbean
2.2

Ecuador

Suriname

São Tomé and...

Peru

B r a z i l

French Polynesia (Fr)

Bolivia

Paraguay

Chile

Uruguay

Argentina

Women's education and gender equality has helped reduce total fertility in South Asia

Countries with low levels of contraceptive use, 2005–2008

Rank	Country	Contraceptive us... (% of married wor... 15–49, 2005–2008
1	Sudan	8
2	Mali	8
3	Sierra Leone	8
4	Burundi	9
5	Guinea	9
6	Mauritania	9
7	Guinea-Bissau	10
8	Niger	11
9	Liberia	11
10	Senegal	12

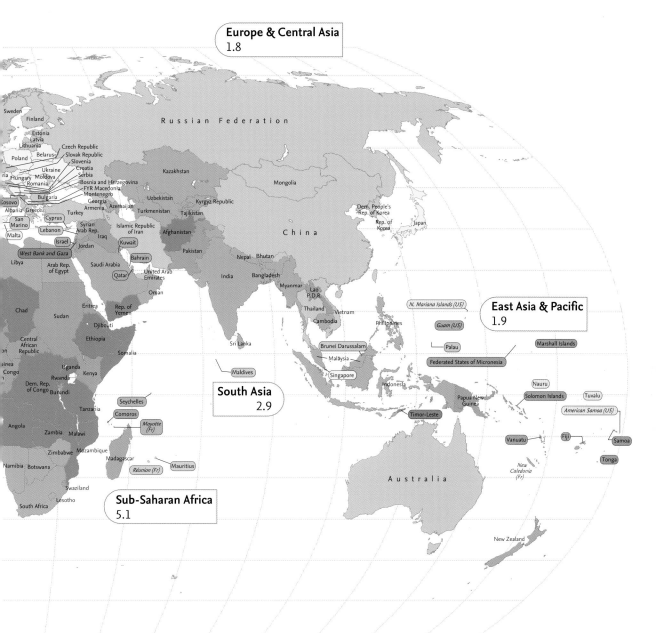

Europe & Central Asia
1.8

East Asia & Pacific
1.9

South Asia
2.9

Sub-Saharan Africa
5.1

Facts	Internet links	
alf a million women die each year because of pregnancy-related uses. For every woman who dies, at least 20 others suffer injuries, fection, and disability. Almost all maternal deaths are preventable.	► UNICEF—Maternal and Newborn Health	www.unicef.org/health/index_maternalhealth.html
	► UNICEF Childinfo—Maternal Health	www.childinfo.org/health.html
ıb-Saharan Africa and South Asia, which bear the greatest burden maternal mortality, also have the lowest levels of skilled birth tendance, at 46 percent and 42 percent respectively.	► World Health Organization—Maternal Health	www.who.int/topics/maternal_health/en
ghty percent of women in the developing world receive antenatal re from a skilled health provider at least once during pregnancy. ıt less than half of all pregnant women benefit from four ıtenatal visits.	► World Bank HNPstats	data.worldbank.org/data-catalog/health-nutrition-and-population-statistics
	► Inter-agency Group on Safe Motherhood	www.safemotherhood.org
50 million abortions performed every year, about 18 million are ısafe. Seventy thousand of them result in death.	► UN MDG Indicators	unstats.un.org/unsd/mdg

Communicable diseases such as HIV/AIDS, tuberculosis, and malaria kill millions of people each year. They exact a terrible toll on society and the economies of developing countries. Although international awareness and funding to fight epidemic diseases have increased, much remains to be done.

Every day, over 7,400 people are infected with HIV, and more than 5,500 die from AIDS. The number of people living with HIV reached 33.4 million in 2008, even though the global spread of HIV appeared to have leveled off in the mid-1990s. The number continues to rise because better care and antiretroviral therapy, which suppresses the HIV virus and stops the progression of HIV to AIDS, have kept more people alive for longer. Antiretroviral therapy expanded by a factor of 10 over the past five years. In 2008, 4 million people in developing countries received antiretroviral therapy.

Almost 70 percent of people living with HIV are in Sub-Saharan Africa, where women and children are especially vulnerable to the disease. Women constitute 60 percent of adults ages 15 to 49 living with HIV, and 86 percent of all HIV-positive children live in the region. Infants are often at high risk of infection through mother-to-child transmission.

Tuberculosis, still a major cause of illness and death worldwide, is becoming more dangerous with the spread of drug-resistant strains. Fifteen countries with the highest tuberculosis incidence rates are located in Asia and Africa. Together they account for 85 percent of all tuberculosis cases. Poor people are especially vulnerable to the disease due to underlying health problems and limited access to treatment. Tuberculosis is the leading cause of death among people who are HIV-positive, accounting for up to half of all AIDS deaths worldwide. Drug-resistant tuberculosis strains are caused by inconsistent or partial treatment, wrong treatment regimens, or unavailability of drugs.

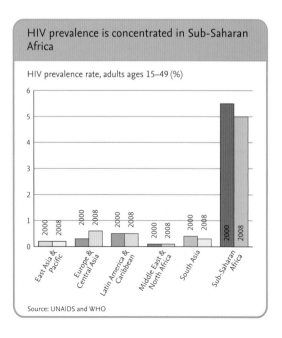

HIV prevalence is concentrated in Sub-Saharan Africa

HIV prevalence rate, adults ages 15–49 (%)

Source: UNAIDS and WHO

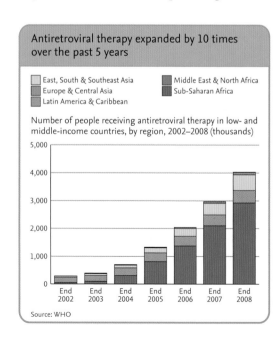

Antiretroviral therapy expanded by 10 times over the past 5 years

Number of people receiving antiretroviral therapy in low- and middle-income countries, by region, 2002–2008 (thousands)

Source: WHO

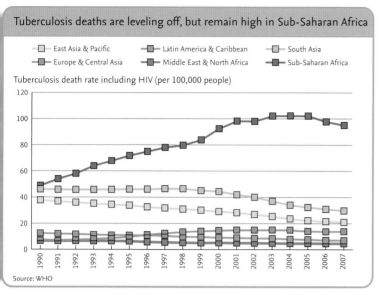

Tuberculosis deaths are leveling off, but remain high in Sub-Saharan Africa

- East Asia & Pacific
- Europe & Central Asia
- Latin America & Caribbean
- Middle East & North Africa
- South Asia
- Sub-Saharan Africa

Tuberculosis death rate including HIV (per 100,000 people)

Source: WHO

Malaria causes nearly 1 million deaths each year, primarily among children below age 5 and pregnant women. Ninety percent of all malaria deaths occur in Sub-Saharan Africa. Insecticide-treated nets are one of the most effective ways to prevent malaria transmission as these nets provide a physical barrier against the bite of an infected mosquito. In addition, a net treated with insecticide provides additional protection by repelling or killing mosquitoes that rest on the net—an important protective effect that extends beyond the individual to the community. The use of treated bednets among children in Sub-Saharan Africa has increased rapidly, from 2 percent in 2000 to 16 percent in 2008, although it is still too low to cover everybody who is at risk. In addition to the use of treated bednets, malaria control depends on surveillance, efficient public health measures, education, and access to medications.

Increase in non-communicable diseases

Urbanization, aging populations, and a globalized lifestyle combine to make chronic and non-communicable diseases, such as diabetes, cancer, cardiovascular diseases, and injuries, increasingly important causes of mortality and morbidity in developing countries. The increase in non-communicable diseases, accompanied by a shift in the distribution of death and disease from younger to older people as the population ages, will affect service delivery and the allocation of health budgets. The rise of chronic, non-communicable diseases

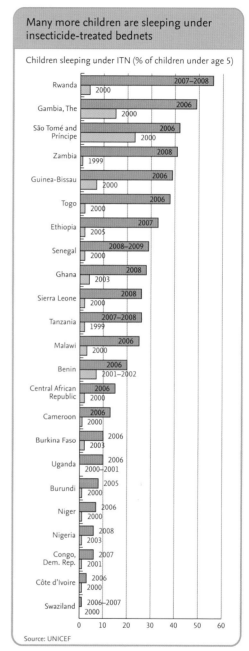

Many more children are sleeping under insecticide-treated bednets

Children sleeping under ITN (% of children under age 5)

Source: UNICEF

comes on top of an unfinished agenda on communicable diseases. This shift of epidemiological burden of diseases will result in many developing countries, especially low-income countries, struggling to allocate their health budgets among old and new priorities.

HIV/AIDS

adult HIV prevalence, 2007

- ■ 15.0% or more
- ■ 5.0–14.9%
- ■ 1.0–4.9%
- ■ 0.5–0.9%
- ■ less than 0.5%
- ■ no data

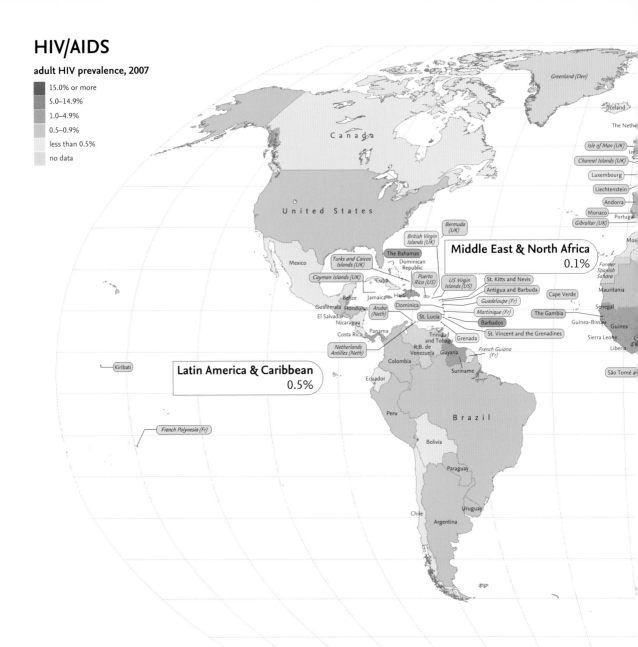

Middle East & North Africa
0.1%

Latin America & Caribbean
0.5%

Campaign to fight HIV/AIDS in Cape Town, South Africa

Rank	Country	Prevalence (% of popu ages 15–
1	Swaziland	26.1
2	Botswana	23.9
3	Lesotho	23.2
4	South Africa	18.1
5	Namibia	15.3
6	Zimbabwe	15.3
7	Zambia	15.2
8	Mozambique	12.5
9	Malawi	11.9
10	Kenya	7.8

Countries with the highest prevalence rates

Europe & Central Asia
0.6%

East Asia & Pacific
0.2%

South Asia
0.3%

Sub-Saharan Africa
5.0%

Facts	Internet links	
3.4 million people were living with HIV in 2008; 2.1 million of them were children under 15 years, and 16 million were women. Every day, over 7,400 persons become infected with HIV and about ,500 persons die from AIDS.	▶ World Health Organization on Tuberculosis, Malaria, and HIV/AIDS	www.who.int/topics/tuberculosis www.who.int/topics/malaria www.who.int/topics/hiv_aids
lmost 90 percent of children living with HIV are in Sub-Saharan Africa.	▶ UNAIDS	www.unaids.org
0 percent of all malaria deaths currently occur in Sub-Saharan Africa, nd most of these deaths are among children under 5.	▶ World Bank HNPstats	data.worldbank.org/data-catalog/health-nutrition-and-population-statistics
One-third of the world's total population has latent tuberculosis nfections. One in every 10 of those people will become sick with ctive TB in his or her lifetime.	▶ UNICEF Childinfo on Malaria and HIV/AIDS	www.childinfo.org/malaria.html www.childinfo.org/hiv_aids.html
Chronic and non-communicable diseases such as heart disease nd stroke, cancer, and diabetes are increasing due to aging and nhealthy lifestyle including, unhealthy food, lack of exercise, and moking, and account for 60 percent of all deaths.	▶ UNICEF on Malaria and HIV/AIDS	www.unicef.org/health/index_malaria.html www.unicef.org/aids/index_documents.html

Services, the most rapidly growing sector of the global economy, now account for almost 70 percent of world output. Developing economies are becoming important producers of manufactured goods; for many, however, the natural resource sectors, especially agriculture and mining, continue to be the main sources of income.

Gross domestic product (GDP) measures the overall output of an economy. It is the sum of value added in agriculture (including forestry and fisheries), industry (including mining and manufacturing), and the service sector (including government and private services). As economies develop, they typically shift from the production and export of agricultural and mining commodities to manufactured goods, and later to services. In many high-income economies more than 70 percent of GDP is produced in the service sector.

Services now account for 53 percent of the output of middle-income economies, although some countries—such as Jordan, Panama, and South Africa—have maintained large service sectors for some time. In low-income

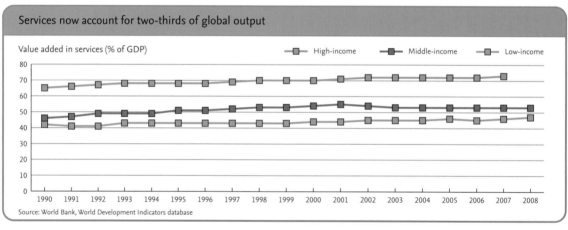

Services now account for two-thirds of global output

Value added in services (% of GDP) — High-income, Middle-income, Low-income

Source: World Bank, World Development Indicators database

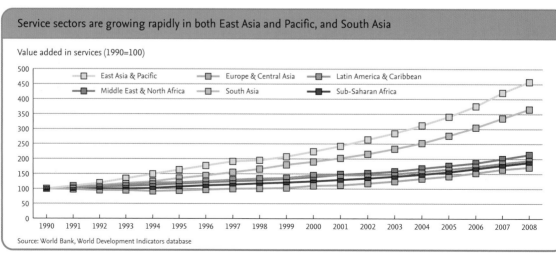

Service sectors are growing rapidly in both East Asia and Pacific, and South Asia

Value added in services (1990=100) — East Asia & Pacific, Europe & Central Asia, Latin America & Caribbean, Middle East & North Africa, South Asia, Sub-Saharan Africa

Source: World Bank, World Development Indicators database

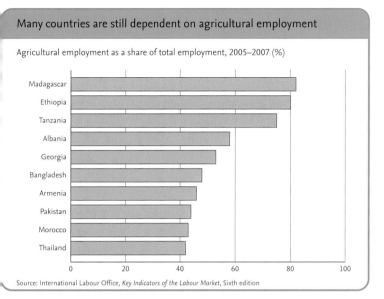

Many countries are still dependent on agricultural employment

Agricultural employment as a share of total employment, 2005–2007 (%)

Madagascar	
Ethiopia	
Tanzania	
Albania	
Georgia	
Bangladesh	
Armenia	
Pakistan	
Morocco	
Thailand	

Source: International Labour Office, *Key Indicators of the Labour Market*, Sixth edition

Although the service sector can contribute more than 70 percent of GDP in high-income economies...

...agriculture is still of major importance in developing countries

economies, the service sectors are growing and now produce almost 50 percent of the output. East Asia and the Pacific, led by China, and South Asia, led by India, have increased their service output in real terms by more than threefold since 1990.

Although the service sector is growing everywhere, agriculture remains of great importance to developing economies. Agriculture not only feeds a growing population, it produces raw materials for industries such as rubber and timber. Increases in oil prices have resulted in additional demand for food crops, such as corn and sugar cane, used to produce biofuels. Higher prices for agricultural products will raise the incomes of producers, but higher food prices also reduce the welfare of consumers.

In 2008, value added in agriculture as a share of GDP was over 40 percent in seven low-income economies, all of them in Africa. Agriculture is also an important source of employment, accounting for over 40 percent of the labor force in 24 countries, over 50 percent in 8 countries, and as much as 82 percent in Madagascar. Not only low-income economies but also some middle-income economies remain dependent on agriculture. In Ethiopia and Tanzania, agriculture accounts for 80 and 75 percent, respectively, of total employment. In comparison, agricultural employment made up 4 percent of total employment in Japan, 2 percent in Germany, 1 percent in the United States and the United Kingdom, and less than 1 percent in Argentina.

Agricultural output

share of value added in agriculture in GDP, 2004–2009, most recent year available

- 25% or more
- 15–24%
- 10–14%
- 3–9%
- less than 3%
- no data

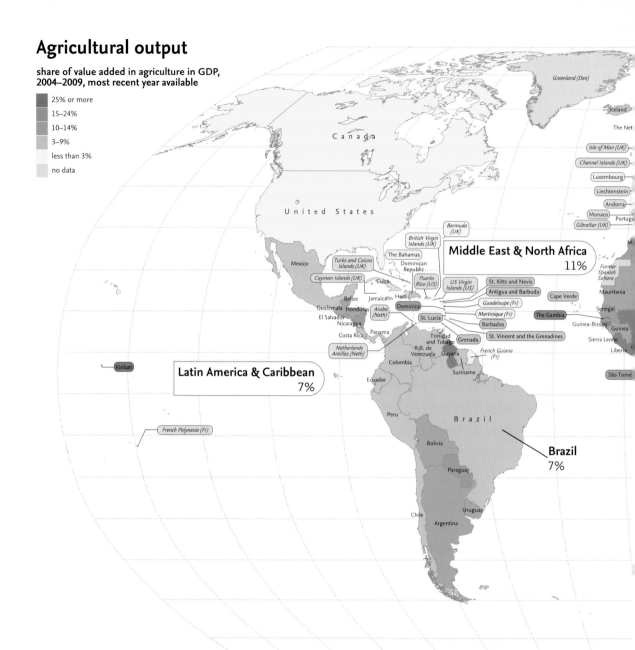

Middle East & North Africa 11%

Latin America & Caribbean 7%

Brazil 7%

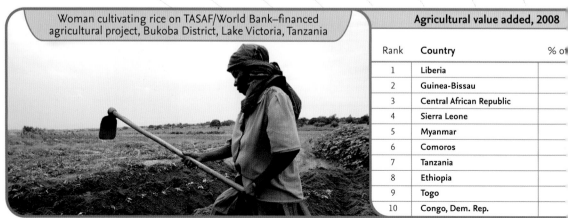

Woman cultivating rice on TASAF/World Bank–financed agricultural project, Bukoba District, Lake Victoria, Tanzania

Agricultural value added, 2008

Rank	Country	% of
1	Liberia	
2	Guinea-Bissau	
3	Central African Republic	
4	Sierra Leone	
5	Myanmar	
6	Comoros	
7	Tanzania	
8	Ethiopia	
9	Togo	
10	Congo, Dem. Rep.	

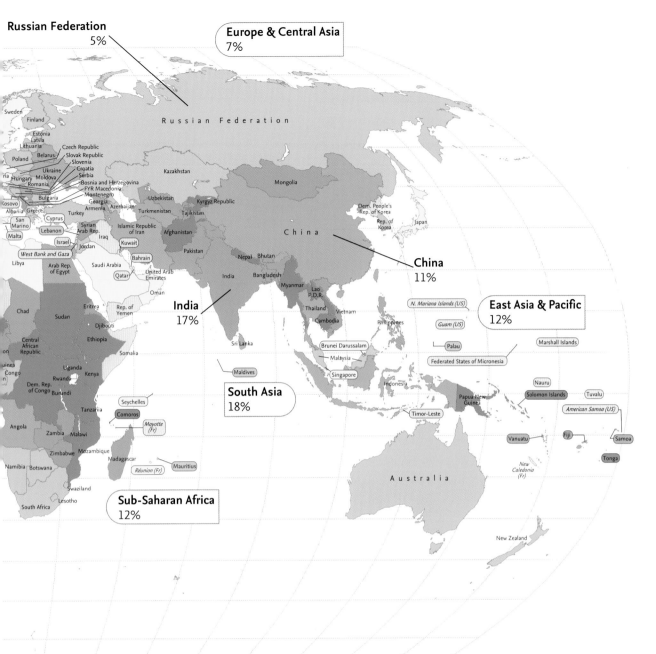

Russian Federation
5%

Europe & Central Asia
7%

China
11%

India
17%

East Asia & Pacific
12%

South Asia
18%

Sub-Saharan Africa
12%

Facts
e world agricultural sector grew by 2.5 percent from 2000 to 2008. e service sector grew by 3.2 percent and the industrial sector by) percent over the same period.
Sub-Saharan Africa the agricultural sector grew by 3.2 percent a year m 2000 to 2008, while the service sector grew by 5.3 percent and the dustrial sector by 5.1 percent.
East Asia and Pacific the industrial sector was the fastest growing with .2 percent annual growth over the period 2000 to 2008. Services were cond, with 9.4 percent growth. Agriculture grew by 4.1 percent.
South Asia the dominant sectors were services, with growth of ' percent, and industry, with 8.2 percent, while agriculture grew by 2 percent over the same period.
n average, services have grown faster than other parts of the economy, cept in East Asia and Pacific, and Europe and Central Asia.

Internet links	
▶ World Bank: World Development Indicators database	data.worldbank.org/ indicator
▶ Organisation for Economic Co-operation and Development	www.oecd.org
▶ IMF Data and Statistics	www.imf.org/external/ data.htm
▶ United Nations Statistics Division, National Accounts Main Aggregates database	unstats.un.org/ unsd/snaama
▶ International Labour Organization Key indicators of the Labor Market	www.ilo.org/KILM.net

Governance describes the way public officials and institutions acquire and exercise authority to provide public goods and services including education, healthcare, infrastructure, and a sound investment climate. Good governance is associated with citizen participation and improved accountability of public officials. It is fundamental to development and economic growth.

Governance has several dimensions:

- the process by which governments are selected, monitored, and replaced;
- the capacity of government to effectively formulate and implement sound policies;
- the respect of citizens and the state for the institutions that govern interactions between them.

Features of good governance—such as free and fair elections, respect for individual liberties and property rights, a free and vibrant press, an open and impartial judiciary, and well-informed and effective legislative structures—all contribute to strong and capable institutions of the state.

Although bad governance is often equated with corruption, the two concepts, while related, are different. Corruption—the abuse of public office for private gain—is an outcome of poor governance, reflecting the breakdown of accountability. A capable and accountable state creates opportunities for poor people, provides better services, and improves development outcomes—which is why the World Bank includes a governance and anticorruption strategy as part of its effort to reduce poverty. There are now several global collaborative governance initiatives, such as the Stolen Asset Recovery (StAR) Initiative, the Extractive Industries Transparency Initiative (EITI), the Construction Sector Transparency Initiative (CoST), and the Business Fighting Corruption Through Collective Action Initiative.

The links among weak institutions, poor development outcomes, and the risk of conflict are often evident in countries that are in fragile situations. These countries are ill-equipped to handle economic shocks,

Countries of the former Soviet Union rank as the worst in controlling corruption

Control of corruption, percentile rank (0–100), 2008

100

80

60

40

20

0

OECD
Eastern Europe & Baltic
Middle East & North Africa
East Asia & Pacific
Latin America
South Asia
Sub-Saharan Africa
Former Soviet Union

Source: Kaufmann D., A. Kraay, and M. Mastruzzi, 2009, *Governance Matters VIII: Governance Indicators for 1996-2008*

South African parliamentary committee at work

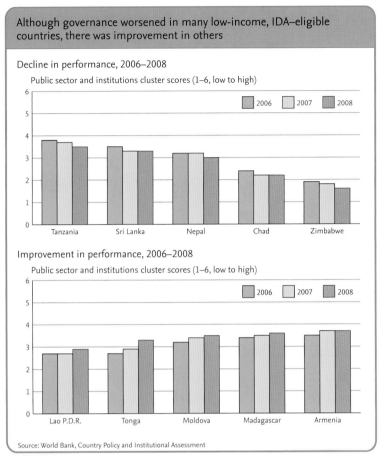

Although governance worsened in many low-income, IDA–eligible countries, there was improvement in others

Decline in performance, 2006–2008

Public sector and institutions cluster scores (1–6, low to high)

Legend: 2006, 2007, 2008

Countries: Tanzania, Sri Lanka, Nepal, Chad, Zimbabwe

Improvement in performance, 2006–2008

Public sector and institutions cluster scores (1–6, low to high)

Legend: 2006, 2007, 2008

Countries: Lao P.D.R., Tonga, Moldova, Madagascar, Armenia

Source: World Bank, Country Policy and Institutional Assessment

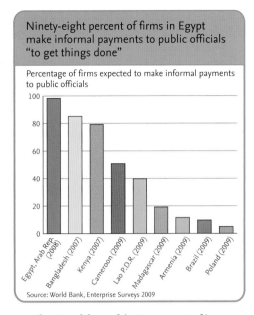

Ninety-eight percent of firms in Egypt make informal payments to public officials "to get things done"

Percentage of firms expected to make informal payments to public officials

Countries: Egypt, Arab Rep. (2008), Bangladesh (2007), Kenya (2007), Cameroon (2009), Lao P.D.R. (2009), Madagascar (2009), Armenia (2009), Brazil (2009), Poland (2009)

Source: World Bank, Enterprise Surveys 2009

natural disasters, and illegal trade or to resist conflict, which increasingly spills across borders. Organized violence, including violent crime, interrupts economic and social development through lost human and social capital, disrupted services, displaced populations, and reduced confidence for future investment. As a result, countries in fragile situations and conflict achieve lower development outcomes and make slower progress toward the Millennium Development Goals.

Measuring the quality of institutions and governance outcomes is difficult and often subject to large margins of error. Data for one dimension of governance—control of corruption—are presented in the map on pages 68–69. The data are aggregate measures derived from several sources of informed views of individuals in both the private and public sectors. The map represents data on control of corruption by percentile ranges, from the best performing (90th to 100th percentile) to the poorest performing (0 to 9th percentile). Some developing countries have better scores on some governance measures than developed countries.

The World Bank's Country Policy and Institutional Assessment (CPIA) is an annual staff effort to measure the extent to which a country's policy and institutional framework supports sustainable growth and poverty reduction. Scores of these assessments are disclosed only for low-income countries that are eligible for lending by the World Bank's International Development Association (IDA). CPIA indicators examine policies and institutions, not development outcomes, which can depend on forces outside a country's control. There are 16 criteria grouped into four clusters; one of the clusters (shown in the top left chart) is the public sector management and institutions cluster. This cluster includes five criteria: property rights and rule-based governance; quality of budgetary and financial management; efficiency of revenue mobilization; quality of public administration; and transparency, accountability, and corruption in the public sector.

Controlling corruption

control of corruption from the Worldwide Governance
Indicators, percentile rank, June 2008

- 90th–100th percentile
- 75th–89th percentile
- 50th–74th percentile
- 25th–49th percentile
- 10th–24th percentile
- 0–9th percentile
- no data

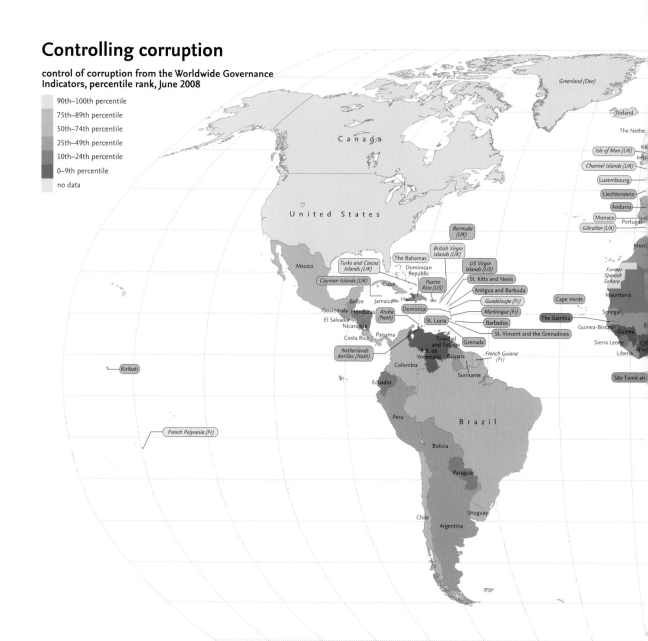

People in many countries are fighting against corruption

Control of corruption

Approximate rank	Developing country, population over 1 million	Percentile rank, 2008
1	Chile	87
2	Uruguay	84
3	Namibia	73
4	Costa Rica	70
5	Jordan	68
6	Poland	68
7	South Africa	65
8	Latvia	65
9	Lithuania	63
10	Malaysia	63

Facts	Internet links	
► Nine Sub-Saharan African countries rank in the 50th percentile or higher in the Worldwide Governance Indicators measure of control of corruption.	► World Bank: Worldwide Governance Indicators	**www.govindicators.org**
	► World Bank: Enterprise Surveys	**www.enterprisesurveys.org**
► Research shows a relationship between low levels of income and higher levels of corruption. But some middle-income countries, such as Botswana, Chile, and Uruguay, perform as well as some high-income countries on measures of governance.	► World Bank: Doing Business	**www.doingbusiness.org**
	► United Nations Development Programme (UNDP): Democratic Governance	**www.undp.org/governance**
► Three key principles for promoting good governance include transparency, accountability, and participation. Participation implies that people have rights that need to be recognized and that they should have a voice in the decisions that affect them.	► Transparency International	**www.transparency.org**
	► World Bank: Public Sector Governance	**www.worldbank.org/ publicsector**

Infrastructure—the basic framework for delivering energy, transport, water and sanitation, and information and communications services to people, directly or indirectly—affects people's lives everywhere. Increased productivity and incomes and improvements in health and education outcomes require investment in infrastructure.

Infrastructure services play a key role in the most important development objective—reducing poverty and improving the lives of billions of people in developing countries. These services affect people in many ways—what they consume and produce; how they heat and light their homes; how they travel to work, to school, or to visit family and friends; and how they communicate. Access to clean water and sanitation reduces infant mortality. Electricity powers hospitals and refrigerators for vaccines. Roads in rural areas boost school attendance and use of medical clinics. And information and communication technologies can improve teacher training and promote better health practices.

Physical isolation is a strong contributor to poverty. People living in remote places have reduced access to health and education services, employment opportunities, and markets. Problems are particularly severe in rural areas that lack good transportation facilities. Transport infrastructure—the roads, bridges, railroads, waterways, ports, and the services they provide—can eliminate growth-constraining bottlenecks and shortages, increase agricultural productivity, improve poor rural farmers' incomes and nutrition, and expand nonfarm employment.

Despite global efforts, improvements in water and sanitation infrastructure have barely kept pace with population growth and migration in the developing world and will require more public and private investment.

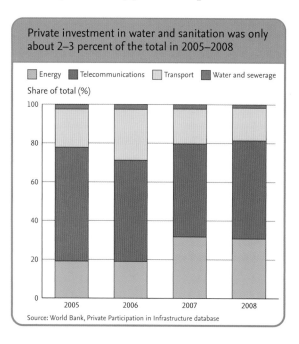

Private investment in water and sanitation was only about 2–3 percent of the total in 2005–2008

Energy ▪ Telecommunications ▫ Transport ▪ Water and sewerage

Share of total (%)

Source: World Bank, Private Participation in Infrastructure database

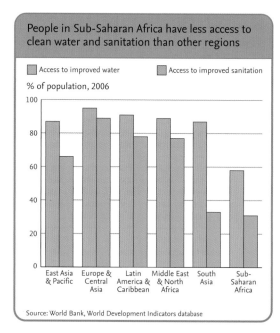

People in Sub-Saharan Africa have less access to clean water and sanitation than other regions

▪ Access to improved water ▪ Access to improved sanitation

% of population, 2006

East Asia & Pacific / Europe & Central Asia / Latin America & Caribbean / Middle East & North Africa / South Asia / Sub-Saharan Africa

Source: World Bank, World Development Indicators database

South Asia and Sub-Saharan Africa have the fewest mobile phone subscriptions, but South Asia's annual increase between 2004 and 2008 was almost 70 percent, while Sub-Saharan Africa's was about 40 percent

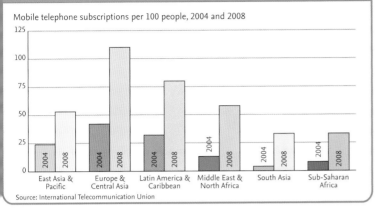

Mobile telephone subscriptions per 100 people, 2004 and 2008

Source: International Telecommunication Union

Developing countries of Europe and Central Asia have the best access to broadband Internet

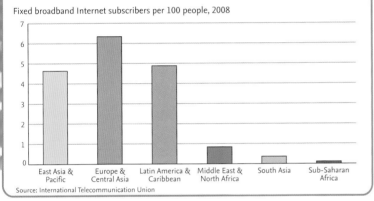

Fixed broadband Internet subscribers per 100 people, 2008

Source: International Telecommunication Union

Yemeni man using a mobile phone

Measured in 2008 constant price dollars, investment commitments in water and sanitation projects with private participation from 2000 to 2008 were $33 billion compared with $517 billion in investments in telecommunications. Globally, approximately 1.1 billion people remain without access to safe water and 2.6 billion without adequate sanitation. Infrastructure is typically an enabler, but rarely the sole solution to development challenges. Reducing disease transmission, for example, requires better water and sanitation facilities, but it also requires good hygiene practices such as routine hand washing.

Information and communication technology has vast potential for fostering growth in developing countries by helping to increase productivity in a wide range of economic activities from agriculture to manufacturing and services. Mobile phones keep families and communities in contact and provide market information for farmers and businesspeople. According to the International Telecommunication Union, by the end of 2009 there were over 4.6 billion mobile cellular subscriptions in the world, or about 67 per 100 people. The Internet delivers information to schools and hospitals, and computers improve public and private services as well as increase productivity and participation.

The global supply of infrastructure services is not able to meet the needs of today. Developing countries need about $900 billion (7–9 percent of GDP) to maintain existing infrastructure and to build new infrastructure, but only half that amount is available. The global financial and economic crisis is expected to severely curtail investment in and maintenance of infrastructure as governments face shrinking budgets and declining private financial flows.

Internet users

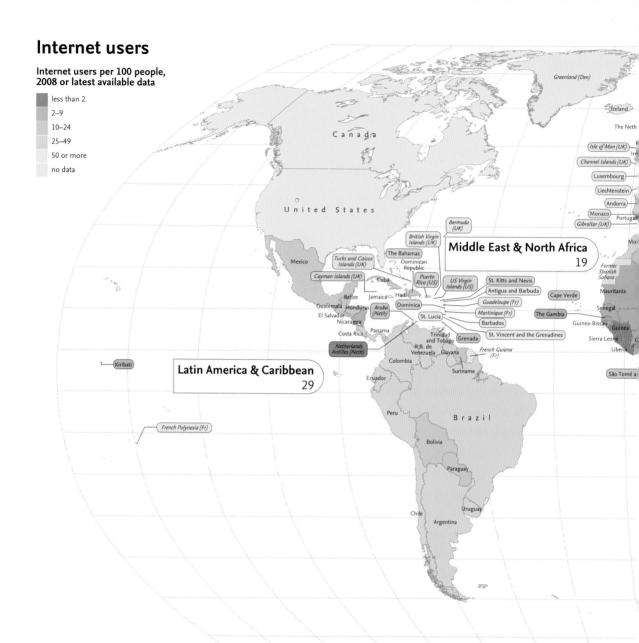

Internet users per 100 people,
2008 or latest available data

- less than 2
- 2–9
- 10–24
- 25–49
- 50 or more
- no data

Middle East & North Africa
19

Latin America & Caribbean
29

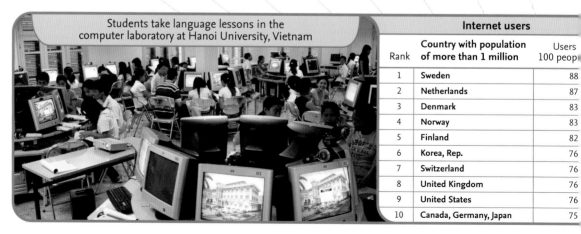

Students take language lessons in the
computer laboratory at Hanoi University, Vietnam

Rank	Country with population of more than 1 million	Users 100 peop...
	Internet users	
1	Sweden	88
2	Netherlands	87
3	Denmark	83
4	Norway	83
5	Finland	82
6	Korea, Rep.	76
7	Switzerland	76
8	United Kingdom	76
9	United States	76
10	Canada, Germany, Japan	75

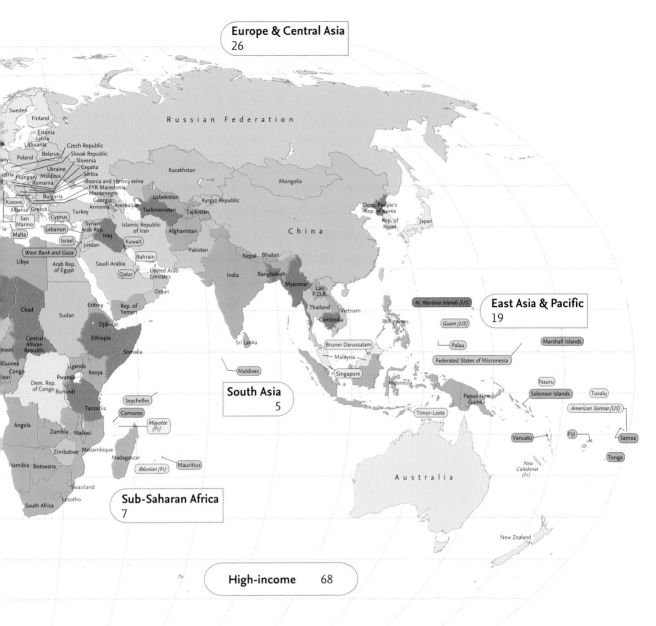

Europe & Central Asia
26

Russian Federation

Sweden
Finland
Estonia
Latvia
Lithuania
Czech Republic
Poland
Belarus
Slovak Republic
Slovenia
Ukraine
Croatia
Hungary
Moldova
Serbia
Bosnia and Herzegovina
FYR Macedonia
Romania
Montenegro
Kosovo
Georgia
Bulgaria
Armenia Azerbaijan
Albania Greece
San Marino
Turkey
Cyprus
Syrian Arab Rep.
Lebanon
Malta
Iraq
West Bank and Gaza
Israel
Jordan
Libya
Arab Rep. of Egypt
Saudi Arabia
Qatar
United Arab Emirates
Oman
Chad
Sudan
Rep. of Yemen
Eritrea
Djibouti
Ethiopia
Central African Republic
Somalia
Guinea
Congo
Uganda
Dem. Rep. of Congo
Rwanda
Burundi
Kenya
Tanzania
Angola
Zambia
Malawi
Zimbabwe
Mozambique
Namibia
Botswana
Madagascar
Swaziland
South Africa
Lesotho

Kazakhstan
Mongolia
Uzbekistan
Kyrgyz Republic
Turkmenistan
Tajikistan
Islamic Republic of Iran
Afghanistan
China
Pakistan
Nepal Bhutan
India
Bangladesh
Myanmar
Lao P.D.R.
Thailand
Cambodia
Vietnam
Sri Lanka
Maldives
Brunei Darussalam
Malaysia
Singapore
Indonesia

Dem. People's Rep. of Korea
Rep. of Korea
Japan

N. Mariana Islands (US)
Guam (US)
Philippines
Palau
Federated States of Micronesia
Marshall Islands

East Asia & Pacific
19

South Asia
5

Seychelles
Comoros
Mayotte (Fr)
Réunion (Fr)
Mauritius

Sub-Saharan Africa
7

Papua New Guinea
Timor-Leste
Nauru
Solomon Islands
Tuvalu
American Samoa (US)
Vanuatu
Fiji
Samoa
Tonga
New Caledonia (Fr)

Australia

New Zealand

High-income   68

Facts	Internet links	
In 2009 there were 1.7 billion people, or 26 percent of the world's population, using the Internet. The average for developing countries was about 18 percent.	► International Telecommunication Union	www.itu.int
There are still wide gaps in the use of the Internet in different regions in the world: Latin America and the Caribbean has about 29 Internet users per 100 people; East Asia and Pacific has about 19; and Sub-Saharan Africa has about 7 users per 100 people. The average for high-income countries is almost 70.	► International Road Federation	www.irfnet.org
	► World Resources Institute— EarthTrends	earthtrends.wri.org (click on Energy and Resources)
	► World Bank— Infrastructure	data.worldbank.org/topic/ infrastructure (click on Topics, then select Sustainable Development)
The cost of fixed broadband Internet service is about $36 a month in developing countries. The tariff ranges from under $10 in the Arab Republic of Egypt and India to more than $500 a month in countries such as Burkina Faso, Guinea, Malawi, and Nigeria.	► Organisation for Economic Co-operation and Development	www.oecd.org (click on By Topic, then select Information and Communications Technologies)
In 2007 broadband Internet services reached just 2 percent of the population in low-income economies, mostly in urban centers.	► WHO—Water, Sanitation, and Health	www.who.int/water_ sanitation_health/en

Investment replenishes assets used up in production and increases the total capital stock; without it there would not be sustainable economic growth. However, high rates of investment alone do not ensure rapid economic growth. A good investment climate is one in which government policies encourage firms and entrepreneurs to invest productively, create jobs, and contribute to growth and poverty reduction. On average, 22 percent of the world output is invested for production purposes.

Physical investment (gross capital formation) takes many forms: buildings, machinery, and equipment; improvements to property; and additions to inventories. Investment is financed out of domestic savings or external savings—the latter is limited and generally more volatile. Countries that have high savings

and investment rates are likely to have high rates of economic growth. Growth is also spurred by improved efficiency brought on by technological advances and investments in people, such as through better education and healthcare. To sustain growth, government policies must create a climate that encourages productive investment.

In most recent years, East Asia and the Pacific has had the highest investment rate, averaging 40 percent of gross domestic product (GDP). South Asia invested 38 percent of its output. Even Sub-Saharan Africa at 23 percent, the lowest investment rate among developing regions, exceeded the rate of 21 percent in high-income economies. Total investment in developing regions in 2008 was $5.2 trillion, about two-thirds that in high-income economies.

Government policies play a key role in shaping the investment climate. They influence the security of property rights, the effectiveness of regulation, the impact of taxation, the quality and accessibility of infrastructure, and the functioning of financial and labor markets. The quality of

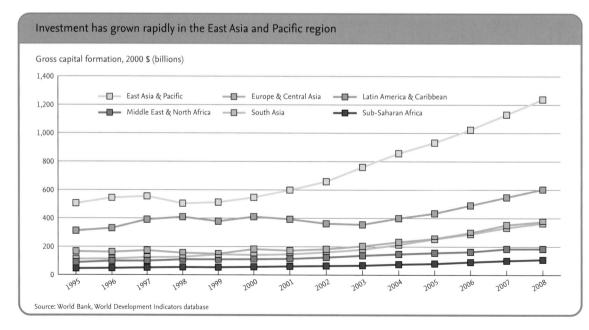

Investment has grown rapidly in the East Asia and Pacific region

Gross capital formation, 2000 $ (billions)

Source: World Bank, World Development Indicators database

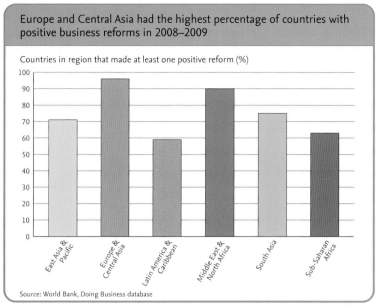

Europe and Central Asia had the highest percentage of countries with positive business reforms in 2008–2009

Countries in region that made at least one positive reform (%)

Source: World Bank, Doing Business database

Although China and some of the other "tigers" in East Asia and Pacific have attained spectacular growth rates, high levels of investment do not guarantee high growth rates. Investment produces growth. Investment may also chase growth. More investment is likely in places where high returns are possible.

Over the period 1995 through 2008, most developing regions invested an average of 19 to 36 percent of their GDP each year. The results have varied, from Latin America and the Caribbean, where an investment ratio of 20 percent produced growth of only 3.2 percent, to South Asia, where an investment ratio of 28 percent resulted in annual growth of 6.4 percent. Sub-Saharan Africa is an interesting exception: an investment ratio of 19 percent led to an annual growth rate of 4.3 percent, on par with or better than several regions with higher investment ratios.

the investment climate also contributes strongly to increased productivity and employment creation, both necessary for poverty reduction. Poor governance increases transaction costs, encourages unproductive activities such as lobbying, and reduces transparency. Hence, it leads to misallocation of resources and discourages new investment.

Economies in Europe and Central Asia were the most active reformers for the sixth year in a row. Between 2008 and 2009, 96 percent of countries in the region made at least one positive reform to make doing business easier, while 75 percent reformed in South Asia.

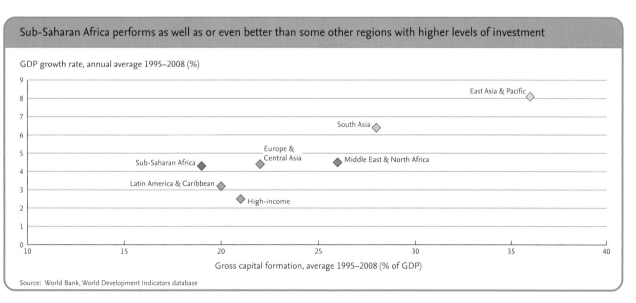

Sub-Saharan Africa performs as well as or even better than some other regions with higher levels of investment

GDP growth rate, annual average 1995–2008 (%)

Gross capital formation, average 1995–2008 (% of GDP)

Source: World Bank, World Development Indicators database

Investment for growth

gross capital formation as share of GDP,
2004–2008, most recent year available

- less than 15%
- 15–19%
- 20–24%
- 25–29%
- 30% or more
- no data

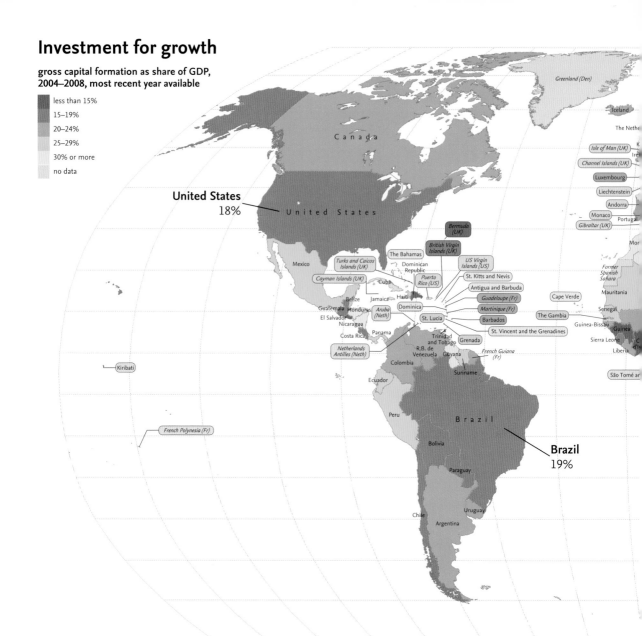

United States
18%

Brazil
19%

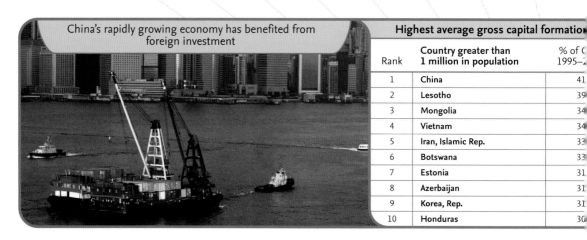

China's rapidly growing economy has benefited from foreign investment

Highest average gross capital formation

Rank	Country greater than 1 million in population	% of G 1995–2
1	China	41
2	Lesotho	39
3	Mongolia	34
4	Vietnam	34
5	Iran, Islamic Rep.	33
6	Botswana	33
7	Estonia	31
8	Azerbaijan	31
9	Korea, Rep.	31
10	Honduras	30

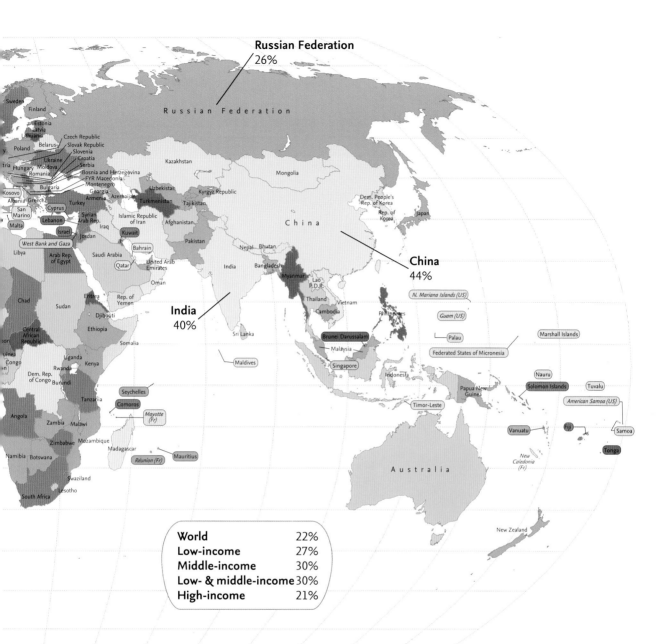

Russian Federation
26%

China
44%

India
40%

World	22%
Low-income	27%
Middle-income	30%
Low- & middle-income	30%
High-income	21%

Facts	Internet links	
...vestment has grown fastest in South Asia. Between 2000 and 2008, ...has been increasing at an average rate of 13.8 percent per year.	▸ World Bank Data and Statistics	**data.worldbank.org**
...vestment has been the slowest in Latin America and the Caribbean, ...eraging 5.7 percent a year between 2000 and 2008.	▸ Organisation for Economic Co-operation and Development	**www.oecd.org**
...vestment declined in 11 countries between 2000 and 2008.		
...mong the top 10 countries with the highest average investment ...te between 1995 and 2008, 2 were from Sub-Saharan Africa.	▸ United Nations Statistics Division	**www.data.un.org**
...China investment grew at an average of 12 percent a year ...etween 2000 and 2008.	▸ IMF—World Economic Outlook	**www.imf.org/weo**

Starting a business

time required to start a new business, June 2009

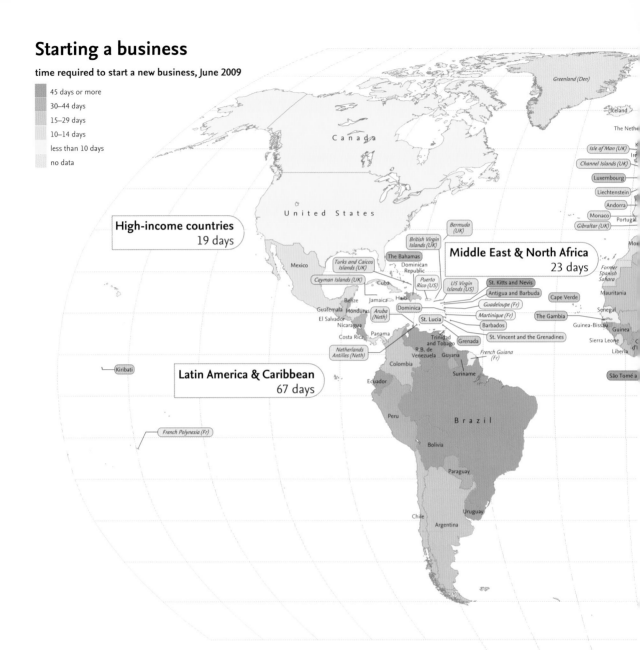

- 45 days or more
- 30–44 days
- 15–29 days
- 10–14 days
- less than 10 days
- no data

High-income countries
19 days

Middle East & North Africa
23 days

Latin America & Caribbean
67 days

Greenland (Den)

Iceland

The Nethe

Canada

Isle of Man (UK)
Ire
Channel Islands (UK)
Luxembourg
Liechtenstein
Andorra
Monaco Portugal
Gibraltar (UK)

United States

Bermuda (UK)

Mo

British Virgin Islands (UK)

Mexico

The Bahamas
Dominican Republic

Turks and Caicos Islands (UK)

Cayman Islands (UK)   Cuba

Puerto Rico (US)

US Virgin Islands (US)

St. Kitts and Nevis
Antigua and Barbuda

Former Spanish Sahara

Mauritania

Belize
Guatemala Honduras
El Salvador
Nicaragua

Haiti
Jamaica
Aruba (Neth)

Dominica

Guadeloupe (Fr)

Cape Verde

Senegal

St. Lucia
Martinique (Fr)
The Gambia
Barbados
Guinea-Bissau   Guinea

Costa Rica   Panama

Netherlands Antilles (Neth)

Colombia

Ecuador

Peru

Kiribati

French Polynesia (Fr)

Trinidad and Tobago   Grenada
R.B. de Venezuela   Guyana

St. Vincent and the Grenadines

French Guiana (Fr)

Suriname

Sierra Leone
d'
Liberia

São Tomé a

B r a z i l

Bolivia

Paraguay

Chile

Uruguay
Argentina

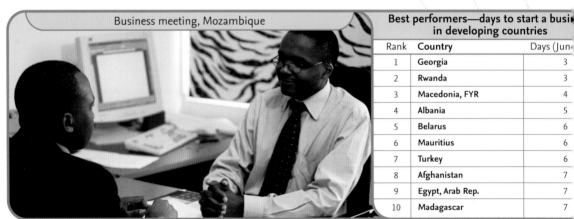

Business meeting, Mozambique

Best performers—days to start a busi
in developing countries

Rank	Country	Days (Jun
1	Georgia	3
2	Rwanda	3
3	Macedonia, FYR	4
4	Albania	5
5	Belarus	6
6	Mauritius	6
7	Turkey	6
8	Afghanistan	7
9	Egypt, Arab Rep.	7
10	Madagascar	7

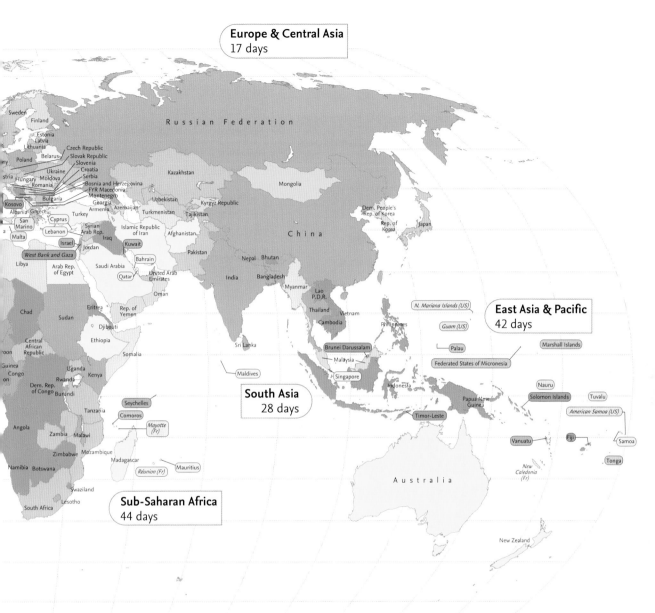

Europe & Central Asia
17 days

East Asia & Pacific
42 days

South Asia
28 days

Sub-Saharan Africa
44 days

Facts	Internet links	
Sixty-one economies made it easier to start a business between 2008 and 2009.	► World Bank— Doing Business database	**www.doingbusiness.org**
Samoa's new company act allows entrepreneurs to choose the amount of capital for their company.	► World Bank— Enterprise Surveys	**www.enterprisesurveys.org**
In 2008–2009, Belarus shortened business startup time by almost [...] weeks by simplifying registration formalities, abolishing the minimum capital requirements, making use of a notary optional, and removing the need for a company seal.	► World Bank— Private Participation in Infrastructure database	**ppi.worldbank.org**
Between 2008 and 2009, Slovenia automated company registration, cutting the time to register a business by 13 days.		
In South Asia, Afghanistan established a new one-stop shop and introduced a flat registration fee.	► World Bank— Privatization database	**rru.worldbank.org/Privatization**
Botswana simplified business licensing and tax registration as part of an ongoing computerization effort.		

Economies have become more dependent on each other for goods, services, labor, and capital. Advances in information and communications technology, expanding financial markets, and cheaper transportation systems enable easier movement of inputs and outputs among economies, accelerating global integration, although many barriers remain. Global integration creates many opportunities, but the benefits need to be shared equitably both among and within economies.

Traditional patterns of production and employment have given way to new modes of production and distribution, which are often spread over multiple locations. Developing economies offering higher returns are attracting foreign investment in manufacturing. Skilled as well as unskilled labor is seeking employment in economies that offer higher wages. High-income economies are looking at the developing world to meet the increasing demand for service and technology workers.

International trade is a critical channel for integration. Goods equivalent to 53 percent of global gross domestic product (GDP) were traded in 2008, up from 32 percent in 1990. Over the same period, trade in services increased from 8 percent to 12 percent of global GDP. The financial crisis, which originated in high-income economies, slowed global trade. Trade in goods decreased to

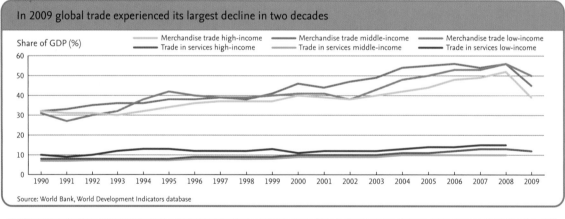

In 2009 global trade experienced its largest decline in two decades

Share of GDP (%)

Merchandise trade high-income — Merchandise trade middle-income — Merchandise trade low-income
Trade in services high-income — Trade in services middle-income — Trade in services low-income

Source: World Bank, World Development Indicators database

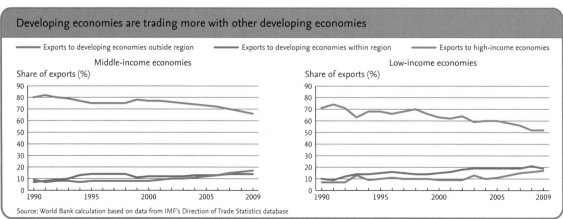

Developing economies are trading more with other developing economies

Exports to developing economies outside region — Exports to developing economies within region — Exports to high-income economies

Middle-income economies
Share of exports (%)

Low-income economies
Share of exports (%)

Source: World Bank calculation based on data from IMF's Direction of Trade Statistics database

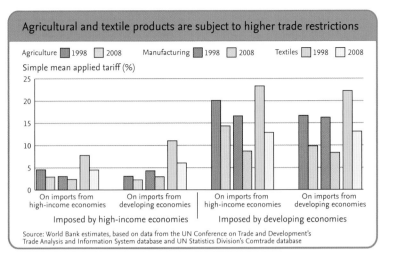

Agricultural and textile products are subject to higher trade restrictions

Agriculture ■ 1998 □ 2008   Manufacturing ■ 1998 □ 2008   Textiles □ 1998 □ 2008

Simple mean applied tariff (%)

Imposed by high-income economies:
- On imports from high-income economies
- On imports from developing economies

Imposed by developing economies:
- On imports from high-income economies
- On imports from developing economies

Source: World Bank estimates, based on data from the UN Conference on Trade and Development's Trade Analysis and Information System database and UN Statistics Division's Comtrade database

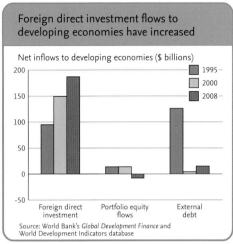

Foreign direct investment flows to developing economies have increased

Net inflows to developing economies ($ billions)

■ 1995 □ 2000 ■ 2008

- Foreign direct investment
- Portfolio equity flows
- External debt

Source: World Bank's *Global Development Finance* and World Development Indicators database

41 percent of global GDP in 2009, and trade in services fell to 11 percent of GDP.

High-income economies remain the principal source and destination of international trade, but more developing economies are participating, and trade with other developing economies is growing. Developing economies now account for almost 30 percent of world trade. Some, such as China, Mexico, and Thailand, are specializing in manufactured goods, but many are still dependent on exports of food, fuel, and raw materials.

The international service sector has grown rapidly in the new century. Between 2005 and 2009, trade in services by developing economies grew at an annual average rate of 20 percent (in nominal terms)—14 percentage points higher than that of high-income economies. South Asia led the way, growing at an average annual rate of 22 percent. But agricultural and industrial goods still dominate world trade, accounting for 78 percent of total trade in 2009.

Reductions in tariff and nontariff barriers have helped to spur trade, but many trade barriers remain. The poorest countries impose higher barriers across a broad range of goods to protect their producers and raise revenues for their governments. Rich countries often impose their highest barriers selectively on the exports of developing countries, especially agricultural and textile products. In addition to tariff protection, they provide subsidies and other forms of support to their farmers, enabling them to sell agricultural products at very low prices that developing country producers cannot match. Total agricultural support in OECD countries exceeded $376 billion in 2008, representing a 3.2 percent increase from 2007, in nominal terms.

Effective global integration requires the free flow of goods, services, investment, labor, and technology, not merely the reduction of tariffs and import quotas. An open and equitable trading system enhances growth opportunities and encourages domestic and foreign investment. During the last decade there have been increasing flows of foreign direct investment (FDI) toward developing economies. It has long been recognized that the benefits of FDI for these countries can be significant, including knowledge and technology transfer to domestic firms and the labor force, productivity spillover, enhanced competition, and improved access for exports abroad. Although slowed by the financial crisis, net FDI received by developing economies increased by 12.3 percent in 2008 to a total of $587 billion.

East Asia and the Pacific received the highest inflow of FDI ($187.1 billion). China received 79 percent of the regional inflows and commanded one-quarter of all FDI inflows in the developing economies.

Merchandise trade

exports and imports as a share of GDP,
2009 or latest available data

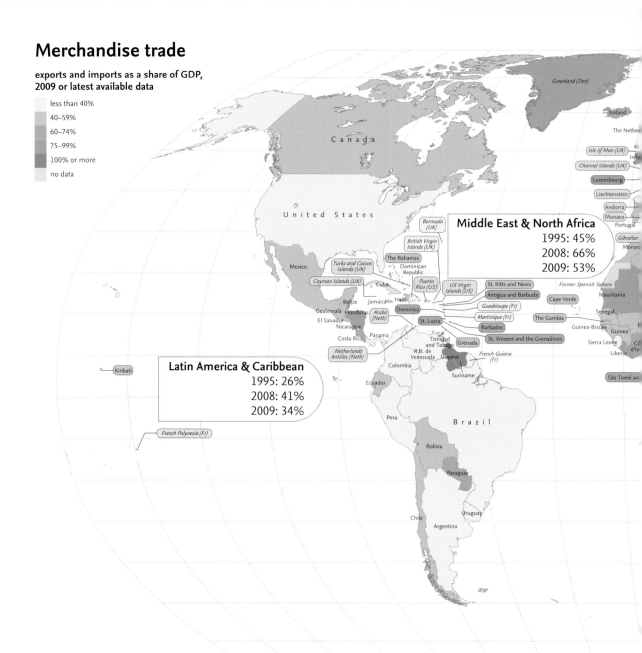

Legend:
- less than 40%
- 40–59%
- 60–74%
- 75–99%
- 100% or more
- no data

Middle East & North Africa
1995: 45%
2008: 66%
2009: 53%

Latin America & Caribbean
1995: 26%
2008: 41%
2009: 34%

Map labels: Greenland (Den), Iceland, The Nether..., Ki..., Isle of Man (UK), Ire..., Channel Islands (UK), Luxembourg, Liechtenstein, Andorra, Monaco, Portugal, Gibraltar, Morocc..., Canada, United States, Mexico, Bermuda (UK), British Virgin Islands (UK), The Bahamas, Dominican Republic, Turks and Caicos Islands (UK), Cayman Islands (UK), Cuba, Puerto Rico (US), US Virgin Islands (US), St. Kitts and Nevis, Antigua and Barbuda, Cape Verde, Former Spanish Sahara, Mauritania, Belize, Jamaica, Haiti, Guadeloupe (Fr), Senegal, Guatemala, Honduras, Aruba (Neth), Dominica, The Gambia, Guinea-Bissau, Guinea, El Salvador, Martinique (Fr), Nicaragua, St. Lucia, Barbados, Sierra Leone, Costa Rica, Panama, Trinidad and Tobago, Grenada, St. Vincent and the Grenadines, Liberia, Côte d'Iv..., Netherlands Antilles (Neth), R.B. de Venezuela, Guyana, French Guiana (Fr), São Tomé an..., Kiribati, Colombia, Suriname, Ecuador, Peru, Brazil, Bolivia, French Polynesia (Fr), Paraguay, Chile, Uruguay, Argentina

Merchandise trade					
Quay cranes on dock, Sri Lanka	Largest merchandise exporters, 2009			Largest merchandise importers,	
	Rank	Developing country	$ billions	Rank	Developing country	b...
	1	China	1,202	1	China	1,...
	2	Russian Federation	304	2	India	
	3	Mexico	230	3	Mexico	
	4	Malaysia	157	4	Russian Federation	
	5	India	155	5	Turkey	

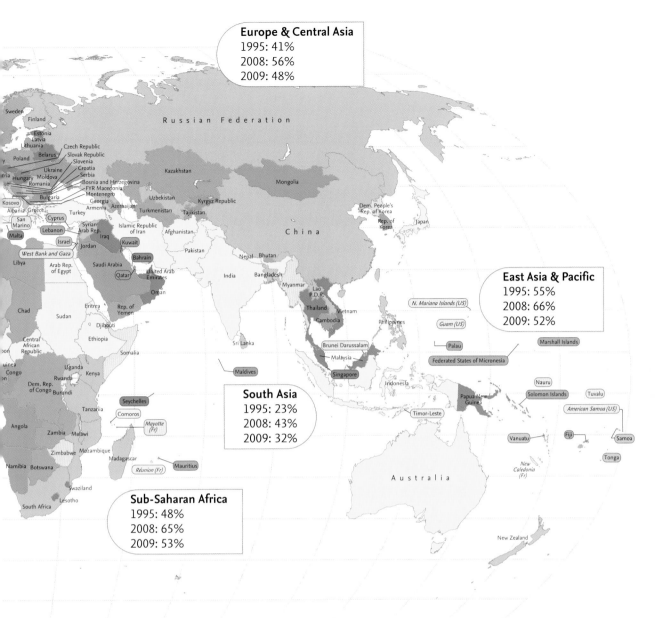

Europe & Central Asia
1995: 41%
2008: 56%
2009: 48%

East Asia & Pacific
1995: 55%
2008: 66%
2009: 52%

South Asia
1995: 23%
2008: 43%
2009: 32%

Sub-Saharan Africa
1995: 48%
2008: 65%
2009: 53%

Facts	Internet links	
The five largest exporters in 2009 accounted for more than half the merchandise exports of developing economies.	▶ OECD—Trade	www.oecd.org/trade
World exports of services grew from $861 billion in 1990 to more than $3.9 trillion in 2008, but declined to $3.4 trillion in 2009 because of the global financial crisis.	▶ IMF—Statistics	www.imfstatistics.org/dot www.imfstatistics.org/bop
Average tariffs imposed by high-income economies have declined, but averaging tariffs across thousands of products can mask high tariffs on certain commodities that are particularly important for developing economies. For some high-income economies the maximum applied tariff rate can be as high as 887 percent.	▶ WTO Trade and Tariff Data	www.wto.org (go to Resources, select Trade and Tariff Statistics)
The United States imports more goods than any other country, followed by China and Germany.	▶ United Nations Conference on Trade and Development—Statistics	www.unctad.org (go to Statistics and select UNCTADstat)
Following the global financial crisis, world merchandise exports declined by 16 percent between 2008 and 2009.	▶ United Nations Trade Statistics	unstats.un.org/unsd/trade unstats.un.org/unsd/servicetrade

Foreign direct investment

foreign direct investment net inflows as a share of GDP, 2008 or latest available data

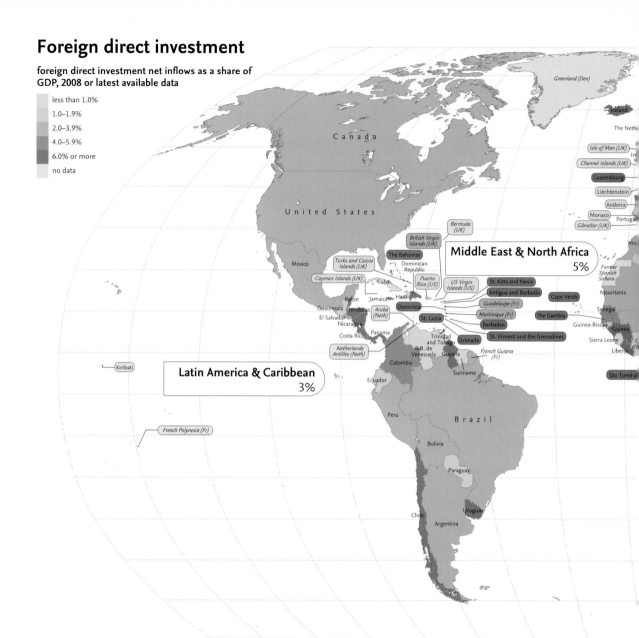

- less than 1.0%
- 1.0–1.9%
- 2.0–3.9%
- 4.0–5.9%
- 6.0% or more
- no data

Middle East & North Africa
5%

Latin America & Caribbean
3%

Greenland (Den)

Iceland

The Neth

Isle of Man (UK)

Channel Islands (UK)

Luxembourg

Liechtenstein

Andorra

Monaco · Portugal

Gibraltar (UK)

Mo

Canada

United States

Mexico

Bermuda (UK)

British Virgin Islands (UK)

The Bahamas

Dominican Republic

Turks and Caicos Islands (UK)

Cayman Islands (UK)

Cuba

Belize

Jamaica

Haiti

Puerto Rico (US)

US Virgin Islands (US)

St. Kitts and Nevis

Antigua and Barbuda

Cape Verde

Guatemala   Honduras   Aruba (Neth)

El Salvador

Nicaragua

Dominica

Guadeloupe (Fr)

Martinique (Fr)

The Gambia

St. Lucia

Barbados

Costa Rica   Panama

Netherlands Antilles (Neth)

Colombia

Trinidad and Tobago

R.B. de Venezuela   Guyana

Grenada

St. Vincent and the Grenadines

French Guiana (Fr)

Mauritania

Senegal

Guinea-Bissau   Guinea

Sierra Leone   Liberia

C'd'I

São Tomé a

Ecuador

Suriname

Peru

Brazil

Kiribati

French Polynesia (Fr)

Bolivia

Paraguay

Chile

Uruguay

Argentina

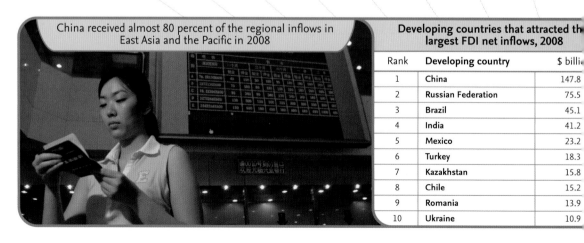

China received almost 80 percent of the regional inflows in East Asia and the Pacific in 2008

Developing countries that attracted th largest FDI net inflows, 2008

Rank	Developing country	$ billi
1	China	147.8
2	Russian Federation	75.5
3	Brazil	45.1
4	India	41.2
5	Mexico	23.2
6	Turkey	18.3
7	Kazakhstan	15.8
8	Chile	15.2
9	Romania	13.9
10	Ukraine	10.9

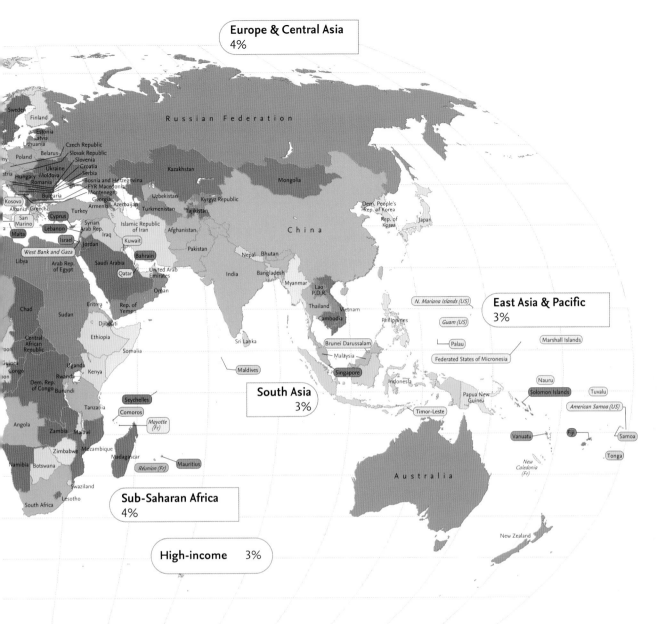

Europe & Central Asia
4%

East Asia & Pacific
3%

South Asia
3%

Sub-Saharan Africa
4%

High-income   3%

Facts	Internet links	
Luxembourg's net outward direct investment in foreign economies in 2008 was nearly 3.8 times its GDP. Iceland's was 63 percent of its GDP.	▶ International Monetary Fund Balance of Payments Statistics	**www.imfstatistics.org/bop**
Risk perceptions in international credit markets during the second half of 2008 affected all the developing regions resulting in negative portfolio investment flows of $53 billion.	▶ World Bank	**data.worldbank.org/topic/ financial-sector**
Notably, China continued to moderately record a positive net flow of portfolio equity by $8.7 billion.		
For the first time in the last five years, foreign investors reduced portfolio investments in Russian corporate securities by $15.3 billion because of the global liquidity crisis.	▶ United Nations Conference on Trade and Development— Statistics	**www.unctad.org** (go to Statistics and select UNCTADstat)
FDI net flows to high-income countries accounted for nearly 68.2 percent of the world total in 2008. Among developing regions, Europe and Central Asia received the highest amount in 2008 ($186.6 billion), having quadrupled in value since 2000.	▶ Multilateral Investment Guarantee Agency, World Bank Group	**www.fdi.net**

The movement of people across national borders is a visible and increasingly important aspect of global integration. Three percent of the world's population—more than 213 million people—now live in countries in which they were not born. The forces driving the flow of migrants from poor economies to rich economies are likely to grow stronger in the future.

Migration is on the rise, especially from poor economies to rich economies. Wage differences and demographic trends encourage migration. In many high-income economies the population is aging and growing slowly, while in many developing countries the population is young and growing rapidly. This imbalance creates a strong demand for developing-economy workers, especially to provide services that can be supplied only locally. Immigrants in high-income economies have increased to 11 percent of the population, up from 8 percent two decades before. There can be other reasons for immigration. After the breakup of the Soviet Union in 1991, many people moved between the newly independent states, raising the number of migrants recorded in middle-income economies.

Migration is often accompanied by a flow of remittances—transfers of gifts and wages and salaries earned abroad—from migrants to their countries of origin. Over the past decade remittances flows have increased rapidly, emerging as an important source of external finance for developing economies. Unlike other kinds of financial flows, remittances do not create liabilities and are often received by people who need financing the most. From 2000 to 2009 remittances inflows to developing economies more than tripled. Global remittances flows exceeded $415 billion in 2009, with 74 percent going to developing economies.

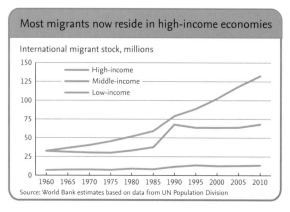

Most migrants now reside in high-income economies

International migrant stock, millions

— High-income
— Middle-income
— Low-income

Source: World Bank estimates based on data from UN Population Division

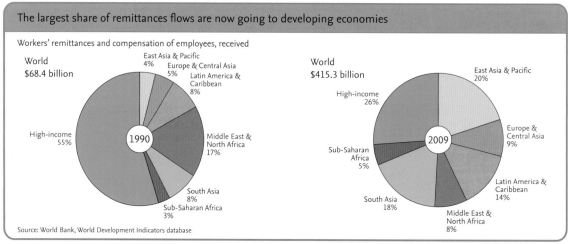

The largest share of remittances flows are now going to developing economies

Workers' remittances and compensation of employees, received

World
$68.4 billion

1990

East Asia & Pacific 4%
Europe & Central Asia 5%
Latin America & Caribbean 8%
Middle East & North Africa 17%
South Asia 8%
Sub-Saharan Africa 3%
High-income 55%

World
$415.3 billion

2009

East Asia & Pacific 20%
Europe & Central Asia 9%
Latin America & Caribbean 14%
Middle East & North Africa 8%
South Asia 18%
Sub-Saharan Africa 5%
High-income 26%

Source: World Bank, World Development Indicators database

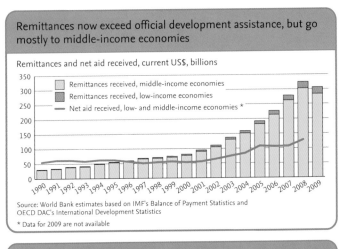

Remittances now exceed official development assistance, but go mostly to middle-income economies

Remittances and net aid received, current US$, billions

Legend:
- Remittances received, middle-income economies
- Remittances received, low-income economies
- Net aid received, low- and middle-income economies *

Source: World Bank estimates based on IMF's Balance of Payment Statistics and OECD DAC's International Development Statistics

* Data for 2009 are not available

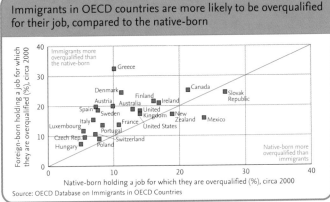

Immigrants in OECD countries are more likely to be overqualified for their job, compared to the native-born

Foreign-born holding a job for which they are overqualified (%), circa 2000

Immigrants more overqualified than the native-born

Native-born holding a job for which they are overqualified (%), circa 2000

Native-born more overqualified than immigrants

Source: OECD Database on Immigrants in OECD Countries

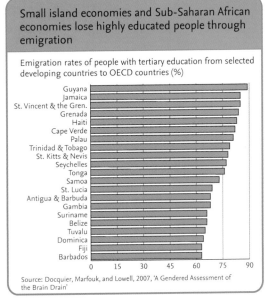

Small island economies and Sub-Saharan African economies lose highly educated people through emigration

Emigration rates of people with tertiary education from selected developing countries to OECD countries (%)

Source: Docquier, Marfouk, and Lowell, 2007, 'A Gendered Assessment of the Brain Drain'

In 2009 the largest share of remittances went to Asia: East Asia and the Pacific received $85 billion in remittances and South Asia received $75 billion. The top remittance-receiving developing economies in 2009 were India ($49.3 billion), China ($47.6 billion), Mexico ($22.2 billion), and the Philippines ($19.8 billion). Among the high-income economies, France ($15.6 billion), Germany ($10.9 billion), Spain ($9.9 billion), and Poland ($8.8 billion) received the largest amount of remittances in the form of compensation of employees.

Empirical studies have found that remittances can raise income levels, especially among the poor. Evidence from some countries suggests that a large proportion of remittances received are invested, which should lead to improvements in the overall economy. Migration opportunities may also encourage higher levels of educational attainment. And increases in income from remittances along with the transfer of knowledge through migrants result in better health outcomes for other household members.

Migration may also have negative effects. Among international migrants are millions of highly educated people who have moved to developed countries from developing countries. By migrating they improve their own prospects and provide valuable services in high-income economies, but the loss of human capital, the so-called brain drain, from developing countries, may increase the concentration of poverty and reduce the social benefits of migration. The regions most affected by brain drain are Sub-Saharan Africa and small island economies. For example, between 1995 and 2002, an estimated 69 percent of medical officers trained in Ghana emigrated, causing health services in the country to deteriorate.

Furthermore, highly skilled emigrants do not always find jobs that match their skills in the destination country. Immigrants in most OECD countries are more likely to be overqualified—working in occupations for which their skills are too high—compared with the native-born population.

Migration

international migrants as a share of population, 2010

- less than 1.0%
- 1.0–2.9%
- 3.0–5.9%
- 6.0–14.9%
- 15.0% or more
- no data

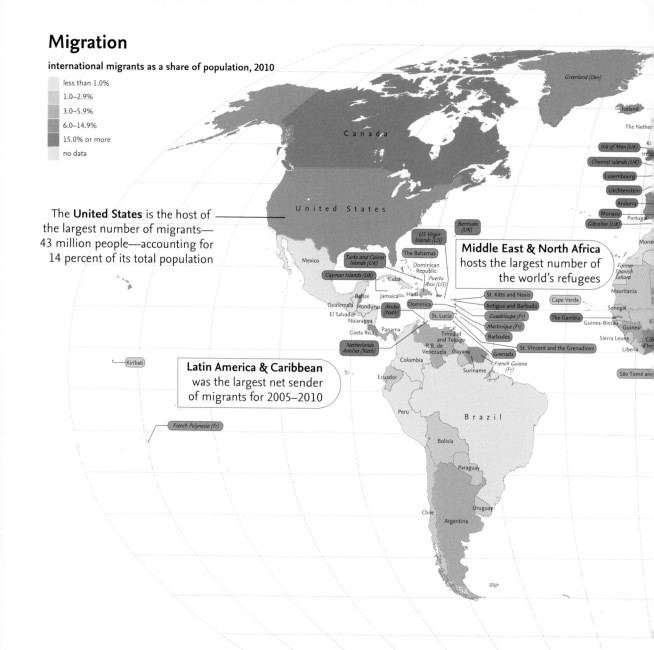

The **United States** is the host of the largest number of migrants—43 million people—accounting for 14 percent of its total population

Middle East & North Africa hosts the largest number of the world's refugees

Latin America & Caribbean was the largest net sender of migrants for 2005–2010

Map labels: Greenland (Den), Iceland, The Nether, Canada, Isle of Man (UK), Ire, Channel Islands (UK), Luxembourg, Liechtenstein, Andorra, United States, Monaco, Portugal, Gibraltar (UK), Bermuda (UK), US Virgin Islands (US), Moro, The Bahamas, Mexico, Turks and Caicos Islands (UK), Dominican Republic, Former Spanish Sahara, Cayman Islands (UK), Cuba, Puerto Rico (US), Mauritania, Belize, Jamaica, Haiti, St. Kitts and Nevis, Cape Verde, Senegal, Guatemala, Honduras, Aruba (Neth), Dominica, Antigua and Barbuda, El Salvador, Guadeloupe (Fr), The Gambia, Guinea-Bissau, Guinea, Nicaragua, St. Lucia, Martinique (Fr), Costa Rica, Panama, Barbados, Sierra Leone, Co d'Ivo, Netherlands Antilles (Neth), Trinidad and Tobago, St. Vincent and the Grenadines, Liberia, R.B. de Venezuela, Guyana, Grenada, Colombia, French Guiana (Fr), São Tomé and, Kiribati, Ecuador, Suriname, Peru, Brazil, French Polynesia (Fr), Bolivia, Paraguay, Chile, Uruguay, Argentina

Immigrants becoming U.S. citizens at a naturalization oath ceremony

Countries with highest migrations, 2005–		
Rank	Country	Net in-migration (thou
1	United States	5,052
2	Spain	1,750
3	Italy	1,650
4	Canada	1,050
5	Afghanistan	1,000
Rank	Country	Net out-migration (thou
1	Mexico	2,430
2	China	1,731
3	Pakistan	1,416
4	India	1,000
5	Philippines	900

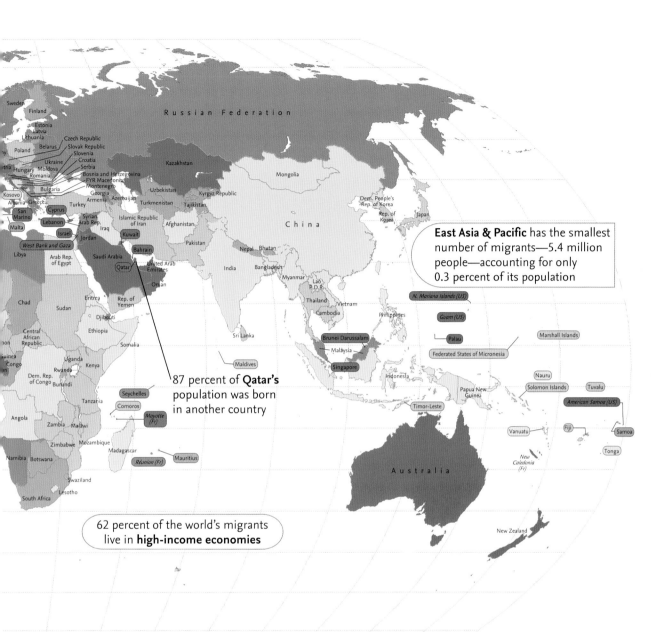

East Asia & Pacific has the smallest number of migrants—5.4 million people—accounting for only 0.3 percent of its population

87 percent of **Qatar's** population was born in another country

62 percent of the world's migrants live in **high-income economies**

Facts	Internet links	
the 1960s the majority of migrants lived in developing countries. day, nearly two-thirds reside in high-income countries.	▶ United Nations Population Division— International Migration	www.un.org/esa/ population/migration
he number of migrants in the world grew from about 72 million in 1960 more than 213 million in 2010. But this remained about 3 percent of the orld's population.	▶ United Nations Refugee Agency—Statistics	www.unhcr.org/ statistics.html
s of 2010, 81 million migrants live in developing countries (about 1.4 percent their population), compared to 132 million in high-income countries (about 2 percent of their population).	▶ OECD—Migration	www.oecd.org/migration
efugees are an important component of the migrant stock. At the end of 2009, e number of refugees, including Palestinian refugees under the mandate of NRWA, stood at 15.2 million, accounting for approximately 7 percent of the igrants in the world.	▶ International Organization for Migration	www.iom.int
ut of 179 countries with migration estimates for 2005–2010, 76 are net igrant recipients and 103 are net migrant senders.	▶ International Labour Organization— Labour Migration	www.ilo.org (go to Themes, select Labour Migration)

Remittances

remittances received as a share of GDP, 2009 or latest available data

- 5.0% or more
- 2.5–4.9%
- 1.0–2.4%
- 0.5–0.9%
- less than 0.5%
- no data

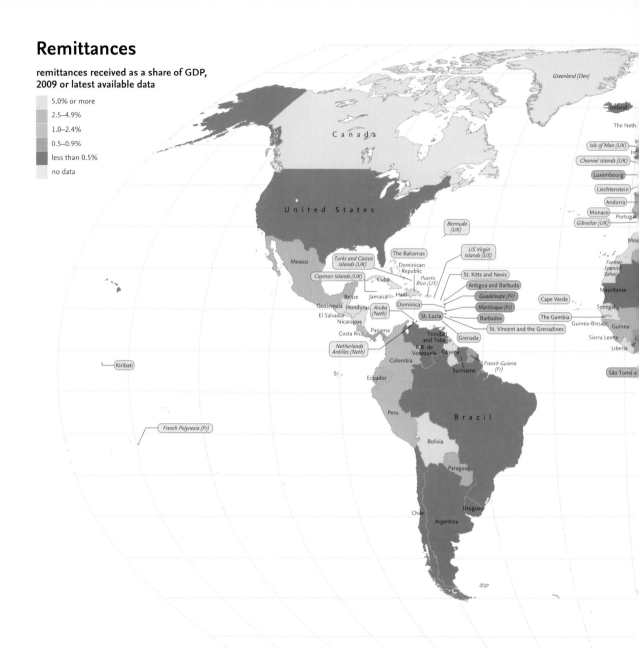

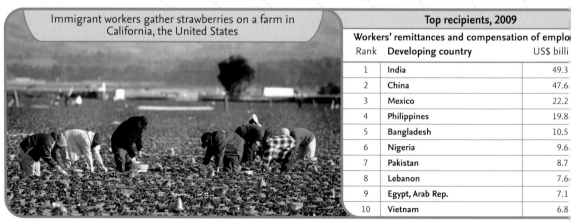

Immigrant workers gather strawberries on a farm in California, the United States

Top recipients, 2009

Workers' remittances and compensation of emplo

Rank	Developing country	US$ billi
1	India	49.3
2	China	47.6
3	Mexico	22.2
4	Philippines	19.8
5	Bangladesh	10.5
6	Nigeria	9.6
7	Pakistan	8.7
8	Lebanon	7.6
9	Egypt, Arab Rep.	7.1
10	Vietnam	6.8

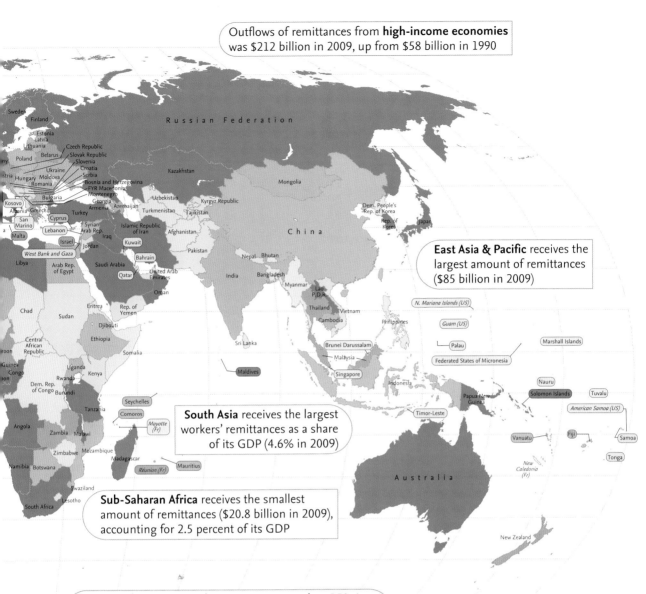

Outflows of remittances from **high-income economies** was $212 billion in 2009, up from $58 billion in 1990

East Asia & Pacific receives the largest amount of remittances ($85 billion in 2009)

South Asia receives the largest workers' remittances as a share of its GDP (4.6% in 2009)

Sub-Saharan Africa receives the smallest amount of remittances ($20.8 billion in 2009), accounting for 2.5 percent of its GDP

In 2009, **Ukraine** received remittances more than 150 times the value in 2000. **Kyrgyz Republic** and **Slovak Republic** received remittances 100 and 93 times the value in 2000

Facts	Internet links	
s a share of GDP, countries such as Tajikistan (35 percent), Tonga (29 percent), ɛsotho (28 percent), and Samoa (27 percent) had the largest receipt of ·mittances in 2009. Chile (0.003 percent), Lao PDR (0.02 percent), Malawi ۱.02 percent), United States (0.02 percent), and Libya (0.03 percent) had ۱e smallest.	▶ World Bank— Migration and Remittances	www.worldbank.org/prospects/migrationandremittances
t the beginning of the 1990s, more than half of remittances went to high-income ɔuntries. In 2009, middle-income countries received nearly 68 percent of all ɛmittances, and low-income countries received 5.4 percent.	▶ OECD—Migration	www.oecd.org/migration
ɛmittances to developing countries increased from 1.1 percent of GDP in ₁990 to 1.9 percent in 2009. In high-income countries it remained constant ‹ 0.3 percent.	▶ International Monetary Fund, Balance of Payments Statistics	www.imfstatistics.org/bop
·Iigh-income countries are the principal source of outward remittance flows. ۱he United States is the largest, with $48.3 billion in outward flows in 2009. ·audi Arabia ($26.0 billion) is the second largest, followed by Switzerland ·۱9.2 billion), Russian Federation ($18.6 billion), and Germany ($15.9 billion).	▶ Development Research Centre on Migration, Globalisation and Poverty	www.migrationdrc.org
	▶ Migration Information Source	www.migrationinformation.org

The global economy has become more integrated than ever before. More people are on the move. Countries are exchanging more goods and services, and international financial flows have increased. But even in an expanding world economy, many countries cannot finance their own development. Aid helps to fill the gap.

Development is a partnership between developing and donor countries. Donor countries help recipient countries build the capacity to foster change; recipient countries invest in their people and create an environment that sustains growth. Countries that have difficulty tapping financial markets must rely on aid flows from wealthier countries to fund development programs. Net official development assistance (ODA) to developing countries reached $128.6 billion in 2008, the highest ever in nominal terms—representing a 13.7 percent increase in real terms from the 2007 level.

Dock workers moving cargo in Ecuadorean port

Who were the largest donors? According to the Organisation for Economic Co-operation and Development's Development Assistance Committee (DAC), the top 10 donors in 2009 contributed 85 percent of all aid provided by DAC members. The top four—the United States, the European Commission, the United Kingdom, and Germany—contributed more than 65 percent.

Aid increased sharply in 2005, as donor countries followed through on promises made at the 2002 United Nations International Conference on Financing for Development, in Monterrey, Mexico, and reinforced at the 2005 Group of Eight (G8) summit at Gleneagles, Scotland. But a large part of this came as debt relief, not new aid flows. Aid in absolute terms and measured as a share of donors' gross national income declined between 2005 and 2007, but has increased since then. Still, a significant increase in donor commitment is required to meet the targets set at Gleneagles.

The form and purpose for which aid is given makes a difference. Debt-related aid provides relief from liabilities that recipient

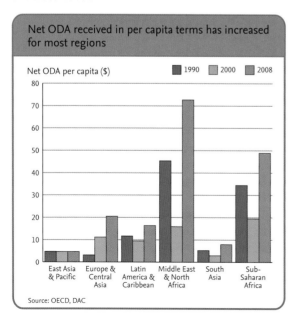

Net ODA received in per capita terms has increased for most regions

Net ODA per capita ($) — 1990 ☐ 2000 ☐ 2008

Source: OECD, DAC

Who were the largest donors in 2009?		Top 10 DAC donors Net bilateral ODA disbursements in 2009	
		$ millions	% of total
1	United States	25,112	25.6
2	European Commission	14,616	14.9
3	United Kingdom	7,769	7.9
4	Germany	6,999	7.1
5	France	6,854	7.0
6	Japan	5,998	6.1
7	Netherlands	4,794	4.9
8	Spain	4,299	4.4
9	Norway	3,163	3.2
10	Canada	3,147	3.2
	Other DAC members	15,209	15.5
	All DAC members	97,961	100.0

Source: OECD, DAC

The social sector received 39 percent of DAC donors' bilateral aid in 2008

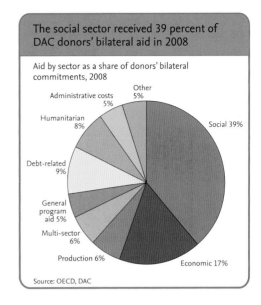

Aid by sector as a share of donors' bilateral commitments, 2008

Source: OECD, DAC

countries have difficulty servicing and can free up public resources for other purposes, but it may not result in an equivalent expansion of development activities. Humanitarian assistance provides relief for sudden disasters and emergency situations, but it does not generally contribute to financing long-term development. Furthermore, the administrative costs of providing aid are mainly spent in the donor economy.

Aid is not the only source of development finance or, for many countries, the most important. Remittances and private capital flows are a growing source of financing for some. But extremely poor countries, especially in Sub-Saharan Africa, still require substantial increases in aid to reach their development goals.

More aid from DAC members is required to meet their target for 2010

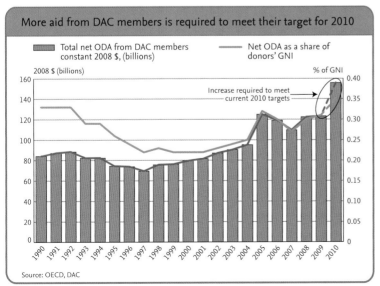

Source: OECD, DAC

Sources of finance for developing countries

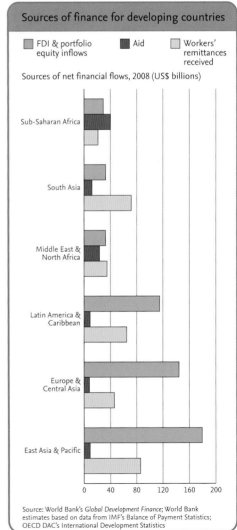

Sources of net financial flows, 2008 (US$ billions)

Source: World Bank's *Global Development Finance*; World Bank estimates based on data from IMF's Balance of Payment Statistics; OECD DAC's International Development Statistics

Aid

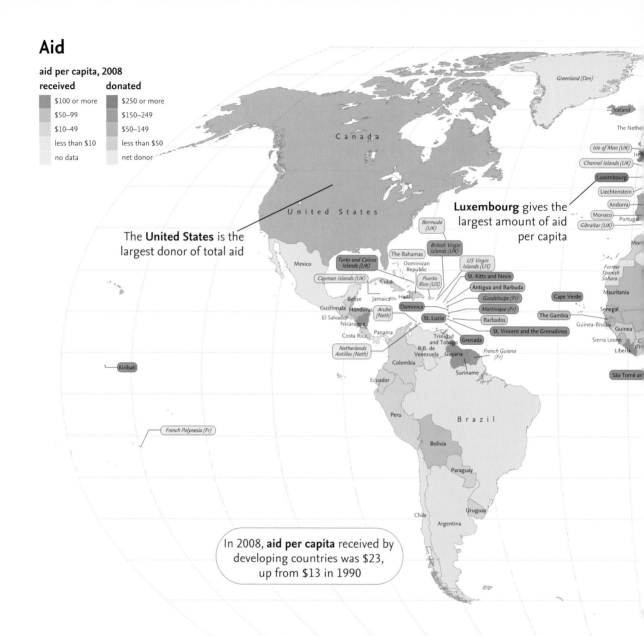

aid per capita, 2008

received
- $100 or more
- $50–99
- $10–49
- less than $10
- no data

donated
- $250 or more
- $150–249
- $50–149
- less than $50
- net donor

The **United States** is the largest donor of total aid

Luxembourg gives the largest amount of aid per capita

In 2008, **aid per capita** received by developing countries was $23, up from $13 in 1990

Greenland (Den)
Iceland
The Nethe
Canada
United States
Mexico
Bermuda (UK)
The Bahamas
Dominican Republic
Turks and Caicos Islands (UK)
Cayman Islands (UK)
Cuba
Belize
Jamaica
Haiti
Guatemala
Honduras
El Salvador
Nicaragua
Aruba (Neth)
Costa Rica
Panama
Netherlands Antilles (Neth)
Colombia
Ecuador
Peru
Bolivia
Paraguay
Chile
Uruguay
Argentina
Brazil
Puerto Rico (US)
British Virgin Islands (UK)
US Virgin Islands (US)
St. Kitts and Nevis
Antigua and Barbuda
Guadeloupe (Fr)
Dominica
Martinique (Fr)
St. Lucia
Barbados
St. Vincent and the Grenadines
Grenada
Trinidad and Tobago
R.B. de Venezuela
Guyana
French Guiana (Fr)
Suriname
Cape Verde
The Gambia
Former Spanish Sahara
Mauritania
Senegal
Guinea-Bissau
Guinea
Sierra Leone
Liberia
Portugal
Gibraltar (UK)
Monaco
Andorra
Liechtenstein
Luxembourg
Channel Islands (UK)
Isle of Man (UK)
Mor
Kiribati
French Polynesia (Fr)
São Tomé ar

A British Chinook helicopter takes UNHCR relief items to the Leepa Valley, in Pakistan-administered Kashmir

Net ODA received as a share of GNI, 2

Rank	Developing country	
1	Liberia	
2	Afghanistan	
3	Burundi	
4	Solomon Islands	
5	Micronesia, Fed. Sts.	
6	Marshall Islands	
7	São Tomé and Príncipe	
8	Palau	
9	Malawi	
10	Mozambique	

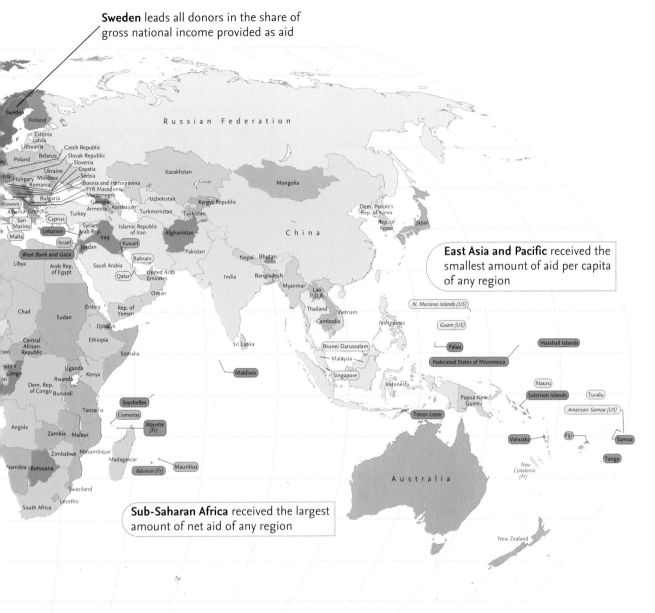

Sweden leads all donors in the share of gross national income provided as aid

East Asia and Pacific received the smallest amount of aid per capita of any region

Sub-Saharan Africa received the largest amount of net aid of any region

Facts	Internet links	
Many donor countries pledged to provide aid equivalent to at least .7 percent of GNI, but the average remains below 0.31 percent. In 009, only five countries—Sweden, Norway, Luxembourg, Denmark, nd the Netherlands—have fulfilled their pledge.	▶ Organisation for Economic Co-operation and Development (OECD), Development Assistance Committee (DAC)	**www.oecd.org/dac**
ince 1990, aid per capita increased by $14 in Sub-Saharan Africa, rom $35 to $49. Aid per capita to the Middle East and North Africa ncreased by $28, from $45 in 1990 to $73 in 2008.	▶ Statistics on aid from OECD DAC	**www.oecd.org/dac/stats**
ying arrangements, which limit where aid can be spent, may prevent id recipients from obtaining the best value for their money. On verage, 87 percent of the aid provided by DAC members was untied n 2008, compared with 81 percent in 2000.	▶ European Commission—Aid	**ec.europa.eu/europeaid**
	▶ World Bank Group, International Development Association	**www.worldbank.org/ida**
id received by low-income countries in 2008 constituted 9.2 percent f their GNI. In middle-income countries aid was only 0.3 percent f GNI.	▶ International Monetary Fund, Poverty Reduction Growth Facility	**www.imf.org** (search for What the IMF Does)

Many countries borrow from abroad to finance development, but when debt exceeds the capacity of a country to service it, the debt burden becomes unsustainable and hinders development. Making debt manageable for poor countries frees up resources that can be used to support social programs.

A country's external debt burden affects its creditworthiness and vulnerability to financial shocks. In 2008, developing countries' external debt was $3.7 trillion, with the 10 largest debtors owing 63 percent of the total. The global financial crisis has had a pronounced impact on capital flows to developing economies. The long-term debt flows from private creditors to developing countries dropped from $315 billion in 2007 to $228 billion in 2008. Another sign of the vulnerability of developing countries to financial uncertainty was the outflow of $12.7 billion of short-term debt. This was partially offset by an increase in financing from official creditors that stepped in with emergency financing to developing countries most affected by the global financial crisis. In 2008 there were net debt inflows from official creditors of $28 billion after five years in a row in which repayments exceeded new borrowing.

All developing regions have experienced improvements in their external debt ratios. Measured against developing countries' gross national income (GNI), the stock of external obligations is now 22.1 percent, compared with 37.2 percent in 2000. The ratio of debt service (principal and interest

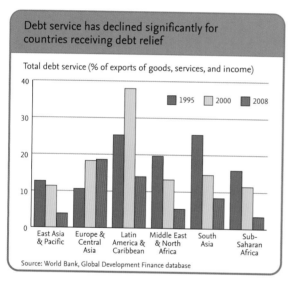

Debt service has declined significantly for countries receiving debt relief

Total debt service (% of exports of goods, services, and income)

Source: World Bank, Global Development Finance database

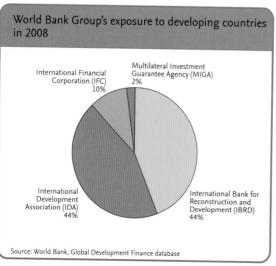

World Bank Group's exposure to developing countries in 2008

International Financial Corporation (IFC) 10%

Multilateral Investment Guarantee Agency (MIGA) 2%

International Development Association (IDA) 44%

International Bank for Reconstruction and Development (IBRD) 44%

Source: World Bank, Global Development Finance database

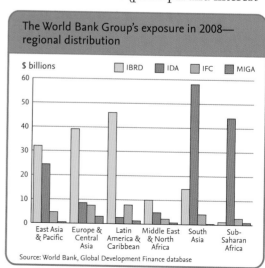

The World Bank Group's exposure in 2008— regional distribution

$ billions

IBRD   IDA   IFC   MIGA

Source: World Bank, Global Development Finance database

payments) to exports has fallen by half, to 9.5 percent. And the ratio of total external debt outstanding to exports has fallen from 90.2 percent in 2000 to 58.7 percent in 2008. East Asia and the Pacific and the Middle East and North Africa have the lowest external debt ratios. Europe and Central Asia is the most indebted region: the ratios of external debt outstanding to GNI (37.3 percent) and to export earnings (93.3 percent) were three times those of the East Asian countries. The debt to export ratio in Sub-Saharan African countries declined to 48 percent at the end of 2008, compared with 180.6 percent in 2000, and the debt service to export ratio fell to 3.3 percent, less than one-third its 2000 level.

Debt relief

Poor countries unable to borrow from private sources have borrowed from official creditors. In 1996 the World Bank and the International Monetary Fund (IMF) launched the Heavily Indebted Poor Countries (HIPC) initiative to provide relief to a group of mostly African countries with recurring debt repayment problems. The initiative aimed to provide permanent relief from unsustainable debt and to redirect the resources going to debt service to social expenditures aimed at poverty reduction. By June 2010, 36 countries had participated in the initiative and received debt relief of $72.3 billion. Since 2005 the World Bank, IMF, African Development Fund, and Inter-American Development Bank have provided additional debt relief under the Multilateral Debt Relief Initiative (MDRI). As of June 2010, 29 HIPC countries, primarily in Sub-Saharan Africa, had received additional assistance of $45.2 billion under the MDRI.

World Bank Group Financing

The World Bank Group through its member institutions— International Bank for Reconstruction and Development (IBRD), International Development Association (IDA), International Financial Corporation (IFC), and Multilateral Investment Guarantee Agency (MIGA)—committed over $40 billion in 2008 to help countries struggling with the global economic crisis, a record for the institution. The World Bank Group's exposure to developing countries at end-2008 (defined as disbursed and undisbursed commitments) totaled $324 billion: IBRD and IDA each had exposure of approximately $143 billion; IFC exposure was $32 billion; and that of MIGA $7 billion. The countries of South Asia accounted for almost 24 percent of the total owed to the World Bank Group. Three

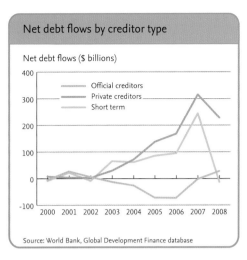

Net debt flows by creditor type

Net debt flows ($ billions)

Official creditors
Private creditors
Short term

Source: World Bank, Global Development Finance database

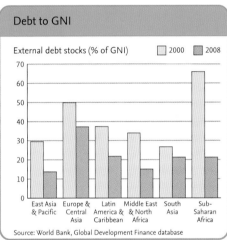

Debt to GNI

External debt stocks (% of GNI) □ 2000 ■ 2008

East Asia & Pacific / Europe & Central Asia / Latin America & Caribbean / Middle East & North Africa / South Asia / Sub-Saharan Africa

Source: World Bank, Global Development Finance database

other regions—East Asia and the Pacific, Europe and Central Asia, and Latin America and the Caribbean— accounted for between 18 and 19 percent each.

IDA provides concessional financing to the world's poorest countries. Its operations are concentrated in South Asia and Sub-Saharan Africa. Together these regions account for 72 percent of the outstanding IDA portfolio. IFC and MIGA are active in all regions but with a concentration in Latin America and the countries of Europe and Central Asia. These two regions combined accounted for 53 and 67 percent of the IFC's and MIGA's portfolios, respectively.

External debt

external debt as a share of GNI, 2008

- 60% or more
- 45–59%
- 30–44%
- 15–29%
- less than 15%
- no data

Guinea-Bissau
274%

Liberia
515%

Turkey is one of the top 10 debtor countries	Highest debtors		
	Rank	Developing country	Total external debt ([Total debt service (9
	1	**Russian Federation**	402 [26%]
	2	**China**	378 [9%]
	3	**Turkey**	277 [35%]
	4	**Brazil**	256 [16%]
	5	**India**	230 [19%]
	6	**Poland**	218 [42%]
	7	**Mexico**	203 [19%]
	8	**Indonesia**	150 [30%]
	9	**Argentina**	128 [40%]
	10	**Kazakhstan**	107 [95%]

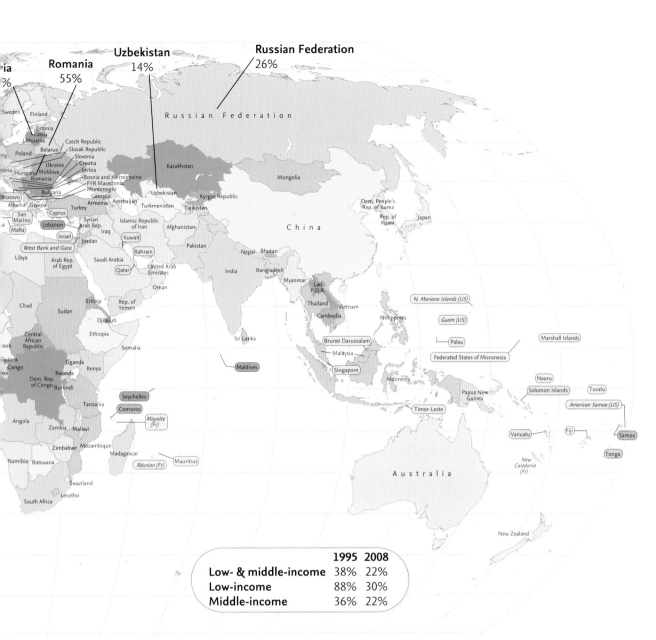

Romania 55%
Uzbekistan 14%
Russian Federation 26%

	1995	2008
Low- & middle-income	38%	22%
Low-income	88%	30%
Middle-income	36%	22%

Facts	Internet links	
n Sub-Saharan Africa, the ratio of debt to GNI fell from an average 5 percent in 2000 to 21 percent in 2008.	► World Bank	data.worldbank.org/topic/economic-policy-and-external-debt
Out of 120 developing countries with available estimates, 99 have lowered heir external debt to GNI ratio between 2000 and 2008.	► Bank for International Settlements External Debt Statistics	www.bis.org (go to Statistics, then select External Debt)
he ratio of debt service to exports fell from 20 percent in 2000 to .5 percent in 2008.	► World Bank—Quarterly External Debt Statistics	www.worldbank.org/qeds
he global financial crisis has squeezed credit from the private sector. hort-term debt together with the flows from private creditors to eveloping countries fell 66 percent in 2008 from 2007.	► OECD—External Debt	www.oecd.org (go to Statistics, then select External Debt)
	► IMF—External Debt	www.imf.org/external/np/sta/ed/ed.htm
he World Bank committed over $40 billion in 2008 to help countries truggling with the global economic crisis.	► Joint External Debt Hub	www.jedh.org

Cities will continue to grow. Cities can be tremendously efficient in many ways—such as easier provision of water and sanitation services, and better access to healthcare, education, and other social and cultural services—but they also face increases in congestion, pollution, costs of meeting basic needs and make demands on the environment and natural resources.

Cities, now home to almost half of the world's people, are growing rapidly in size and number, especially in developing countries. People flock to cities for work, access to public services, and a higher standard of living. By

2050, the world's urban population is expected to almost double, from 3.4 billion in 2009 to 6.3 billion. Sub-Saharan Africa will experience a drastic increase in its urban population, from 298 million to more than a billion over the next four decades.

Among developing regions, urbanization has gone farthest in Latin America and the Caribbean, where 79 percent of the people now live in urban areas; this number is expected to increase to 89 percent by 2050. By 2050, 70 percent of the world's population will live in urban areas, in some countries placing tremendous pressure on the capacity of the natural and human-made environment to support them. The consequences are deteriorating living conditions, the growth of slums, the destruction of habitat, and air and water pollution.

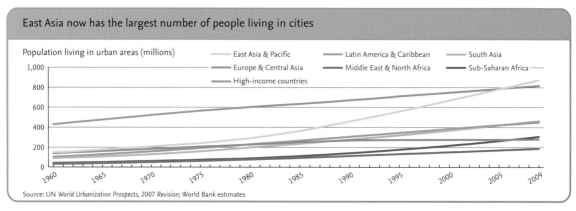

East Asia now has the largest number of people living in cities

Source: UN World Urbanization Prospects, 2007 Revision; World Bank estimates

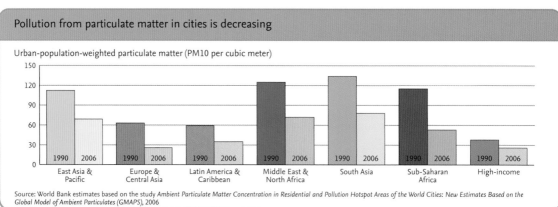

Pollution from particulate matter in cities is decreasing

Source: World Bank estimates based on the study Ambient Particulate Matter Concentration in Residential and Pollution Hotspot Areas of the World Cities: New Estimates Based on the Global Model of Ambient Particulates (GMAPS), 2006

Cities house half the world's population, but basic services are often lacking in poor areas

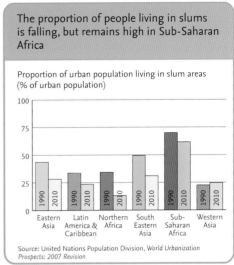
The proportion of people living in slums is falling, but remains high in Sub-Saharan Africa

Proportion of urban population living in slum areas (% of urban population)

Source: United Nations Population Division, *World Urbanization Prospects: 2007 Revision*

UN Habitat defines a slum dwelling as a household that lacks one or more of the following:

- Durable housing of a permanent nature
- Sufficient living space
- Easy access to safe water
- Access to adequate sanitation
- Security of tenure that prevents forced evictions.

By this definition more than 900 million people in developing regions live in slums—about one in three people living in urban areas or one of every six people worldwide. To achieve significant improvements in the lives of slum dwellers, public and private investment in durable, affordable housing is required.

Urbanization and the environment

The cost of urbanization to human health comes from a variety of sources. Diarrheal diseases from inadequate sanitation account for an estimated 4 percent of the global burden of disease. The proximity to industrial works and roadways and the use of inefficient and polluting sources of energy can result in exposure to high levels of soot and small, airborne particles (PM10—fine, suspended particles less than 10 microns in diameter) that contribute to lung cancer, other respiratory diseases, and heart disease.

Air and water pollution in many of the world's major cities cause moderate to severe sickness and death, and cost billions of dollars in lost productivity and damages. Although all the world's large cities share these problems, water pollution tends to be most serious in South, Southeast, and Central Asia. Air

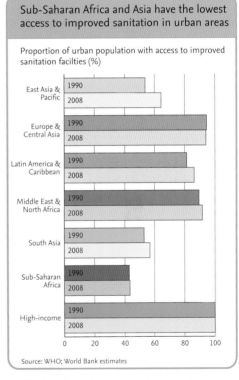
Sub-Saharan Africa and Asia have the lowest access to improved sanitation in urban areas

Proportion of urban population with access to improved sanitation facilties (%)

Source: WHO; World Bank estimates

pollution has the biggest impact in China, Latin America and the Caribbean, and Eastern Europe. Not only are the human and financial costs of pollution high, they tend to fall disproportionately on poor people. So addressing pollution is justified on equity, economic, and environmental grounds.

Urbanization

urban population as a share of total population, 2009

- less than 35%
- 35–49%
- 50–64%
- 65–79%
- 80% or more
- no data

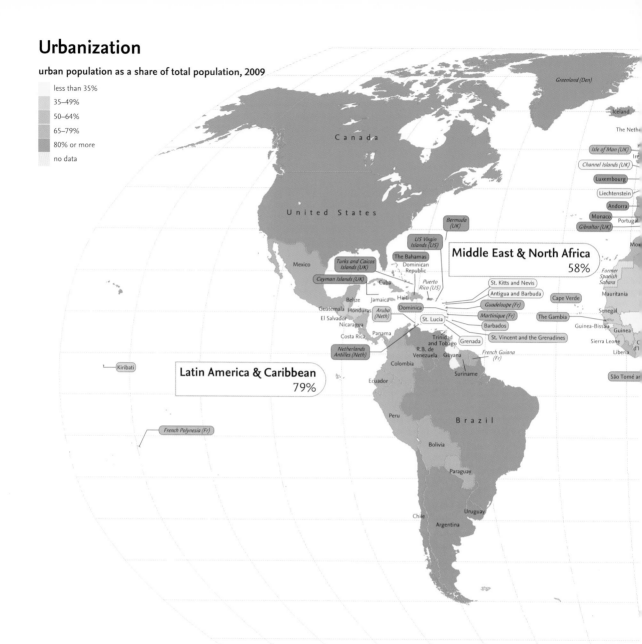

Greenland (Den)

Iceland

The Neth

Isle of Man (UK)

Ire

Channel Islands (UK)

Luxembourg

Liechtenstein

Andorra

Monaco

Portugal

Gibraltar (UK)

Canada

United States

Mexico

Bermuda (UK)

US Virgin Islands (US)

The Bahamas

Dominican Republic

Turks and Caicos Islands (UK)

Cayman Islands (UK)

Cuba

Puerto Rico (US)

Belize

Jamaica

Haiti

Guatemala

Honduras

Aruba (Neth)

Dominica

El Salvador

Nicaragua

Costa Rica

Panama

Netherlands Antilles (Neth)

Colombia

Ecuador

Peru

Bolivia

Paraguay

Chile

Uruguay

Argentina

Brazil

St. Kitts and Nevis

Antigua and Barbuda

Cape Verde

Guadeloupe (Fr)

Martinique (Fr)

The Gambia

St. Lucia

Barbados

St. Vincent and the Grenadines

Trinidad and Tobago

Grenada

R.B. de Venezuela

Guyana

French Guiana (Fr)

Suriname

Middle East & North Africa
58%

Former Spanish Sahara

Mauritania

Senegal

Guinea-Bissau

Guinea

Sierra Leone

Liberia

d'I

São Tomé ar

Mo

Latin America & Caribbean
79%

Kiribati

French Polynesia (Fr)

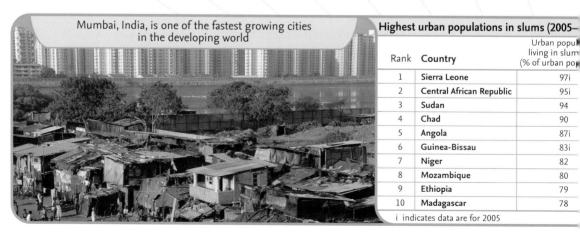

Mumbai, India, is one of the fastest growing cities in the developing world

Highest urban populations in slums (2005–

Rank	Country	Urban popul living in slum (% of urban po)
1	Sierra Leone	97i
2	Central African Republic	95i
3	Sudan	94
4	Chad	90
5	Angola	87i
6	Guinea-Bissau	83i
7	Niger	82
8	Mozambique	80
9	Ethiopia	79
10	Madagascar	78

i indicates data are for 2005

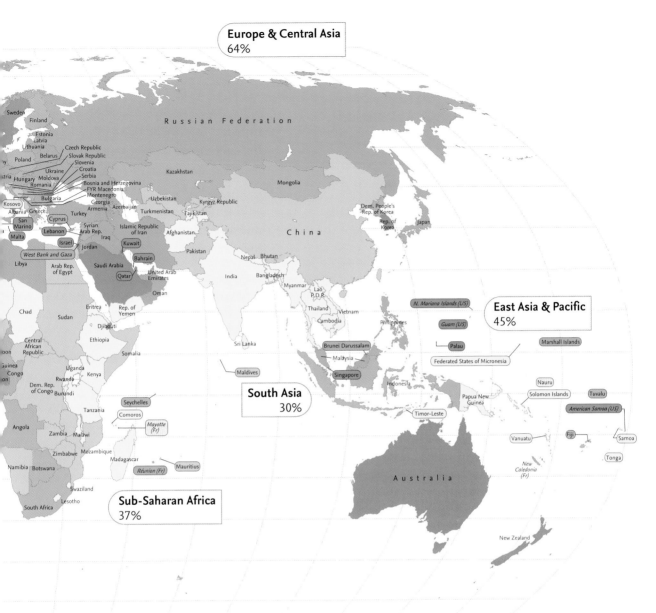

Europe & Central Asia
64%

Russian Federation

Sweden
Finland
Estonia
Latvia
Lithuania
Poland
Belarus
Czech Republic
Slovak Republic
Slovenia
Croatia
Ukraine
Serbia
Moldova
Bosnia and Herzegovina
FYR Macedonia
Montenegro
Georgia
Armenia
Azerbaijan
Turkmenistan
Kyrgyz Republic
Tajikistan

Kazakhstan

Mongolia

Kosovo
Albania Greece
Turkey
Syrian Arab Rep.
Islamic Republic of Iran
Afghanistan

Dem. People's Rep. of Korea
Rep. of Korea
Japan

San Marino
Cyprus
Malta
Lebanon
Israel
Jordan
Kuwait
Bahrain
West Bank and Gaza
Qatar
United Arab Emirates
Pakistan

China

Libya
Arab Rep. of Egypt
Saudi Arabia
Oman
Nepal Bhutan
India
Bangladesh
Myanmar
Lao P.D.R.

Chad
Sudan
Eritrea
Rep. of Yemen
Djibouti
Ethiopia
Somalia
Thailand
Cambodia
Vietnam
Philippines

Central African Republic
Uganda
Kenya
Sri Lanka
Brunei Darussalam
Malaysia
Singapore

N. Mariana Islands (US)
Guam (US)
Palau
Federated States of Micronesia
Marshall Islands

East Asia & Pacific
45%

Guinea
Congo
Dem. Rep. of Congo
Rwanda
Burundi
Tanzania

Maldives

South Asia
30%

Indonesia
Papua New Guinea

Nauru
Solomon Islands
Tuvalu

Angola
Zambia Malawi
Seychelles
Comoros
Mayotte (Fr)
Timor-Leste
American Samoa (US)
Vanuatu
Fiji
Samoa

Zimbabwe Mozambique
Madagascar
Réunion (Fr)
Mauritius
New Caledonia (Fr)
Tonga

Namibia Botswana
Australia

Swaziland
South Africa Lesotho
Sub-Saharan Africa
37%

New Zealand

Facts	Internet links	
Latin America and the Caribbean has the highest share of people living in urban areas.	▶ United Nations Population Information Network	**www.un.org/popin**
Urban areas cover only 3 percent of the world's land area.	▶ Population Reference Bureau	**www.prb.org**
The urban population of Sub-Saharan Africa is growing at 3.8 percent, faster than any other region.	▶ World Bank Urban Development	**www.worldbank.org/urban**
In 1800, 3 percent of the world's people lived in urban areas; by 1900 14 percent did; and today more than 50 percent do.	▶ United Nations, *World Urbanization Prospects, 2007 Revision*	**esa.un.org/unup**
Almost 70 percent of greenhouse gas emissions come from cities.		

The world is producing enough food to feed all, but 1 billion people lack adequate nutrition to meet their daily needs. Lack of food—along with poor quality food that does not supply vital nutrients—takes a pervasive toll on health and productivity in developing countries, especially in Sub-Saharan Africa.

The demand for food will continue to grow because of population growth, income growth, accelerating changes in dietary habits, and industrial demand for commodities such as corn (maize) and soybeans. By 2050 there will be 9 billion people living on Earth, almost 3 billion more than today. Most will live in cities, but all will depend on rural areas to feed them.

Meeting the growing demand for food and improving the quality of life of those who produce it require increasing the productivity of farmers and their land. Agricultural output has grown more rapidly than population, but so has the demand for agricultural products. Since 2000 the world's food production per capita has grown by 1.3 percent annually. Production in the developing regions of Asia and South America has grown even faster, around 2 percent. But in Africa, with some of the highest rates of undernourishment, food production has barely kept pace with population increase.

Food consumption patterns in developing countries are changing as incomes rise. Traditional meals, based on cereals and vegetables, are being replaced by more input-intensive and higher-priced meat products.

Producing more food requires more efficient use of the agricultural inputs— land, water, and soil fertility. Intensified cultivation through the use of fertilizers, pesticides, irrigation, and new plant varieties can make limited land more productive. Such practices, however, may also cause further environmental

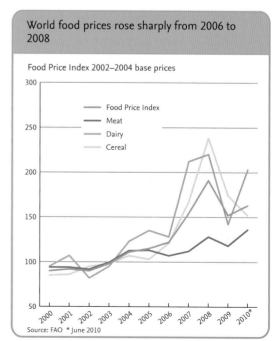

Food production per capita in Southeast Asia and South America has risen steadily

Food production per capita index, 1999–2001=100

— World
— Africa
— South America
— Southeast Asia

Source: FAO

World food prices rose sharply from 2006 to 2008

Food Price Index 2002–2004 base prices

— Food Price Index
— Meat
— Dairy
— Cereal

Source: FAO * June 2010

Overgrazing is one of many causes of land degradation

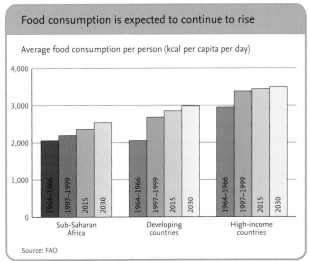

Food consumption is expected to continue to rise

Average food consumption per person (kcal per capita per day)

Sub-Saharan Africa | Developing countries | High-income countries
1964–1966, 1997–1999, 2015, 2030

Source: FAO

degradation. The effects of climate change represent a further challenge to efforts to raise the productivity of plants and animals.

Many poor farmers subsist on fragile lands, poorly suited to intensive farming. They lack access to fertilizers, farm equipment, irrigation systems, high-yielding plant varieties, and markets for their produce. Overgrazing, deforestation, improper crop rotation, and poor soil and water management contribute to land degradation. The degradation of land reduces its productivity, encouraging growing populations to move on to new and poorer land, converting forests and fragile, semi-arid areas into low-productivity cultivated areas.

In 2002, almost 1.4 billion people were living on fragile lands, more than three-quarters of them in Asia and Africa. On these lands, yields are low, the risks of crop failure are high, and a large portion of the population is undernourished. Many, especially in Africa, are vulnerable to climate variability and associated floods and droughts that are likely to become more pronounced as a result of climate change, leading to local famines and increased levels of malnutrition. Sustainable production methods, based on environmentally sound practices, along with the development of more efficient markets for farm inputs and outputs and off-farm activities, are the keys to improving rural livelihoods and expanding the global food supply.

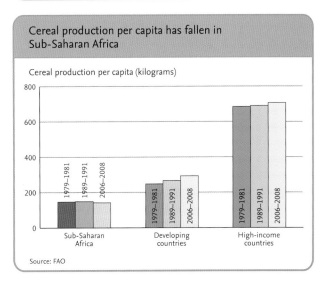

Cereal production per capita has fallen in Sub-Saharan Africa

Cereal production per capita (kilograms)

Sub-Saharan Africa | Developing countries | High-income countries
1979–1981, 1989–1991, 2006–2008

Source: FAO

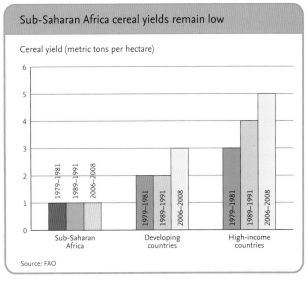

Sub-Saharan Africa cereal yields remain low

Cereal yield (metric tons per hectare)

Sub-Saharan Africa | Developing countries | High-income countries
1979–1981, 1989–1991, 2006–2008

Source: FAO

Undernourishment

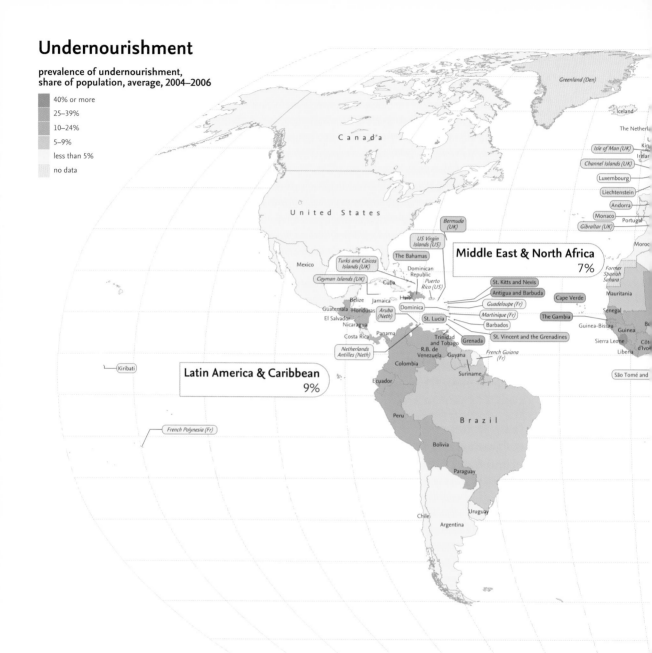

prevalence of undernourishment,
share of population, average, 2004–2006

- 40% or more
- 25–39%
- 10–24%
- 5–9%
- less than 5%
- no data

Greenland (Den)

Iceland

The Netherl
Isle of Man (UK)   Kin
Channel Islands (UK)   Irelar
Luxembourg
Liechtenstein
Andorra
Monaco   Portugal
Bermuda
(UK)   Gibraltar (UK)
US Virgin   Moroc
Islands (US)
The Bahamas
Canada   Former
Spanish
Middle East & North Africa   Sahara
7%   Mauritania
Mexico
United States
Turks and Caicos
Islands (UK)
Dominican
Republic   St. Kitts and Nevis
Cayman Islands (UK)   Puerto   Antigua and Barbuda
Cuba   Rico (US)   Cape Verde
Haiti   Guadeloupe (Fr)   Senegal
Belize   Jamaica   Dominica   Martinique (Fr)   The Gambia
Guatemala Honduras Aruba   St. Lucia   Guinea-Bissau   Guinea
El Salvador   (Neth)   Barbados   Sierra Leone   Côte
Nicaragua   St. Vincent and the Grenadines   d'Ivo
Costa Rica Panama Trinidad   Liberia
and Tobago   Grenada
Kiribati   Netherlands   R.B. de
Antilles (Neth) Venezuela   Guyana   French Guiana   São Tomé and
Latin America & Caribbean Colombia   (Fr)
9%
Ecuador   Suriname

Peru   B r a z i l

French Polynesia (Fr)   Bolivia

Paraguay

Chile   Uruguay
Argentina

Feeding centers are important in preventing
undernourishment in many countries

Countries with the highest levels of undernourishm

Rank	Country	% of popul. 2004–20
1	Congo, Dem. Rep.	75
2	Eritrea	66
3	Burundi	63
4	Haiti	58
5	Comoros	51
6	Sierra Leone	46
7	Zambia	45
8	Angola	44
9	Ethiopia	44
10	Central African Republic	41

Europe & Central Asia
6%

Sweden
Finland
Estonia
Latvia
Lithuania
Czech Republic
Poland
Belarus
Slovak Republic
Slovenia
Croatia
Ukraine
Serbia
Bosnia and Herzegovina
stria
Hungary
Moldova
FYR Macedonia
Romania
Montenegro
Bulgaria
Kosovo
Georgia
Albania
Greece
Armenia
Azerbaijan
Turkmenistan
Turkey
Cyprus
San Marino
Syrian Arab Rep.
Islamic Republic of Iran
Afghanistan
Malta
Lebanon
Israel
Jordan
Kuwait
West Bank and Gaza
Libya
Arab Rep. of Egypt
Qatar
Bahrain
Saudi Arabia
United Arab Emirates
Oman

Russian Federation
Kazakhstan
Mongolia
Uzbekistan
Kyrgyz Republic
Tajikistan
China
Dem. People's Rep. of Korea
Rep. of Korea
Japan
Pakistan
Nepal
Bhutan
India
Bangladesh
Myanmar
Lao P.D.R.
Thailand
Vietnam
Cambodia
Sri Lanka
Philippines
Maldives
Brunei Darussalam
Malaysia
Singapore
Indonesia
Timor-Leste

N. Mariana Islands (US)

East Asia & Pacific
12%

Guam (US)
Palau
Marshall Islands
Federated States of Micronesia
Nauru
Solomon Islands
Tuvalu
Papua New Guinea
American Samoa (US)
Vanuatu
Fiji
Samoa
Tonga
New Caledonia (Fr)

Chad
Sudan
Eritrea
Rep. of Yemen
Djibouti
Central African Republic
Ethiopia
Somalia
uinea
Congo
on
Uganda
Kenya
Rwanda
Dem. Rep. of Congo
Burundi
Tanzania
Seychelles
Comoros
Mayotte (Fr)
Angola
Zambia
Malawi
Madagascar
Mauritius
Zimbabwe
Mozambique
Réunion (Fr)
Namibia
Botswana
Swaziland
South Africa
Lesotho

South Asia
22%

Sub-Saharan Africa
28%

Australia

New Zealand

Facts	Internet links	
Worldwide 1.02 billion people were estimated to be undernourished in 2009.	▶ FAO—Hunger	**www.fao.org** (click on Hunger)
More than 100 million people were deprived of access to adequate food because of the food crises in 2006–2008.	▶ World Health Organization	**www.who.org**
According to FAO, about 642 million people in East Asia and Pacific and 65 million people in Sub-Saharan Africa are suffering from chronic hunger.	▶ World Food Programme	**www.wfp.org**
	▶ Consultative Group on International Agricultural Research	**www.cgiar.org**
bout 30 percent of people in developing countries are affected by vitamin nd mineral deficiencies.	▶ International Fund for Agricultural Development	**www.ifad.org**

Water is crucial to economic growth and development—and to the survival of terrestrial and aquatic ecosystems. Demand for water is increasing for food production, for industrial uses, and for human consumption. Meanwhile, nearly 900 million people lack convenient access to safe drinking water.

With the projected growth in population and economic activity, the share of the world's population facing water shortages will increase more than fivefold by 2050. Human needs for water in daily life compete with demands from agriculture, energy production, and other industrial uses. Urbanization and changes in lifestyle have led to higher per capita use. Climate change is also expected to influence the availability and distribution of freshwater supplies. These trends pose a significant challenge for meeting the Millennium Development Goals and sustaining the growth of developing countries.

Although the Earth's water resources are estimated at about 1.4 billion cubic kilometers, only a fraction is available for human needs. Freshwater makes up only 2.5 percent of total water resources, or about 35 million cubic kilometers. Most freshwater occurs in the form of permanent ice or snow, locked up in Antarctica and Greenland, or in deep groundwater aquifers. The principal sources of water for human use are lakes, rivers, soil moisture, and relatively shallow groundwater basins. The

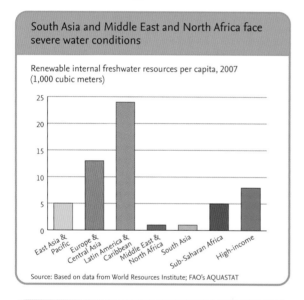

South Asia and Middle East and North Africa face severe water conditions

Renewable internal freshwater resources per capita, 2007 (1,000 cubic meters)

Source: Based on data from World Resources Institute; FAO's AQUASTAT

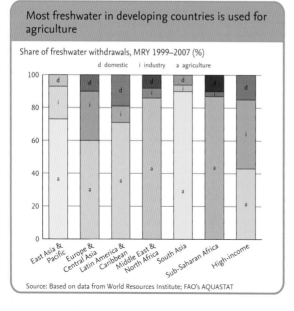

Most freshwater in developing countries is used for agriculture

Share of freshwater withdrawals, MRY 1999–2007 (%)

d domestic   i industry   a agriculture

Source: Based on data from World Resources Institute; FAO's AQUASTAT

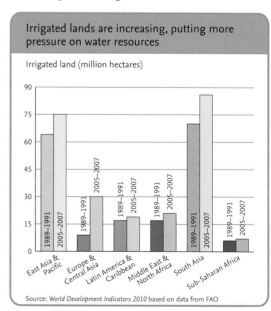

Irrigated lands are increasing, putting more pressure on water resources

Irrigated land (million hectares)

Source: *World Development Indicators 2010* based on data from FAO

The diversion of water for irrigation has resulted in the Aral Sea shrinking, causing health problems and destroying the fishing industry

usable portion is less than 1 percent of all freshwater and only 0.03 percent of all water on Earth. Much of that is located far from human populations.

Humans compete with ecosystems in the use of freshwater. Extraction of water for human needs diminishes the amount available to maintain the integrity of terrestrial and marine ecosystems. The three major factors leading to increased water demand over the past century have been population growth, industrial development, and the expansion of irrigated land in agriculture. Agriculture accounts for more than 70 percent of freshwater withdrawals—90 percent in low-income countries. Most of this water is used for irrigation to provide about 40 percent of world food production. Pollution of water bodies causes further degradation of natural systems and reduces the supply fit for human consumption.

Although domestic use of water for drinking and washing is the smallest part of the demand for water—usually less than 5 percent of the total—providing safe water for human consumption is of great importance for health and wellbeing. Water supplies should be free of chemical and biological contaminants and delivered in such a way that their cleanliness is protected. They should also be regularly and conveniently available.

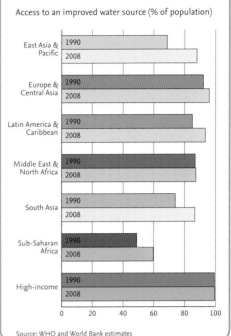

Despite progress, more than 40 percent of the population of Sub-Saharan Africa lacks access to an improved water source

Access to an improved water source (% of population)

Source: WHO and World Bank estimates

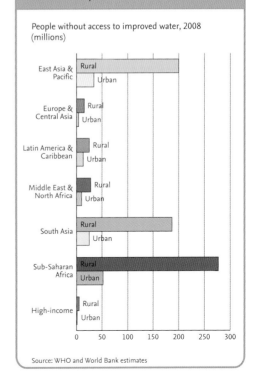

People in rural areas are more likely to lack access to improved water sources

People without access to improved water, 2008 (millions)

Source: WHO and World Bank estimates

Access to water

share of population with access to an improved
water source, 2008

- less than 50%
- 50–69%
- 70–89%
- 90–99%
- 100%
- no data

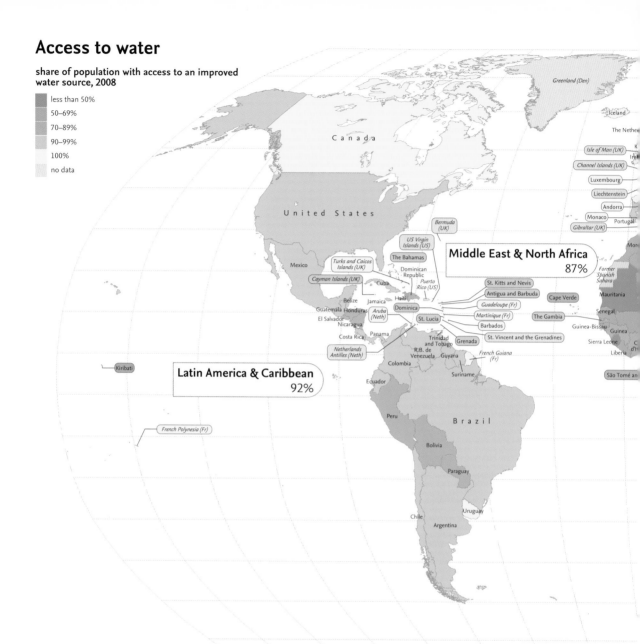

Greenland (Den)

Iceland

The Nethe

Isle of Man (UK)

Channel Islands (UK)

Luxembourg

Liechtenstein

Andorra

Monaco   Portugal

Gibraltar (UK)

Canada

United States

Bermuda (UK)

US Virgin Islands (US)

The Bahamas

Mexico

Turks and Caicos Islands (UK)

Cayman Islands (UK)

Cuba

Dominican Republic

Puerto Rico (US)

Middle East & North Africa
87%

Former Spanish Sahara

Mor

Mauritania

St. Kitts and Nevis

Antigua and Barbuda

Cape Verde

Belize   Jamaica   Haiti

Guadeloupe (Fr)

Senegal

Guatemala Honduras   Aruba (Neth)   Dominica

Martinique (Fr)

The Gambia

El Salvador

Nicaragua

St. Lucia

Guinea-Bissau   Guinea

Barbados

Costa Rica   Panama

Trinidad and Tobago

Grenada

St. Vincent and the Grenadines

Sierra Leone

C d'I'

Netherlands Antilles (Neth)

R.B. de Venezuela   Guyana

French Guiana (Fr)

Liberia

Kiribati

Colombia

Suriname

São Tomé an

Latin America & Caribbean
92%

Ecuador

Peru

B r a z i l

French Polynesia (Fr)

Bolivia

Paraguay

Chile

Uruguay

Argentina

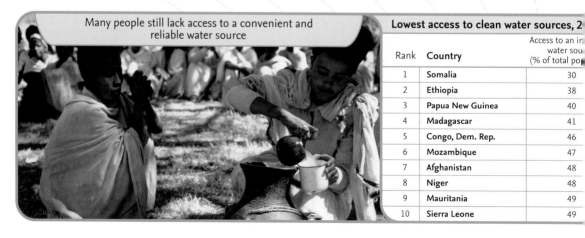

Many people still lack access to a convenient and
reliable water source

Lowest access to clean water sources, 2

Rank	Country	Access to an ir water sou (% of total po
1	Somalia	30
2	Ethiopia	38
3	Papua New Guinea	40
4	Madagascar	41
5	Congo, Dem. Rep.	46
6	Mozambique	47
7	Afghanistan	48
8	Niger	48
9	Mauritania	49
10	Sierra Leone	49

Europe & Central Asia
95%

East Asia & Pacific
86%

South Asia
84%

Sub-Saharan Africa
58%

Facts	Internet links	
While population has increased from 1.6 billion to 6 billion, water withdrawals have increased from about 500 cubic kilometers to ,830 cubic kilometers during 1900–2000.	► AQUASTAT, Food and Agriculture Organization	**www.fao.org/nr/water/aquastat/ main/index.stm** (click on Statistical Databases)
y 2050 the world's water will have to support the agricultural ystems that will feed and create livelihoods for an additional .7 billion people.	► UN Environment Programme	**www.unep.org**
atin America, with 31 percent, and East Asia, with 22 percent, ave more than half of the world's freshwater resources.		
outh Asia uses 90 percent of total freshwater withdrawals for gricultural use.	► World Resources Institute	**www.wri.org**

Forests contribute to the livelihood of poor people and nourish the natural systems on which many more people depend. About 30 percent of global land area is forest, which accounts for as much as 90 percent of terrestrial biodiversity. In most countries, however, forests are shrinking.

Forest loss is taking a terrible toll on both the natural and economic resources of many countries. Forests meet many people's basic, everyday needs, providing food, fuel, building materials, and clean water. Forests also provide essential public goods of global value. They facilitate the hydrological and nutrient cycles and act as carbon sinks, reducing the accumulation of greenhouse gases in the atmosphere.

Deforestation is the main cause of biodiversity loss. *Biodiversity* refers to the variety of plants and animal species on earth, the genetic variability within each

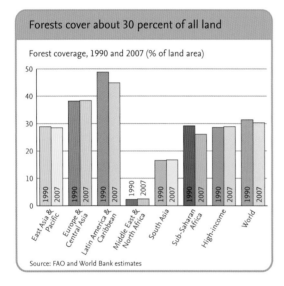

Forests cover about 30 percent of all land

Forest coverage, 1990 and 2007 (% of land area)

Source: FAO and World Bank estimates

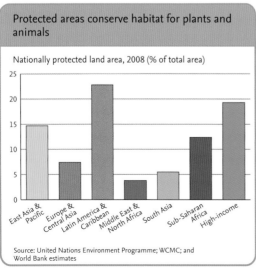

Protected areas conserve habitat for plants and animals

Nationally protected land area, 2008 (% of total area)

Source: United Nations Environment Programme; WCMC; and World Bank estimates

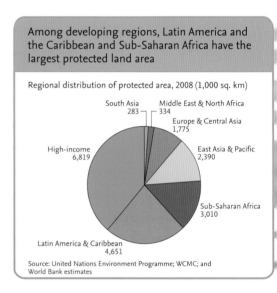

Among developing regions, Latin America and the Caribbean and Sub-Saharan Africa have the largest protected land area

Regional distribution of protected area, 2008 (1,000 sq. km)

South Asia 283
Middle East & North Africa 334
Europe & Central Asia 1,775
East Asia & Pacific 2,390
Sub-Saharan Africa 3,010
Latin America & Caribbean 4,651
High-income 6,819

Source: United Nations Environment Programme; WCMC; and World Bank estimates

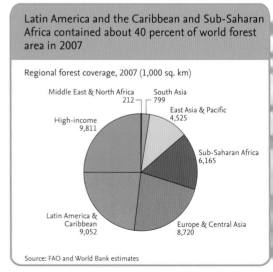

Latin America and the Caribbean and Sub-Saharan Africa contained about 40 percent of world forest area in 2007

Regional forest coverage, 2007 (1,000 sq. km)

Middle East & North Africa 212
South Asia 799
East Asia & Pacific 4,525
Sub-Saharan Africa 6,165
Europe & Central Asia 8,720
Latin America & Caribbean 9,052
High-income 9,811

Source: FAO and World Bank estimates

A bend in the Ganga River, India

species, and the variety of ecosystems in which they live. Tropical forests are particularly rich in diversity of life. In addition, forest loss in the tropics is responsible for 10 to 30 percent of global greenhouse gas emissions.

Deforestation is largely driven by human action. Because many services provided by forests are not valued, they are subject to destructive and unsustainable exploitation that is not economically or environmentally justified. Forests are cleared to expand agricultural land or allow the exploitation of minerals. Timber is used to provide fuel and raw material for manufacturing and construction. In many cases, a proper accounting would show that forests are more valuable than these destructible uses.

Global deforestation is proceeding at 13 million hectares a year, but because of reforestation the net forest loss will add up to about 5 million hectares between 2000 and 2010. New incentives and careful regulation are needed to stop deforestation. Forest areas may be designated as protected areas to prevent illegal and unsustainable exploitation. About 13 percent, including some lower density forest areas, of global forest area is under protection. Generally the least well protected forests are located in Africa.

Rainforest protected from destruction within the Argentinian sector of Iguazú National Park

Forest lost and gained

average annual change in forest area, between 1990 and 2007

- decrease of 1.0% or more
- decrease of 0.1–0.9%
- no significant change
- increase of 0.1–0.9%
- increase of 1.0% or more
- no data

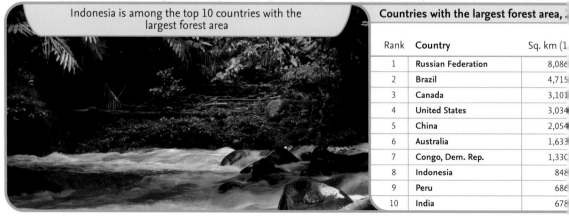

Indonesia is among the top 10 countries with the largest forest area

Countries with the largest forest area,

Rank	Country	Sq. km (1
1	**Russian Federation**	8,086
2	**Brazil**	4,715
3	**Canada**	3,101
4	**United States**	3,034
5	**China**	2,054
6	**Australia**	1,633
7	**Congo, Dem. Rep.**	1,330
8	**Indonesia**	848
9	**Peru**	686
10	**India**	678

Facts	Internet links	
Between 1990 and 2007, the world lost about 140 million hectares of forest, more than 8 million hectares per year.	▶ Food and Agriculture Organization—Forestry	**www.fao.org** (click on Forestry)
China added an average of about 2.9 million hectares of forest each year from 1990 to 2007.	▶ International Union for Conservation of Nature	**www.iucn.org**
The forest area in Brazil decreased by more than 48 million hectares, about 35 percent of the world's forest loss, between 1990 and 2007.		
At the global level, deforestation seems to be slowing: the estimate of forest cover change indicates an annual loss of 7.3 million hectares during the years 2000 to 2007, compared with 8.9 million hectares annually between 1990 and 2007.	▶ Food and Agriculture Organization's *Global Forest Resources Assessment 2010*	**www.fao.org/forestry/fra2010**

Protected areas

nationally protected areas as a share of
total land area, 2008

- ■ less than 2%
- ■ 2–4%
- ■ 5–9%
- ■ 10–19%
- □ 20% or more
- □ no data

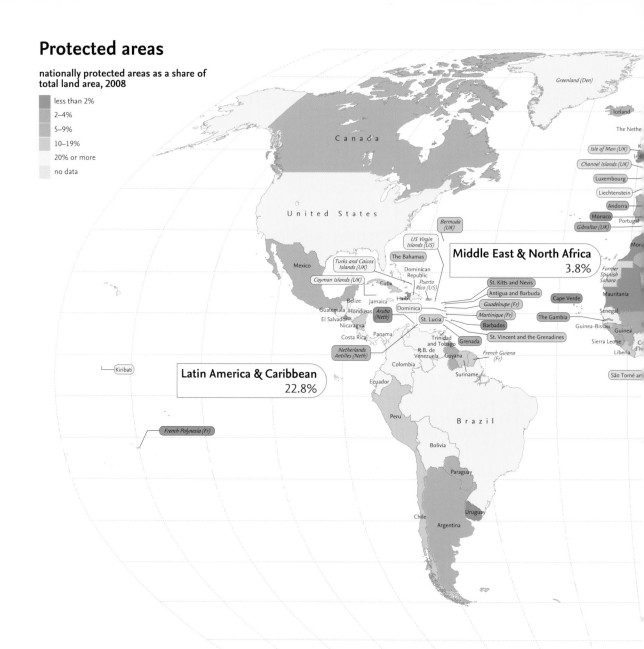

Greenland (Den)

Iceland

The Nethe

Canada

Isle of Man (UK)

Channel Islands (UK)

Luxembourg

Liechtenstein

Andorra

United States

Monaco   Portugal

Gibraltar (UK)

Bermuda (UK)

US Virgin Islands (US)

The Bahamas

Mexico

Middle East & North Africa
3.8%

Former Spanish Sahara

Mauritania

Turks and Caicos Islands (UK)

Dominican Republic

Cayman Islands (UK)

Puerto Rico (US)

Cuba

Haiti

St. Kitts and Nevis

Antigua and Barbuda

Cape Verde

Senegal

Belize

Jamaica

Guadeloupe (Fr)

The Gambia

Guinea-Bissau

Guatemala Honduras

Dominica

Aruba (Neth)

Martinique (Fr)

Guinea

El Salvador

St. Lucia

Barbados

Nicaragua

Costa Rica

Panama

Trinidad and Tobago

St. Vincent and the Grenadines

Sierra Leone

Liberia

Grenada

Kiribati

Netherlands Antilles (Neth)

R.B. de Venezuela

Guyana

French Guiana (Fr)

São Tomé an

Colombia

Suriname

Ecuador

Latin America & Caribbean
22.8%

Peru

B r a z i l

French Polynesia (Fr)

Bolivia

Paraguay

Chile

Uruguay

Argentina

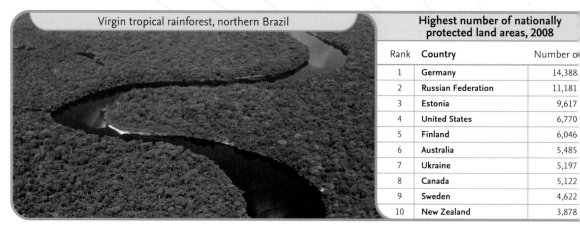

Virgin tropical rainforest, northern Brazil

Highest number of nationally protected land areas, 2008

Rank	Country	Number o
1	Germany	14,388
2	Russian Federation	11,181
3	Estonia	9,617
4	United States	6,770
5	Finland	6,046
6	Australia	5,485
7	Ukraine	5,197
8	Canada	5,122
9	Sweden	4,622
10	New Zealand	3,878

Europe & Central Asia
7.8%

East Asia & Pacific
14.7%

South Asia
5.5%

Sub-Saharan Africa
12.4%

Facts	Internet links	
The world's nationally protected areas were about 19 million square kilometers or 14 percent of the total surface area in 2008.	▶ United Nations Environment Programme World Conservation Monitoring Centre	www.unep-wcmc.org/protected_areas
Marine surface areas were about 2.2 million square kilometers or 1.7 percent of the world's total surface area in 2008.	▶ International Union for Conservation of Nature	www.iucn.org
About 112,000 terrestrial areas were registered with the International Union for Conservation of Nature in 2008, an increase from 1,000 in 1962.	▶ World Wildlife Fund for Nature	www.wwf.org
About 10 percent, or about 400 million hectares, of the world's forest area has been declared protected.	▶ Food and Agriculture Organization's *Global Forest Resources Assessment 2010*	www.fao.org/forestry/fra2010

World demand for energy is surging. The share of energy production from alternative sources has increased slightly since 1990, but fossil fuels supplied more than 80 percent of the world's total energy production in 2007. Fossil fuels are the primary source of carbon dioxide emissions, which, along with the other greenhouse gases, are believed to be the principal cause of global climate change. Producing the energy needed for growth while mitigating its effects on the world's climate is a global challenge for everyone.

Developing countries contain five-sixths of the world's population and use about half the world's energy, but their demand is growing faster than richer countries'. Global energy use increased by about 2.6 percent from 2006 to 2007, but in fast-growing East Asia and the Pacific, energy use grew by 5.6 percent.

As economies develop, technological progress and a shift away from energy-intensive activities help to increase energy efficiency, but rising incomes and growing populations increase the demand for energy. As a result, between 1990 and 2007 worldwide energy use increased by about 36 percent, while the population rose by only 25 percent.

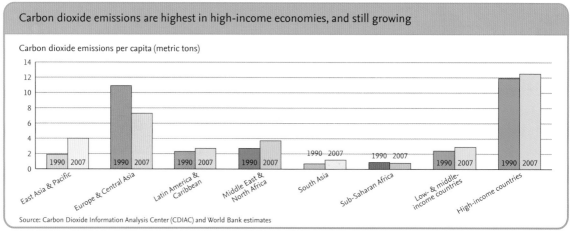

Carbon dioxide emissions are highest in high-income economies, and still growing

Carbon dioxide emissions per capita (metric tons)

Source: Carbon Dioxide Information Analysis Center (CDIAC) and World Bank estimates

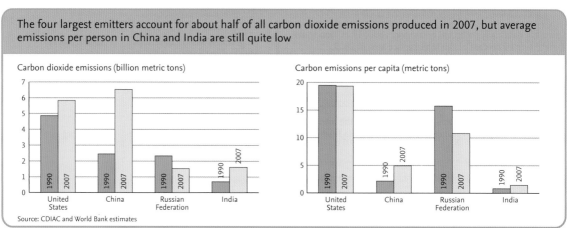

The four largest emitters account for about half of all carbon dioxide emissions produced in 2007, but average emissions per person in China and India are still quite low

Carbon dioxide emissions (billion metric tons)

Carbon emissions per capita (metric tons)

Source: CDIAC and World Bank estimates

data.worldbank.org/atlas-global/energy
See pp. 6–7 for more information

The way energy is generated determines its environmental consequences. The extensive use of fossil fuels in recent decades has boosted emissions of carbon dioxide, the principal greenhouse gas that traps heat in the atmosphere. Burning coal releases twice as much carbon dioxide as burning the equivalent amount of natural gas. It is estimated that half the amount of carbon released each year by human activities stays in the atmosphere, contributing to climate change; half of the remaining carbon is being dissolved in the ocean and the other half is absorbed on land by vegetation and soils. Clearing of forests has reduced their ability to trap carbon dioxide.

The level of carbon dioxide in the atmosphere has increased by more than 30 percent since the beginning of the industrial revolution. According to the Intergovernmental Panel on Climate Change, the rate and duration of global warming in the 20th century are unprecedented in the past thousand years. The global average surface temperature has increased by about 0.6 degrees Celsius since 1861, the year instrument records became available, and the 1990s were the warmest decade yet recorded. Increases in the maximum temperature and the number of hot days have been observed in nearly all regions. Warming is expected to continue, with increases in the range of 1.4 to 5.8 degrees Celsius over the next 100 years.

Global warming shrinks glaciers, changes the frequency and intensity of rainfall, shifts growing seasons, advances the flowering of trees and emergence of insects, and causes the sea level to rise. The magnitude and effect of climate change vary across regions, but developing countries are likely to suffer most because of their dependence on climate-sensitive activities such as agriculture and fishing. They also have more limited capacity to respond to the effects of climate change.

Solar panel powering telecommunications satellite dish on a remote island in Fiji

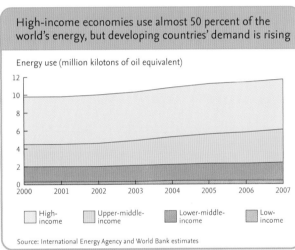
High-income economies use almost 50 percent of the world's energy, but developing countries' demand is rising

Energy use (million kilotons of oil equivalent)

High-income   Upper-middle-income   Lower-middle-income   Low-income

Source: International Energy Agency and World Bank estimates

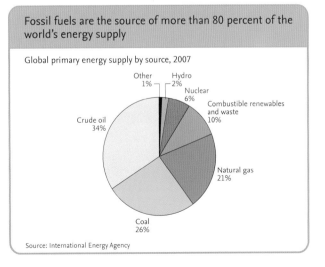
Fossil fuels are the source of more than 80 percent of the world's energy supply

Global primary energy supply by source, 2007

Other 1%   Hydro 2%   Nuclear 6%   Combustible renewables and waste 10%   Crude oil 34%   Natural gas 21%   Coal 26%

Source: International Energy Agency

Energy use

**energy use per capita,
kilograms of oil equivalent, 2007**

- 5,000 or more
- 2,500–4,999
- 1,000–2,499
- 500–999
- less than 500
- no data

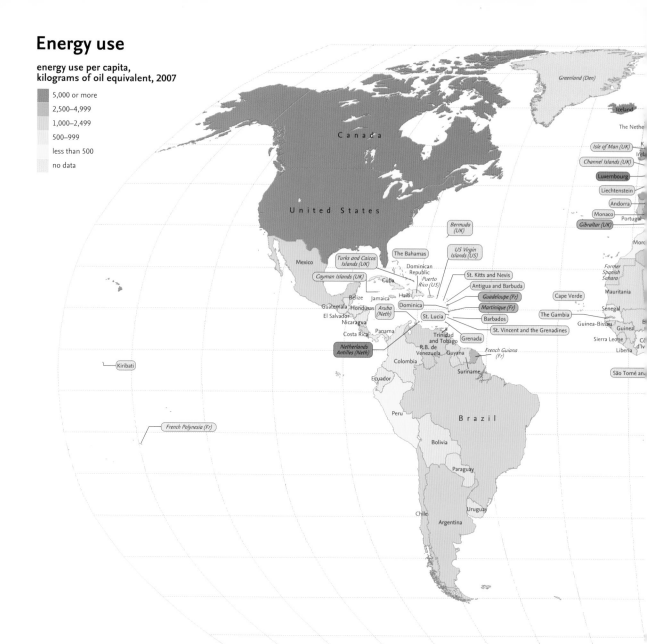

Hydropower plant in Thailand

Countries with highest energy consumption, 2007

Rank	Country	Million metric ton of oil equivalent
1	United States	2,340
2	China	1,956
3	Russian Federation	672
4	India	595
5	Japan	514
6	Germany	331
7	Canada	269
8	France	264
9	Brazil	236
10	Korea, Rep.	222

Sweden
Finland
Estonia
Latvia
Lithuania
Czech Republic
Slovak Republic
Belarus
Slovenia
Poland
Croatia
Ukraine
Serbia
Hungary Moldova
Bosnia and Herzegovina
Romania
FYR Macedonia
Bulgaria
Montenegro
Kosovo
Georgia
Albania Greece
Armenia Azerbaijan
San Marino
Cyprus
Turkey
Syrian Arab Rep.
Lebanon
Israel
West Bank and Gaza
Jordan
Malta
Libya
Arab Rep. of Egypt
Saudi Arabia
Kuwait
Bahrain
Qatar
United Arab Emirates
Oman
Chad
Sudan
Eritrea
Rep. of Yemen
Djibouti
Central African Republic
Ethiopia
Somalia
Guinea
Congo
Uganda
Kenya
Dem. Rep. of Congo
Rwanda
Burundi
Tanzania
Angola
Zambia
Malawi
Zimbabwe
Mozambique
Namibia Botswana
Madagascar
Swaziland
Lesotho
South Africa

Russian Federation
Kazakhstan
Mongolia
Uzbekistan
Kyrgyz Republic
Turkmenistan
Tajikistan
Islamic Republic of Iran
Afghanistan
Pakistan
Nepal
Bhutan
India
Bangladesh
Myanmar
Lao P.D.R.
Thailand
Vietnam
Cambodia
China
Dem. People's Rep. of Korea
Rep. of Korea
Japan
Philippines

Sri Lanka
Maldives
Seychelles
Comoros
Mayotte (Fr)
Réunion (Fr)
Mauritius

N. Mariana Islands (US)
Guam (US)
Palau
Marshall Islands
Federated States of Micronesia
Brunei Darussalam
Malaysia
Singapore
Indonesia
Nauru
Solomon Islands
Tuvalu
Papua New Guinea
Timor-Leste
American Samoa (US)
Vanuatu
Fiji
Samoa
New Caledonia (Fr)
Tonga
Australia
New Zealand

Facts	Internet links	
In 2007, petroleum, coal, and natural gas were the top sources of the world's energy consumption, accounting for 34, 26, and 21 percent, respectively.	▶ Intergovernmental Panel on Climate Change	www.ipcc.ch
Renewable energy from nuclear, hydro, and solar sources constituted less than 10 percent of the world's energy consumption in 2007.	▶ International Energy Agency	www.iea.org
Sub-Saharan Africa still gets more than half of its energy from traditional combustible renewable sources and waste.	▶ United Nations Statistics Division	unstats.un.org/unsd
China, Brazil, Canada, the United States, and the Russian Federation produced more than half of the world's hydropower energy in 2007.		
Latin America and the Caribbean produces more than 55 percent of its electricity from hydropower.	▶ The World Bank Group Energy Program	www.worldbank.org/energy
About 1.5 billion people in the world lived without access to electricity in 2008.	▶ U.S. Energy Information Administration	www.eia.doe.gov
In Sub-Saharan Africa, more than 70 percent of people live without access to electricity.		

Greenhouse gases

carbon dioxide emissions per capita, 2007

- 15.0 metric tons or more
- 10.0–14.9 metric tons
- 5.0–9.9 metric tons
- 1.0–4.9 metric tons
- less than 1.0 metric ton
- no data

Greenland (Den)

Iceland

The Nether

Isle of Man (UK)

Channel Islands (UK)

Luxembourg

Liechtenstein

Andorra

Monaco

Gibraltar (UK)

Portugal

Canada

United States

Morc

Former
Spanish
Sahara

Mauritania

Bermuda
(UK)

US Virgin
Islands (US)

Middle East & North Africa
3.7 metric tons

Mexico

Turks and Caicos
Islands (UK)

The Bahamas

Dominican
Republic

Cayman Islands (UK)

Cuba

Puerto
Rico (US)

St. Kitts and Nevis

Antigua and Barbuda

Cape Verde

Senegal

Belize

Jamaica

Haiti

Guadeloupe (Fr)

The Gambia

Guinea-Bissau

Guinea

Guatemala

Honduras

Aruba
(Neth)

Dominica

Martinique (Fr)

El Salvador

Nicaragua

St. Lucia

Barbados

Sierra Leone

Cô
d'I

Costa Rica

Panama

Trinidad
and Tobago

Grenada

St. Vincent and the Grenadines

Liberia

Netherlands
Antilles (Neth)

R.B. de
Venezuela

Guyana

French Guiana
(Fr)

Kiribati

Latin America & Caribbean
2.7 metric tons

Colombia

Suriname

São Tomé an

Ecuador

Peru

Brazil

French Polynesia (Fr)

Bolivia

Paraguay

Chile

Uruguay

Argentina

Coal-fired power stations are major contributors to atmospheric pollution	Greatest increase in emissions between 1990 and 2	
	Rank	**Country**	Increase in carbon dioxide em (million metric tons of oil equi

Rank	Country	Increase in carbon dioxide em (million metric tons of oil equi
1	China	4,074
2	United States	971
3	India	921
4	Germany	787
5	Iran, Islamic Rep.	269
6	Korea, Rep.	261
7	Indonesia	247
8	Saudi Arabia	187
9	Thailand	182
10	Brazil	159

Europe & Central Asia
7.2 metric tons

East Asia & Pacific
4.0 metric tons

South Asia
1.2 metric tons

Sub-Saharan Africa
0.8 metric tons

Facts	Internet links	
Between 1990 and 2007, the world's carbon dioxide energy-related emissions rose by 36 percent to 30 billion metric tons.	► Intergovernmental Panel on Climate Change	**www.ipcc.ch**
High-income economies emit more than four times as much carbon dioxide per person as developing economies.	► Carbon Dioxide Information Analysis Center	**cdiac.ornl.gov**
Developing countries emitted more than half the world's 30 billion metric tons of total carbon dioxide emissions in 2007.		
Carbon dioxide concentrations in the atmosphere have increased from 280 parts per million in preindustrial times to 382 in 2006—an increase of 36 percent.	► World Resources Institute	**www.wri.org**
Carbon dioxide constitutes about 75 percent of global greenhouse gas emissions.	► The IEA Greenhouse Gas R&D Programme	**www.ieaghg.org**

Economic wellbeing is derived from a country's assets. Development can be seen as a process of building and managing this diversified portfolio of assets. For wellbeing to be sustainable, the total value of assets must be maintained at a constant level over time or growing. Adjusted net saving is a measure of the net change in a country's total wealth and thus a powerful indicator of sustainability.

A country's wealth includes not only physical capital such as buildings and machinery. It also includes natural capital, such as oil deposits, forests and crop land, and human and social capital. The capacity of a country to sustain and increase wellbeing depends on how well these assets are managed. Adjusted net saving (ANS) provides a measure of net change in wealth. It is defined as gross saving plus investment in human capital (education expenditures), minus depreciation of produced capital, depletion of natural capital (subsoil assets, forest, and land), and damage from global and local pollution. If ANS is negative, it means that the country is exhausting its resources at the cost of future generations; hence it is on a path of unsustainable development.

Countries rich in natural resources have an advantage over others in financing

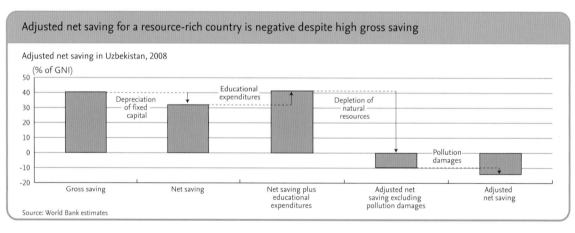

Adjusted net saving for a resource-rich country is negative despite high gross saving

Adjusted net saving in Uzbekistan, 2008

Source: World Bank estimates

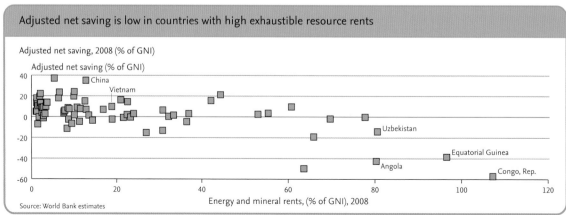

Adjusted net saving is low in countries with high exhaustible resource rents

Adjusted net saving, 2008 (% of GNI)

Source: World Bank estimates

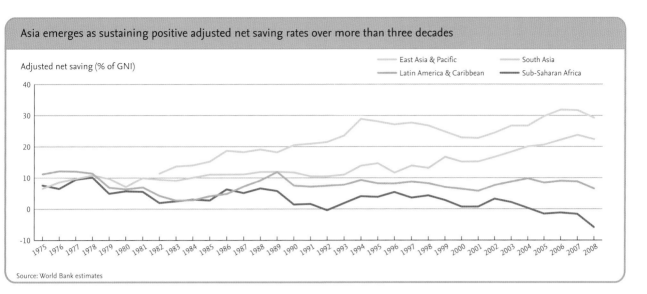

Asia emerges as sustaining positive adjusted net saving rates over more than three decades

Adjusted net saving (% of GNI)

East Asia & Pacific South Asia
Latin America & Caribbean Sub-Saharan Africa

Source: World Bank estimates

development. Natural resource rents can be effectively deployed for this purpose, but it is important to reinvest such rents in other types of capital, notably human capital and institutions. The data show that natural resource abundance often leads to low or negative ANS. This is true for many resource-rich countries in the developing world. Adjusted net saving as a percent of GNI often has a negative relationship with the share of energy and mineral resource rents in GNI. Countries such as Angola, the Republic of Congo, Equatorial Guinea, and Uzbekistan with resource rents greater than 80 percent of GNI have negative ANS rates of –20 to –60 percent of GNI. With relatively fewer natural resource endowments, China has achieved a high ANS rate by investing in produced and human capital. But natural resource abundance need not be a curse. At the other end of the spectrum are countries such as Botswana and Vietnam, rich in mineral wealth and energy resources but with positive ANS rates. They are good examples of how reinvesting resource rents can go a long way in boosting social and institutional capital with positive results on growth. Among the low-income countries, Vietnam's GDP grew by 7.51 percent per year during 1990–2008 and per capita income increased by 6.0 percent per year. Botswana has been the fastest-growing economy in Sub-Saharan Africa during the last 18 years, with an average annual per capita growth rate of 3.9 percent.

Adjusted net saving trends across regions have varied widely over time. Sub-Saharan Africa, and Europe and Central Asia have declining trends in ANS. These two regions are on an unsustainable development path. But if we look more closely, distinct stories emerge. In Sub-Saharan Africa, a relatively small handful of countries has dragged down performance for the entire region, relative to the rest of the world. But nearly two-thirds of African countries have had positive saving rates over the decade. This group was led by the largest African economy, South Africa, and includes others such as Botswana, Ethiopia, Kenya, Mauritius, Namibia, and Uganda. Other resource-rich regions, such as Latin America and the Caribbean, and the Middle East and North Africa, do not show a clear trend. Asian regions stand out as achieving almost steadily increasing ANS rates generated mostly via their high gross saving rates in recent years.

Wealth of nations

adjusted net saving, including particulate
emission damage, as a share of GNI,
2008 or latest available data

- less than -5.0%
- -5.0–0.0%
- 0.1–4.9%
- 5.0–9.9%
- 10% or more
- no data

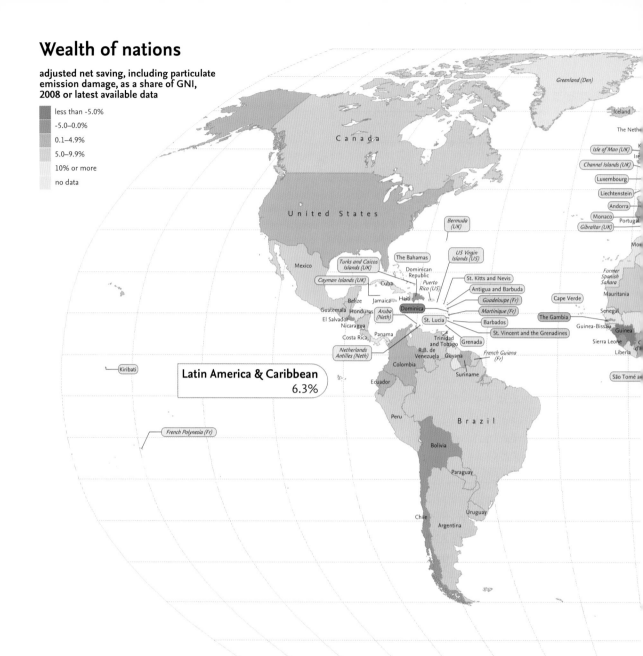

Latin America & Caribbean
6.3%

Countries with the highest share of natural capital on total wealth			
Rank	Country, population over 30 million	Natural capital as share of wealth (2005)	Adjusted net (% of GNI,
1	Congo, Dem. Rep.	69%	-2.5
2	Sudan	56%	-13.1
3	Nigeria	55%	..
4	Iran, Islamic Rep.	53%	7.5*
5	Algeria	52%	21.4
6	Russian Federation	43%	1.5
7	Vietnam	39%	9.7
8	Tanzania	35%	5.1*
9	Ethiopia	32%	8.9
10	Pakistan	28%	6.1
* 2007 **2006			

Natural capital as a share of comprehensive
wealth is most important in low- and lower-
middle-income countries. But countries differ
substantially in terms of adjusted net saving.

Europe & Central Asia
3.2%

East Asia & Pacific
28.6%

South Asia
21.6%

Sub-Saharan Africa
-6.2%

Facts	Internet links	
Natural capital constitutes a major component of wealth and is a principal source of income in developing countries.	▶ Where Is the Wealth of Nations?	go.worldbank.org/ 2QTH26ULQ0
If Trinidad and Tobago had reinvested all resource rents from oil and gas into manufactured capital, it would have accumulated more than three times as much manufactured capital as it did.	▶ Report of the Commission on the Measurement of Economic and Social Progress	www.stiglitz-sen-fitoussi.fr
In 2008 resource-rich Kazakhstan had a gross saving rate of 46 percent of GNI and an adjusted net saving rate of 3 percent of GNI.		
In 2008 the adjusted net savings was 7 percent of GNI for the world as a whole, 13 percent for low- and middle-income countries, and 0.8 percent for high-income countries.	▶ Environmental Economics at the World Bank	www.worldbank.org/ environmentaleconomics

Key indicators of development

Economy	Total population millions 2009	Life expectancy at birth years 2008	Under-5 mortality rate per 1,000 2008	Access to an improved water source % of population 2008	Gross national income (GNI)[a] $ billions 2009	per capita $ 2009
Afghanistan	29.80	44	257	48	10.6	370
Albania	3.16	77	14	97	12.5	3,950
Algeria	34.90	72	41	83	154.2	4,420
American Samoa	0.07	..	..	..	..	.. d
Andorra	0.09	..	4	100	3.4	41,130
Angola	18.50	47	220	50	64.5	3,490
Antigua and Barbuda	0.09	..	12	..	1.1	12,070
Argentina	40.28	75	16	97	304.7	7,570
Armenia	3.08	74	23	96	9.5	3,100
Aruba	0.11	75	..	100	..	.. e
Australia	21.87	81	6	100	957.5	43,770
Austria	8.36	80	4	100	391.8	46,850
Azerbaijan	8.78	70	36	80	42.5	4,840
Bahamas, The	0.34	73	13	..	7.1	21,390
Bahrain	0.79	76	12	..	19.7	25,420
Bangladesh	162.22	66	54	80	95.4	590
Barbados	0.26	77	11	100	..	.. e
Belarus	9.66	71	13	100	53.5	5,540
Belgium	10.79	80	5	100	488.8	45,310
Belize	0.33	76	19	99	1.2	3,740
Benin	8.93	61	121	75	6.7	750
Bermuda	0.06	79	..	..	..	.. e
Bhutan	0.70	66	81	92	1.4	2,020
Bolivia	9.86	66	54	86	16.0	1,620
Bosnia and Herzegovina	3.77	75	15	99	17.7	4,700
Botswana	1.95	54	31	95	12.2	6,240
Brazil	193.73	72	22	97	1,557.2	8,040
Brunei Darussalam	0.40	77	7	..	10.2	27,050
Bulgaria	7.59	73	11	100	43.7	5,770
Burkina Faso	15.76	53	169	76	8.0	510
Burundi	8.30	50	168	72	1.2	150
Cambodia	14.81	61	90	61	9.7	650
Cameroon	19.52	51	131	74	22.8	1,170
Canada	33.74	81	6	100	1,423.0	42,170
Cape Verde	0.51	71	29	84	1.5	3,010
Cayman Islands	0.05	..	..	95	..	.. e
Central African Republic	4.42	47	173	67	2.0	450
Chad	11.21	49	209	50	6.9	610
Channel Islands	0.15	79	..	..	10.2	68,610
Chile	16.97	79	9	96	159.9	9,420
China	1,331.46	73	21	89	4,815.8	3,620
Hong Kong SAR, China	7.00	82	..	..	219.2	31,420
Macao SAR, China	0.54	81	..	..	18.1	35,360
Colombia	45.66	73	20	92	225.2	4,930
Comoros	0.66	65	105	95	0.6	870
Congo, Dem. Rep.	66.02	48	199	46	10.7	160
Congo, Rep.	3.68	54	127	71	6.7	1,830
Costa Rica	4.58	79	11	97	28.5	6,230
Côte d'Ivoire	21.08	57	114	80	22.4	1,060
Croatia	4.43	76	6	99	61.2	13,810
Cuba	11.20	79	6	94	..	.. d
Cyprus	0.87	80	4	100	21.4 f	26,940 f
Czech Republic	10.49	77	4	100	181.5	17,310
Denmark	5.53	79	4	100	325.8	58,930
Djibouti	0.86	55	95	92	1.1	1,280
Dominica	0.07	..	11	95	0.4	4,870
Dominican Republic	10.09	73	33	86	45.5	4,510
Ecuador	13.63	75	25	94	53.4	3,920
Egypt, Arab Rep.	83.00	70	23	99	172.0	2,070
El Salvador	6.16	71	18	87	20.8	3,370
Equatorial Guinea	0.68	50	148	43	8.4	12,420
Eritrea	5.07	59	58	61	1.5	300
Estonia	1.34	74	6	98	18.8	14,060
Ethiopia	82.82	55	109	38	27.0	330
Faeroe Islands	0.05	79	..	..	..	.. e
Fiji	0.85	69	18	..	3.4	3,950
Finland	5.34	80	3	100	243.9	45,680
France	62.62	82	4	100	2,754.6	43,990
French Polynesia	0.27	74	..	100	..	.. e
Gabon	1.47	60	77	87	10.9	7,370
Gambia, The	1.71	56	106	92	0.7	440
Georgia	4.26	72	30	98	11.1 g	2,530 g
Germany	81.88	80	4	100	3,484.7	42,560
Ghana	23.84	57	76	82	16.6	700
Gibraltar	0.03	..	..	..	..	.. e
Greece	11.28	80	4	100	323.1	28,630
Greenland	0.06	68	..	..	1.9	32,960
Grenada	0.10	75	15	..	0.6	5,550
Guam	0.18	76	..	100	..	.. e

Total debt service % of exports of goods, services and income[b] 2008	Merchandise trade % of GDP 2009	Foreign direct investment net inflows, % of GDP 2008	Starting a business time required in days June 2009	Internet users[c] per 100 people 2008	Carbon dioxide emissions per capita metric tons 2007	Economy
..	35.3	2.8	7	1.7	0.0	Afghanistan
3.0	47.6	7.3	5	23.9	1.4	Albania
..	58.9	1.5	24	11.9	4.1	Algeria
..	..	..	..	..	..	American Samoa
..	..	..	..	70.5	6.6	Andorra
2.5	81.1	2.0	68	3.1	1.4	Angola
..	64.0	21.1	21	75.0	5.1	Antigua and Barbuda
10.7	30.6	3.0	27	28.1	4.6	Argentina
12.7	45.9	7.8	15	6.2	1.6	Armenia
..	..	..	..	22.8	23.0	Aruba
..	34.5	4.5	2	70.8	17.7	Australia
..	72.9	2.9	28	71.2	8.3	Austria
0.9	65.2	0.0	10	28.2	3.7	Azerbaijan
..	52.0	9.9	31	31.5	6.4	Bahamas, The
..	126.3	8.2	9	51.9	29.6	Bahrain
3.9	41.3	1.3	44	0.3	0.3	Bangladesh
..	63.8	6.8	..	73.7	5.3	Barbados
3.1	101.8	3.6	6	32.1	6.9	Belarus
..	153.8	20.8	4	68.1	9.7	Belgium
10.5	84.4	14.0	44	10.6	1.4	Belize
..	42.1	1.8	31	1.8	0.5	Benin
..	19.4	..	..	79.4	8.0	Bermuda
..	65.0	2.4	46	6.6	0.9	Bhutan
11.3	53.4	3.1	50	10.8	1.4	Bolivia
4.4	74.5	5.7	60	34.7	7.7	Bosnia and Herzegovina
..	72.6	0.8	61	6.2	2.6	Botswana
22.7	18.2	2.7	120	37.5	1.9	Brazil
..	81.2	0.8	116	55.3	19.7	Brunei Darussalam
14.7	84.4	18.4	18	34.7	6.8	Bulgaria
..	33.2	1.7	14	0.9	0.1	Burkina Faso
28.1	35.8	0.3	32	0.8	0.0	Burundi
0.6	99.1	7.9	85	0.5	0.3	Cambodia
..	31.6	0.2	34	3.8	0.3	Cameroon
..	48.3	3.7	5	75.3	16.9	Canada
3.5	48.1	13.8	24	20.6	0.6	Cape Verde
..	..	..	..	42.4	10.1	Cayman Islands
..	20.4	6.1	22	0.4	0.1	Central African Republic
..	71.9	10.0	75	1.2	0.0	Chad
..	..	..	..	..	..	Channel Islands
18.2	58.3	8.9	27	32.5	4.3	Chile
2.0	45.0	3.3	37	22.5	5.0	China
..	354.4	27.7	6	67.0	5.8	Hong Kong SAR, China
..	42.5	27.1	..	49.2	3.0	Macao SAR, China
16.2	28.5	4.4	20	38.5	1.4	Colombia
..	29.7	1.5	24	3.6	0.2	Comoros
..	60.3	8.6	149	..	0.0	Congo, Dem. Rep.
..	96.6	24.5	37	4.3	0.4	Congo, Rep.
10.5	69.0	6.8	60	32.3	1.8	Costa Rica
9.2	68.6	1.7	40	3.2	0.3	Côte d'Ivoire
..	50.3	8.6	22	50.5	5.6	Croatia
..	..	..	..	12.9	2.4	Cuba
..	49.3	15.5	8	38.8	9.6	Cyprus
..	114.7	3.0	15	57.8	12.1	Czech Republic
..	56.8	0.9	6	83.3	9.1	Denmark
6.3	46.2	25.7	37	2.3	0.6	Djibouti
..	66.2	13.9	14	37.6	1.7	Dominica
..	38.0	6.3	19	21.6	2.1	Dominican Republic
..	50.3	1.8	64	28.8	2.2	Ecuador
4.7	35.1	5.8	7	16.6	2.3	Egypt, Arab Rep.
9.9	49.8	3.5	17	10.6	1.1	El Salvador
..	129.6	..	136	1.8	7.5	Equatorial Guinea
..	33.0	2.2	84	4.1	0.1	Eritrea
..	100.7	8.3	7	66.2	15.2	Estonia
2.8	30.8	0.4	9	0.4	0.1	Ethiopia
..	69.5	..	..	..	14.4	Faeroe Islands
..	69.9	8.7	46	12.2	1.7	Fiji
..	51.6	-1.1	14	82.5	12.1	Finland
..	38.7	3.5	7	67.9	6.0	France
..	..	..	..	..	3.1	French Polynesia
..	66.0	0.1	58	6.2	1.4	Gabon
..	44.3	8.8	27	6.9	0.2	Gambia, The
4.2	51.4	12.2	3	23.8	1.4	Georgia
..	61.3	0.7	18	75.5	9.6	Germany
3.2	87.5	12.7	33	4.3	0.4	Ghana
..	..	..	..	..	13.1	Gibraltar
..	24.0	1.5	19	43.1	8.8	Greece
..	77.8	..	..	63.9	9.2	Greenland
..	47.8	23.8	20	23.2	2.3	Grenada
..	..	..	..	48.4	..	Guam

Economy	Total population millions 2009	Life expectancy at birth years 2008	Under-5 mortality rate per 1,000 2008	Access to an improved water source % of population 2008	Gross national income (GNI)[a] $ billions 2009	per capita $ 2009
Guatemala	14.03	70	35	94	36.8	2,620
Guinea	10.07	58	146	71	3.8	370
Guinea-Bissau	1.61	48	195	61	0.8	510
Guyana	0.76	67	61	94	1.1	1,450
Haiti	10.03	61	72	63	..	.. h
Honduras	7.47	72	31	86	13.6	1,820
Hungary	10.02	74	7	100	130.1	12,980
Iceland	0.32	82	3	100	13.8	43,220
India	1,155.35	64	69	88	1,368.7	1,180
Indonesia	229.96	71	41	80	513.4	2,230
Iran, Islamic Rep.	72.90	71	32	..	330.6	4,530
Iraq	31.49	68	44	79	69.7	2,210
Ireland	4.45	80	4	100	197.2	44,310
Isle of Man	0.08	..	..	..	4.0	49,310
Israel	7.44	81	5	100	191.6	25,740
Italy	60.22	82	4	100	2,112.5	35,080
Jamaica	2.70	72	31	94	13.5	4,990
Japan	127.56	83	4	100	4,830.3	37,870
Jordan	5.95	73	20	96	22.3	3,740
Kazakhstan	15.89	66	30	95	107.1	6,740
Kenya	39.80	54	128	59	30.7	770
Kiribati	0.10	61	48	61	0.2	1,890
Korea, Dem. People's Rep.	23.91	67	55	100	..	.. h
Korea, Rep.	48.75	80	5	98	966.6	19,830
Kosovo	1.81	69	..	..	5.8	3,240
Kuwait	2.79	78	11	99	117.0	43,930
Kyrgyz Republic	5.32	67	38	90	4.6	870
Lao P.D.R.	6.32	65	61	57	5.6	880
Latvia	2.26	72	9	99	27.9	12,390
Lebanon	4.22	72	13	100	33.6	7,970
Lesotho	2.07	45	79	85	2.1	1,030
Liberia	3.95	58	145	68	0.6	160
Libya	6.42	74	17	..	77.2	12,020
Liechtenstein	0.04	83	2	..	4.0	113,210
Lithuania	3.34	72	7	..	38.1	11,410
Luxembourg	0.50	81	3	100	37.1	74,430
Macedonia, FYR	2.04	74	11	100	9.0	4,400
Madagascar	19.63	60	106	41	7.9	420
Malawi	15.26	53	100	80	4.2	280
Malaysia	27.47	74	6	100	198.7	7,230
Maldives	0.31	72	28	91	1.2	3,870
Mali	13.01	48	194	56	8.9	680
Malta	0.41	80	6	100	6.8	16,690
Marshall Islands	0.06	..	36	94	0.2	3,060
Mauritania	3.29	57	118	49	3.2	960
Mauritius	1.28	73	17	99	9.2	7,240
Mayotte	0.20	76	..	..	..	.. d
Mexico	107.43	75	17	94	958.3	8,920
Micronesia, Fed. Sts.	0.11	69	39	94	0.2	2,220
Moldova	3.60	68	17	90	5.7 i	1,590 i
Monaco	0.03	..	4	100	6.7	203,900
Mongolia	2.67	67	41	76	4.4	1,630
Montenegro	0.62	74	8	98	4.1	6,550
Morocco	31.99	71	36	81	90.7 j	2,790 j
Mozambique	22.89	48	130	47	10.0	440
Myanmar	50.02	62	98	71	..	.. h
Namibia	2.17	61	42	92	9.3	4,290
Nepal	29.33	67	51	88	13.0	440
Netherlands	16.53	80	5	100	815.8	49,350
Netherlands Antilles	0.20	76	..	..	..	.. e
New Caledonia	0.25	76	..	..	..	.. e
New Zealand	4.32	80	6	100	114.5	26,830
Nicaragua	5.74	73	27	85	5.8	1,000
Niger	15.29	51	167	48	5.2	340
Nigeria	154.73	48	186	58	175.8	1,140
Northern Mariana Islands	0.09	..	..	98	..	.. e
Norway	4.83	81	4	100	417.3	86,440
Oman	2.85	76	12	88	49.8	17,890
Pakistan	169.71	67	89	90	172.9	1,020
Palau	0.02	69	15	84	0.2	8,940
Panama	3.45	76	23	93	23.2	6,710
Papua New Guinea	6.73	61	69	40	7.9	1,180
Paraguay	6.35	72	28	86	14.4	2,270
Peru	29.16	73	24	82	120.9	4,150
Philippines	91.98	72	32	91	164.5	1,790
Poland	38.15	76	7	100	467.5	12,260
Portugal	10.63	79	4	99	222.6	20,940
Puerto Rico	3.97	79	..	..	..	.. e
Qatar	1.41	76	10	100	..	.. e

Total debt service % of exports of goods, services and income[b] 2008	Merchandise trade % of GDP 2009	Foreign direct investment net inflows, % of GDP 2008	Starting a business time required in days June 2009	Internet users[c] per 100 people 2008	Carbon dioxide emissions per capita metric tons 2007	Economy
12.2	51.3	1.9	29	14.3	1.0	Guatemala
9.6	58.0	10.1	41	0.9	0.1	Guinea
..	41.8	1.8	213	2.4	0.2	Guinea-Bissau
2.0	179.5	14.5	34	26.9	2.0	Guyana
1.9	40.2	0.5	195	10.1	0.2	Haiti
..	89.3	6.2	14	13.1	1.2	Honduras
..	125.2	41.0	4	58.5	5.6	Hungary
..	62.8	7.2	5	90.0	7.5	Iceland
8.7	30.4	3.4	30	4.5	1.4	India
13.4	39.1	1.8	60	7.9	1.8	Indonesia
..	39.1	0.4	9	32.0	7.0	Iran, Islamic Rep.
..	116.2	..	77	1.0	3.3	Iraq
..	77.7	-7.5	13	62.7	10.2	Ireland
..	..	..	..	..	..	Isle of Man
..	49.7	5.4	34	47.9	9.3	Israel
..	38.6	0.7	10	41.8	7.7	Italy
14.2	43.0	9.8	8	57.3	5.2	Jamaica
..	22.3	0.5	23	75.2	9.8	Japan
16.0	89.7	9.3	13	27.4	3.8	Jordan
41.8	65.6	11.8	20	10.9	14.7	Kazakhstan
4.5	46.4	0.3	34	8.7	0.3	Kenya
..	53.1	..	21	2.1	0.3	Kiribati
..	..	..	..	0.0	3.0	Korea, Dem. People's Rep.
..	82.5	0.4	14	75.8	10.4	Korea, Rep.
..	..	..	52	..	..	Kosovo
..	75.9	0.0	35	36.7	32.3	Kuwait
8.2	97.8	4.5	11	16.1	1.2	Kyrgyz Republic
..	42.1	4.2	100	8.5	0.3	Lao P.D.R.
37.7	65.8	4.0	16	60.4	3.4	Latvia
14.0	60.3	12.1	9	22.5	3.2	Lebanon
2.5	145.0	13.4	40	3.6	..	Lesotho
131.3	91.9	17.1	20	0.5	0.2	Liberia
..	72.9	4.4	..	5.1	9.3	Libya
..	..	..	..	66.0	..	Liechtenstein
30.6	92.7	3.8	26	54.4	4.5	Lithuania
..	86.2	170.9	24	79.2	22.6	Luxembourg
8.7	83.9	6.3	4	41.5	5.5	Macedonia, FYR
..	44.7	15.6	7	1.7	0.1	Madagascar
..	51.5	0.9	39	2.1	0.1	Malawi
..	146.8	3.3	11	55.8	7.3	Malaysia
6.2	82.7	1.2	9	23.5	3.0	Maldives
..	52.2	2.1	15	1.6	0.0	Mali
..	105.2	13.6	..	48.3	6.7	Malta
..	72.6	..	17	3.7	1.7	Marshall Islands
..	91.4	2.9	19	1.9	0.6	Mauritania
2.8	65.5	4.1	6	22.2	3.1	Mauritius
..	..	..	..	..	..	Mayotte
12.1	53.9	2.1	13	22.2	4.5	Mexico
..	61.1	..	16	14.5	0.6	Micronesia, Fed. Sts.
11.3	84.7	11.7	10	23.4	1.3	Moldova
..	..	..	..	..	..	Monaco
..	96.0	13.0	13	12.5	4.0	Mongolia
..	60.1	19.3	13	47.2	..	Montenegro
10.3	51.3	2.8	12	33.0	1.5	Morocco
1.2	58.2	6.0	26	1.6	0.1	Mozambique
..	..	..	..	0.2	0.3	Myanmar
..	87.2	6.1	66	5.3	1.5	Namibia
3.6	33.8	0.0	31	1.7	0.1	Nepal
..	119.2	-0.3	10	87.0	10.6	Netherlands
..	..	..	..	..	32.4	Netherlands Antilles
..	..	..	..	34.5	11.7	New Caledonia
..	40.4	4.7	1	71.4	7.7	New Zealand
7.3	76.9	9.8	39	3.3	0.8	Nicaragua
..	45.5	2.7	17	0.5	0.1	Niger
..	54.1	2.4	31	15.9	0.6	Nigeria
..	..	..	..	..	..	Northern Mariana Islands
..	49.6	-0.3	7	82.5	9.1	Norway
..	100.9	4.9	12	20.0	13.7	Oman
8.7	29.7	3.3	20	11.1	1.0	Pakistan
..	65.6	..	28	..	10.5	Palau
9.2	35.1	10.4	12	27.5	2.2	Panama
..	101.5	-0.4	56	1.8	0.5	Papua New Guinea
4.8	67.5	1.1	35	14.3	0.7	Paraguay
12.5	38.3	3.2	41	24.7	1.5	Peru
15.5	52.4	0.9	52	6.2	0.8	Philippines
25.0	65.4	2.8	32	49.0	8.3	Poland
..	49.4	1.9	6	42.1	5.5	Portugal
..	..	..	7	25.3	..	Puerto Rico
..	92.1	..	6	34.0	55.4	Qatar

Economy	Total population millions 2009	Life expectancy at birth years 2008	Under-5 mortality rate per 1,000 2008	Access to an improved water source % of population 2008	Gross national income (GNI)[a] $ billions 2009	per capita $ 2009
Romania	21.48	73	14	..	178.9	8,330
Russian Federation	141.85	68	13	96	1,329.7	9,370
Rwanda	10.00	50	112	65	4.6	460
Samoa	0.18	72	26	88	0.5	2,840
San Marino	0.03	82	2	..	1.6	50,670
São Tomé and Principe	0.16	66	98	89	0.2	1,140
Saudi Arabia	25.39	73	21	..	439.0	17,700
Senegal	12.53	56	108	69	12.9	1,030
Serbia	7.32	74	7	99	43.8	5,990
Seychelles	0.09	73	12	..	0.7	8,480
Sierra Leone	5.70	48	194	49	1.9	340
Singapore	4.99	81	3	100	185.7	37,220
Slovak Republic	5.42	75	8	100	87.4	16,130
Slovenia	2.04	79	4	99	48.1	23,520
Solomon Islands	0.52	66	36	69	0.5	910
Somalia	9.13	50	200	30	..	.. h
South Africa	49.32	51	67	91	284.5	5,770
Spain	45.96	81	4	100	1,464.7	31,870
Sri Lanka	20.30	74	15	90	40.4	1,990
St. Kitts and Nevis	0.05	..	16	99	0.5	10,100
St. Lucia	0.17	73	13	98	0.9	5,170
St. Vincent and the Grenadines	0.11	72	13	..	0.6	5,110
Sudan	42.27	58	109	57	51.6	1,220
Suriname	0.52	69	27	93	2.5	4,760
Swaziland	1.18	46	83	69	2.8	2,350
Sweden	9.30	81	3	100	455.2	48,930
Switzerland	7.73	82	5	100	431.1	56,370
Syrian Arab Republic	21.09	74	16	89	50.9	2,410
Tajikistan	6.95	67	64	70	4.8	700
Tanzania	43.74	56	104	54	21.3 k	500 k
Thailand	67.76	69	14	98	254.7	3,760
Timor-Leste	1.13	61	93	69	2.7	2,460
Togo	6.62	63	98	60	2.9	440
Tonga	0.10	72	19	100	0.3	3,260
Trinidad and Tobago	1.34	69	35	94	22.1	16,490
Tunisia	10.43	74	21	94	38.8	3,720
Turkey	74.82	72	22	99	653.1	8,730
Turkmenistan	5.11	65	48	..	17.5	3,420
Turks and Caicos Islands	0.03	..	23	100	..	.. e
Tuvalu	..	..	36	97	..	.. l
Uganda	32.71	53	135	67	15.0	460
Ukraine	46.01	68	16	98	128.8	2,800
United Arab Emirates	4.60	78	8	100	..	.. e
United Kingdom	61.84	80	6	100	2,567.5	41,520
United States	307.01	78	8	99	14,502.6	47,240
Uruguay	3.34	76	14	100	31.3	9,360
Uzbekistan	27.77	68	38	87	30.5	1,100
Vanuatu	0.24	70	33	83	0.6	2,620
Venezuela, R.B. de	28.38	74	18	93	288.1	10,150
Vietnam	87.28	74	14	94	88.0	1,010
Virgin Islands (U.S.)	0.11	79	..	..	..	.. e
West Bank and Gaza	4.04	73	27	91	..	.. l
Yemen, Rep.	23.58	63	69	62	25.0	1,060
Zambia	12.94	45	148	60	12.6	970
Zimbabwe	12.52	44	96	82	..	.. h
World	6,775.24 s	69 w	67 w	87 w	59,257.7 t	8,746 w
Low-income	846.14	57	127	64	425.1	502
Middle-income	4,812.54	69	57	88	16,269.1	3,381
Lower-middle-income	3,810.80	68	64	86	8,795.9	2,308
Upper-middle-income	1,001.74	71	24	95	7,483.6	7,471
Low- and middle-income	5,658.68	67	73	84	16,709.3	2,953
East Asia & Pacific	1,943.76	72	29	88	6,147.7	3,163
Europe & Central Asia	404.22	69	23	95	2,746.1	6,793
Latin America & Caribbean	572.47	73	23	93	3,970.9	6,936
Middle East & North Africa	330.89	71	34	87	1,189.2	3,594
South Asia	1,567.72	64	76	87	1,704.9	1,088
Sub-Saharan Africa	839.62	52	144	60	919.4	1,095
High-income	1,116.55	80	7	100	42,583.9	38,139
Euro area	327.31	81	4	100	12,701.1	38,805

See page 142 for explanation of symbols.
Notes: Figures in *italics* are for years other than those specified.
a. Calculated using the World Bank Atlas method.
b. Exports include workers' remittances.
c. Data are from the International Telecommunication Union's (ITU) World Telecommunication/ICT Indicators database. Please cite ITU for third-party use of these data.
d. Estimated to be upper-middle-income ($3,946–$12,195).
e. Estimated to be high-income ($12,196 or more).

Total debt service % of exports of goods, services and income[b] 2008	Merchandise trade % of GDP 2009	Foreign direct investment net inflows, % of GDP 2008	Starting a business time required in days June 2009	Internet users[c] per 100 people 2008	Carbon dioxide emissions per capita metric tons 2007	Economy
25.3	58.7	6.9	10	28.8	4.4	Romania
11.5	40.3	4.5	30	31.9	10.8	Russian Federation
..	38.6	2.3	3	3.1	0.1	Rwanda
..	41.5	1.0	9	5.0	0.9	Samoa
..	..	..	..	54.8	..	San Marino
..	67.5	19.0	144	15.5	0.8	São Tomé and Principe
..	76.0	8.3	5	31.3	16.6	Saudi Arabia
..	56.6	5.3	8	8.4	0.5	Senegal
13.9	56.2	6.1	13	44.9	..	Serbia
..	163.5	39.3	38	39.0	7.3	Seychelles
..	36.6	-0.2	12	0.3	0.2	Sierra Leone
..	282.9	11.8	3	69.6	11.8	Singapore
..	126.8	3.3	16	66.0	6.8	Slovak Republic
..	108.3	3.5	6	55.7	7.5	Slovenia
..	63.1	11.8	57	2.0	0.4	Solomon Islands
..	..	..	..	1.1	0.1	Somalia
4.4	47.1	3.5	22	8.6	9.0	South Africa
..	34.8	4.7	47	55.4	8.0	Spain
9.3	41.1	1.8	38	5.8	0.6	Sri Lanka
..	45.5	15.4	45	32.5	5.1	St. Kitts and Nevis
..	69.1	10.6	14	58.8	2.3	St. Lucia
..	68.0	20.5	11	60.5	1.8	St. Vincent and the Grenadines
2.5	29.3	4.5	36	10.2	0.3	Sudan
..	100.5	-7.7	694	9.7	4.8	Suriname
..	100.5	0.4	61	6.9	0.9	Swaziland
..	61.4	7.0	15	87.7	5.4	Sweden
..	76.7	1.3	20	75.9	5.0	Switzerland
..	51.2	3.9	17	17.3	3.5	Syrian Arab Republic
3.1	71.9	7.3	25	8.8	1.1	Tajikistan
1.2	43.1	3.6	29	1.2	0.1	Tanzania
7.7	108.5	3.1	32	23.9	4.1	Thailand
..	..	..	83	..	0.2	Timor-Leste
..	76.4	2.3	75	5.4	0.2	Togo
..	53.7	1.7	25	8.1	1.7	Tonga
..	91.1	4.0	43	17.0	27.9	Trinidad and Tobago
..	84.8	6.5	11	27.1	2.3	Tunisia
29.5	39.4	2.5	6	34.4	4.0	Turkey
..	66.9	4.8	..	1.5	9.2	Turkmenistan
..	..	..	..	..	4.9	Turks and Caicos Islands
..	..	..	..	..	..	Tuvalu
1.7	50.6	5.6	25	7.9	0.1	Uganda
19.4	75.1	6.1	27	10.5	6.8	Ukraine
..	159.2	..	15	65.2	31.0	United Arab Emirates
..	38.2	3.5	13	76.0	8.8	United Kingdom
..	18.7	2.2	6	75.8	19.3	United States
14.6	34.1	7.1	65	40.2	1.9	Uruguay
..	53.2	3.3	15	9.0	4.3	Uzbekistan
..	50.5	5.5	39	7.3	0.4	Vanuatu
5.6	30.6	0.1	141	25.7	6.0	Venezuela, R.B. de
1.9	136.6	10.6	50	24.2	1.3	Vietnam
..	..	..	..	27.3	..	Virgin Islands (U.S.)
..	..	..	49	9.0	0.6	West Bank and Gaza
2.4	69.0	5.8	12	1.6	1.0	Yemen, Rep.
3.2	63.0	6.4	18	5.5	0.2	Zambia
..	..	..	96	11.4	0.8	Zimbabwe
.. w	40.9 w	3.1 w	36 u	23.9 w	4.6 w	World
4.4	49.7	3.8	44	2.3	0.3	Low-income
9.0	45.0	3.5	40	17.0	3.3	Middle-income
5.3	47.2	3.4	34	13.7	2.8	Lower-middle-income
13.6	42.4	3.5	47	29.9	5.3	Upper-middle-income
8.9	45.1	3.5	41	15.0	2.9	Low- and middle-income
3.9	52.1	3.2	42	19.4	4.0	East Asia & Pacific
17.2	48.4	4.8	19	26.4	7.2	Europe & Central Asia
14.0	33.8	2.9	67	29.0	2.7	Latin America & Caribbean
5.3	53.3	3.1	23	18.9	3.7	Middle East & North Africa
8.4	31.3	3.2	28	4.7	1.2	South Asia
3.3	53.1	3.6	44	6.5	0.8	Sub-Saharan Africa
..	39.2	2.9	19	68.3	12.5	High-income
..	56.7	3.1	15	62.6	8.2	Euro area

f. Data are for the area controlled by the Government of the Republic of Cyprus.
g. Data exclude Abkhazia and South Ossetia.
h. Estimated to be low-income ($995 or less).
i. Data exclude Transnistria.
j. Data include Former Spanish Sahara.
k. Data refer to mainland Tanzania only.
l. Estimated to be lower-middle-income ($996–$3,945).

Rank	Economy	Atlas methodology $	Purchasing power parity international $	PPP rank
1	Monaco	203,900 a	..	..
2	Liechtenstein	113,210 a	..	..
3	Norway	86,440	56,050	7
4	Luxembourg	74,430	57,640	3
5	Channel Islands	68,610 a	..	..
6	Qatar	.. a	..	..
7	Bermuda	.. a	..	..
8	Denmark	58,930	37,720	26
9	Switzerland	56,370 a	41,830 a	19
10	Kuwait	43,930 a	53,590 a	6
11	Isle of Man	49,310 a	..	..
12	San Marino	50,670 a	..	..
13	United Arab Emirates	.. a	..	..
14	Netherlands	49,350	40,510	22
15	Sweden	48,930	38,560	23
16	Cayman Islands	.. a	..	..
17	United States	47,240	46,730	14
18	Austria	46,850	38,550	24
19	Finland	45,680	34,430	36
20	Macao SAR, China	35,360 a	52,410 a	8
21	Belgium	45,310	36,520	34
23	Ireland	44,310	33,280	39
24	France	43,990	35,020	35
25	Australia	43,770	38,210	25
26	Iceland	43,220	33,390	38
27	Germany	42,560	36,960	32
28	Canada	42,170	37,590	28
29	Andorra	41,130 a	..	..
30	United Kingdom	41,520	37,360	29
32	Japan	37,870	33,280	39
33	Singapore	37,220	49,850	11
35	Italy	35,080	31,330	42
37	Brunei Darussalam	27,050 a	50,920 a	10
38	Greenland	32,960 a	..	..
40	Hong Kong SAR, China	31,420 a	44,070 a	16
41	Spain	31,870	31,630	41
42	Greece	28,630	28,440	46
43	Cyprus	26,940 a,c	28,050 a,c	45
44	New Zealand	26,830 a	26,430 a	50
45	Bahrain	25,420 a	33,480 a	37
46	Israel	25,740	27,040	51
49	Slovenia	23,520	26,340	53
50	Bahamas, The	21,390 a	..	..
51	Portugal	20,940	22,870	60
54	Korea, Rep.	19,830	27,310	48
55	Malta	16,690 a	22,640 a	57
56	Oman	17,890 a	24,370 a	55
57	Saudi Arabia	17,700 a	24,000 a	56
58	Czech Republic	17,310	23,610	59
59	Trinidad and Tobago	16,490	25,100 b	54
60	Slovak Republic	16,130	21,600	63
63	Estonia	14,060	18,890	66
65	Croatia	13,810	19,170	65
66	Hungary	12,980	18,570	67
67	Equatorial Guinea	12,420	19,350	64
68	Latvia	12,390	16,510	73
69	Poland	12,260	18,440	68
70	Antigua and Barbuda	12,070	17,690 b	70
71	Libya	12,020	16,430 b	74
72	Lithuania	11,410	16,740	72
73	Venezuela, R.B. de	10,150	12,370	91
74	St. Kitts and Nevis	10,100	13,660 b	79
75	Chile	9,420	13,430	81
76	Russian Federation	9,370	18,390	69
77	Uruguay	9,360	12,910	85
78	Palau	8,940	..	..
79	Mexico	8,920	14,110	77
80	Turkey	8,730	13,730	78
81	Seychelles	8,480	16,820 b	71
82	Romania	8,330	14,460	75
84	Brazil	8,040	10,260	99
85	Lebanon	7,970	13,230	83
86	Argentina	7,570	14,120	76
87	Gabon	7,370	12,460	88
88	Mauritius	7,240	13,270	82
89	Malaysia	7,230	13,530	80
90	Kazakhstan	6,740	10,270	98
91	Panama	6,710	12,530 b	87
92	Montenegro	6,550	13,130	84
93	Botswana	6,240	12,860	86
94	Costa Rica	6,230	10,940 b	96
95	Serbia	5,990	11,420	95
96	Bulgaria	5,770	12,290	92
96	South Africa	5,770	10,060	100
99	Grenada	5,550	7,720 b	114
100	Belarus	5,540	12,380	90
101	St. Lucia	5,170	8,880 b	103
102	St. Vincent and the Grenadines	5,110	8,840 b	104
103	Jamaica	4,990	7,320 b	117
104	Colombia	4,930	8,500	106
105	Suriname	4,760 a	6,690 a,b	119
106	Dominica	4,870	8,470 b	107
107	Azerbaijan	4,840	9,030	102
108	Bosnia and Herzegovina	4,700	8,740	105
110	Iran, Islamic Rep.	4,530	11,490	94
111	Dominican Republic	4,510	8,100 b	111
112	Algeria	4,420	8,130 b	110
113	Macedonia, FYR	4,400	10,550	97
114	Namibia	4,290	6,410	121
115	Peru	4,150	8,140	109
116	Albania	3,950	8,170	108
116	Fiji	3,950	4,570	141
118	Ecuador	3,920	8,040	112
119	Maldives	3,870	5,230	130
120	Belize	3,740 a	5,950 a,b	124
121	Thailand	3,760	7,640	115
122	Jordan	3,740	5,840	125
123	Tunisia	3,720	7,820	113
124	China	3,620	6,710	120
125	Angola	3,490	4,970	131
126	Turkmenistan	3,420	6,990 b	118
127	El Salvador	3,370	6,360 b	122
128	Tonga	3,260	4,580 b	139
129	Kosovo	3,240	..	..
131	Armenia	3,100	5,420	128
132	Marshall Islands	3,060	..	..
133	Cape Verde	3,010	3,530	150
134	Samoa	2,840	4,270 b	145
135	Ukraine	2,800	6,190	123
136	Morocco	2,790 d	4,450 d	142
137	Guatemala	2,620	4,590 b	138
137	Vanuatu	2,620	4,280 b	144
139	Georgia	2,530 e	4,700 e	136
140	Timor-Leste	2,460 a	4,700 a,b	134
141	Syrian Arab Republic	2,410	4,620	137
142	Swaziland	2,350	4,580	139
143	Paraguay	2,270	4,430	143
144	Indonesia	2,230	4,060	147

Rank	Economy	Atlas methodology $	Purchasing power parity international $	PPP rank
145	Micronesia, Fed. Sts.	2,220	2,810 b	161
146	Iraq	2,210	3,340	152
147	Egypt, Arab Rep.	2,070	5,690	126
148	Bhutan	2,020	5,300	129
149	Sri Lanka	1,990	4,720	135
150	Kiribati	1,890	3,350 b	151
151	Congo, Rep.	1,830	2,940	157
152	Honduras	1,820	3,730	148
153	Philippines	1,790	3,540	149
154	Mongolia	1,630	3,330	153
155	Bolivia	1,620	4,260	146
156	Moldova	1,590 f	3,060 f	156
157	Guyana	1,450 a	3,030 a,b	155
159	Djibouti	1,280	2,480	163
160	Sudan	1,220	2,000	170
161	India	1,180	3,270	154
161	Papua New Guinea	1,180	2,270 b	166
163	Cameroon	1,170	2,200	168
164	Nigeria	1,140	1,980	171
164	São Tomé and Principe	1,140	1,850	176
166	Uzbekistan	1,100	2,890 b	158
167	Côte d'Ivoire	1,060	1,640	179
167	Yemen, Rep.	1,060	2,340	165
169	Lesotho	1,030	1,960	172
169	Senegal	1,030	1,790	178
171	Pakistan	1,020	2,710	162
172	Vietnam	1,010	2,850	160
173	Nicaragua	1,000	2,450 b	164
174	Zambia	970	1,280	189
175	Mauritania	960	1,960	172
176	Solomon Islands	910	1,860 b	175
177	Lao P.D.R.	880	2,210	167
178	Comoros	870	1,300	187
178	Kyrgyz Republic	870	2,200	168
180	Kenya	770	1,570	181
181	Benin	750	1,510	182
182	Ghana	700	1,480	183
182	Tajikistan	700	1,950	174
184	Mali	680	1,190	191
185	Cambodia	650	1,850	176
187	Chad	610	1,230	190
188	Bangladesh	590	1,580	180
190	Burkina Faso	510	1,170	194
190	Guinea-Bissau	510	1,060	197
192	Tanzania	500 g	1,350 g	185
193	Rwanda	460	1,060	197
193	Uganda	460	1,190	191
195	Central African Republic	450	750	206
196	Gambia, The	440	1,330	186
196	Mozambique	440	880	202
196	Nepal	440	1,180	193
196	Togo	440	850	203
200	Madagascar	420 a	1,050 a	196
202	Afghanistan	370 a	1,110 a,b	195
203	Guinea	370	940	200
204	Niger	340	660	208
204	Sierra Leone	340	790	204
206	Ethiopia	330	930	201
207	Eritrea	300 a	640 a,b	208
209	Malawi	280	760	205
211	Congo, Dem. Rep.	160	300	212
211	Liberia	160	290	213
213	Burundi	150	390	211

Note: Rankings include all 213 economies presented in the key indicators table, but only those that have confirmed World Bank Atlas GNI per capita estimates or rank in the top 20 are shown.

Estimated ranges for economies that do not have confirmed World Bank Atlas GNI per capita figures are:

High-income ($12,196 or more):

    Aruba

    Barbados

    Faeroe Islands

    French Polynesia

    Gibraltar

    Guam

    Netherlands Antilles

    New Caledonia

    Northern Mariana Islands

    Puerto Rico

    Turks and Caicos Islands

    Virgin Islands (U.S.)

Upper-middle-income ($3,946–$12,195):

    American Samoa

    Cuba

    Mayotte

Lower-middle-income ($996–$3,945):

    Tuvalu

    West Bank and Gaza

Low-income ($995 or less):

    Haiti

    Korea, Dem. Rep.

    Myanmar

    Somalia

    Zimbabwe

.. Not available. Figures in *italics* are for an earlier year.

a. 2009 data are not available; ranking is approximate.

b. Estimate is based on regression; other PPP figures are extrapolated from the 2005 International Comparison Program benchmark estimates.

c. Data are for the area controlled by the Government of the Republic of Cyprus.

d. Data include Former Spanish Sahara.

e. Data exclude Abkhazia and South Ossetia.

f. Data exclude Transnistria.

g. Data refer to mainland Tanzania only.

Definitions, sources, notes, and abbreviations

Adjusted net saving Net saving plus education expenditure minus energy depletion, mineral depletion, net of forest depletion, and carbon dioxide and particulate emissions damage. (World Bank)

Agricultural support, total The value of gross transfers from taxpayers and consumers arising from policy measures, net of associated budgetary receipts, regardless of the objectives and impacts on farm production and income or production of farm products. (OECD)

Agricultural products Commodities classified in SITC revision 2, sections 0,1, 2, excluding 27, 28, and 4.

Aid, net Aid flows classified as official development assistance, net of repayments. (OECD DAC)

Aid, untied Bilateral official development assistance commitment not subject to restrictions by donors on procurement sources. (OECD)

Attendance ratio, net Number of children attending school who are of official primary school age, expressed as a percentage of the total number of children of official primary school age. (UNICEF)

Bilateral ODA commitments Firm obligations, expressed in writing and backed by the necessary funds, undertaken by official bilateral donors to provide specified assistance to a recipient country or a multilateral organization. Bilateral commitments are recorded in the full amount of expected transfer, irrespective of the time required for completing disbursements. (OECD DAC)

Birth at health facility Percentage of live births that took place at a health facility in the three years preceding the survey. (Household surveys)

Births attended by skilled health staff The proportion of deliveries attended by personnel trained to give the necessary supervision, care, and advice to women during pregnancy, labor, and the postpartum period; to conduct deliveries on their own; and to care for newborns. (Household surveys)

Bonds Securities issued with a fixed rate of interest for a period of more than one year. They include net flows through cross-border public and publicly guaranteed and private nonguaranteed bond issues. (World Bank)

Business, time to start up The time, in calendar days, needed to complete all the procedures required to legally operate a business. If a procedure can be speeded up at additional cost, the fastest procedure, regardless of cost, is chosen. Time spent gathering information about the registration process is excluded. (World Bank)

Carbon dioxide emissions Emissions from the burning of fossil fuels (including the consumption of solid, liquid, and gas fuels and gas flaring) and the manufacture of cement. (CDIAC)

Cereal yield The production of wheat, rice, maize, barley, oats, rye, millet, sorghum, buckwheat, and mixed grains, measured in kilograms per hectare of harvested land. Refers to crops harvested for dry grain only. Cereal crops harvested for hay or harvested green for food, feed, or silage, and those used for grazing, are excluded. The FAO allocates production data to the calendar year in which the bulk of the harvest took place. Most of a crop harvested near the end of the year will be used in the following year. (FAO)

Child labor Children ages 7–14 who are involved in economic activity for at least one hour in the reference week of the survey. (UCW)

Child labor, Agriculture Children ages 7–14 who are involved in economic activity in the agricultural sector. Agriculture corresponds to division 1 (ISIC revision 2) or categories A and B (ISIC revision 3) and includes agriculture and hunting, forestry and logging, and fishing. (UCW)

Child labor, Manufacturing Children ages 7–14 who are involved in economic activity in the manufacturing sector. Manufacturing corresponds to division 3 (ISIC revision 2) or category D (ISIC revision 3). (UCW)

Child labor, Service Children ages 7–14 who are involved in economic activity in the service sector. Services correspond to divisions 6–9 (ISIC revision 2) or categories G–P (ISIC revision 3) and include wholesale and retail trade, hotels and restaurants, transport, financial intermediation, real estate, public administration, education, health and social work, other community services, and private household activity. (UCW)

Child labor, paid workers Children ages 7–14 who are involved in economic activity and hold the type of jobs defined as "paid employment jobs." (UCW)

Child labor, self-employed workers Children ages 7–14 who are involved in economic activity and hold the type of jobs defined as "self-employment jobs," working on their own account or with one or a few partners. (UCW)

Child labor, unpaid family workers Children ages 7–14 who are involved in economic activity and work without pay in a market-oriented establishment or activity operated by a related person living in the same household. (UCW)

Children out of school, primary school age children The number of children of primary school age who are not enrolled in primary or secondary school. (UIS)

Commercial bank and other lending Net flows of commercial bank lending (public and publicly guaranteed and private nonguaranteed) and other private credits. (World Bank)

Contraceptive prevalence rate The percentage of women married or in-union ages 15–49 who are practicing, or whose sexual partners are practicing, any form of contraception. (Household surveys)

Corruption The abuse of public office for private gain, which is an outcome of poor governance reflecting the breakdown of accountability. (World Bank)

Debt, private nonguaranteed The long-term external obligations of private debtors that are not guaranteed for repayment by a public entity. (World Bank)

Debt, public and publicly guaranteed The long-term external obligations of public debtors, including the national governments and political subdivisions (or an agency of either) and autonomous public bodies, and the external obligations of private debtors that are guaranteed for repayment by a public entity. (World Bank)

Debt, short term All debt having an original maturity of one year or less and interest in arrears on long-term debt. (World Bank)

Debt, total external Debt owed to nonresidents repayable in foreign currency, goods, or services. It is the sum of public, publicly guaranteed, and private nonguaranteed long-term debt, use of International Monetary Fund credit, and short-term debt. (World Bank)

Debt service, public The sum of principal repayments and interest actually paid in foreign currency, goods, or services for long-term public and publicly guaranteed debt and repayments (repurchases and charges) to the International Monetary Fund. (World Bank)

Debt service, total The sum of principal repayments and interest actually paid in foreign currency, goods, or services on long-term debt, interest paid on short-term debt, and repayments (repurchases and charges) to the International Monetary Fund. (World Bank)

Deforestation The permanent conversion of natural forest area to other uses, including shifting cultivation, permanent agriculture, ranching, settlements, and infrastructure development. Deforested areas do not include areas logged but intended for regeneration or areas degraded by fuel wood gathering, acid precipitation, or forest fires. Negative numbers indicate an increase in forest area. (FAO)

Education, primary The level of education that provides children with basic reading, writing, and mathematics skills along with an elementary understanding of such subjects as history, geography, natural science, social science, art, and music. (UIS)

Education, secondary The level of education that completes the provision of basic education aimed at laying the foundations for lifelong learning and human development by offering more subject- or skill-oriented instruction using more specialized teachers. (UIS)

Education, tertiary The level of education, leading to an advanced research qualification that normally requires, as a minimum condition of admission, the successful completion of education at the secondary level. (UIS)

Emigration of people with tertiary education to OECD countries Adults ages 25 and older, residing in an OECD country other than that in which they were born, with at least one year of tertiary education. (Docquier, Marfouk, and Lowell, 2007, "A Gendered Assessment of the Brain Drain")

Energy and minerals rents The product of unit resource rents and the physical quantities of energy extracted. Energy covers coal, crude oil, and natural gas and minerals including bauxite, copper, iron, lead, nickel, phosphate, tin, gold, silver, and zinc. (World Bank)

Energy use The use of primary energy before transformation to other end-use fuels, which is equal to indigenous production plus imports and stock changes, minus exports and fuels supplied to ships and aircraft engaged in international transport. (IEA)

Enrollment rate, gross The ratio of children who are enrolled in an education level, regardless of age, to the population of the corresponding official school age, as defined by the International Standard Classification of Education 1997 (ISCED97). (UIS)

Enrollment rate, net The ratio of children of official school age, as defined by the International Standard Classification of Education 1997 (ISCED97), who are enrolled in school, to the population of the corresponding official school age. (UIS)

Exchange rate, official The exchange rate (local currency units relative to the U.S. dollar) determined by national authorities or the rate determined in the legally sanctioned exchange market. It is calculated as an annual average based on monthly averages. (IMF)

Exports of goods, services, and income International transactions involving a change in ownership of general merchandise, goods sent for processing and repairs, nonmonetary gold, services, receipts of employee compensation for nonresident workers, and investment income. (IMF)

Exports to developing economies outside region The sum of merchandise exports from the reporting economy to other developing economies in other World Bank regions as a percentage of total merchandise exports by the economy. (World Bank)

Exports to developing economies within region The sum of merchandise exports from the reporting economy to other developing economies in the same World Bank region as a percentage of total merchandise exports by the economy. (World Bank)

Exports to high-income economies The sum of merchandise exports from the reporting economy to high-income economies as a percentage of total merchandise exports by the economy. (World Bank)

Female-to-male enrollments in primary and secondary schools The ratio of female-to-male gross enrollment rates in primary and secondary schools. (UIS)

Fertility rate, total The number of children that would be born to a woman if she were to live to the end of her childbearing years and bear children in accordance with current age-specific fertility rates. (World Bank)

Financing from abroad (obtained from nonresidents) and domestic financing (obtained from residents) The means by which a government provides financial resources to cover a budget deficit or allocates financial resources arising from a budget surplus. Includes all government liabilities—other than those for currency issues or demand, time, or savings deposits with government—or claims on others held by government, and changes in government holdings of cash and deposits. Excludes government guarantees of the debt of others. (IMF)

Food consumption per person The amount of food, in terms of quantity, expressed in kilocalories (kcal) per capita per day. It is estimated as the amount of food available for human consumption. The actual food consumption may be lower because of food waste and losses during storage, preparation, and cooking; quantities fed to domestic animals; and food thrown or given away. (FAO)

Food price index Includes the average of six commodity group price indexes of meat, dairy, cereals, oil and fats, and sugar. These commodities are weighted with the average export shares of each of the groups for 2002–2004. (FAO)

Food production per capita Covers food crops that are considered edible and that contain nutrients. To construct the index, production quantities of each commodity are weighted by international prices with the base period of 1999–2001. This method assigns a single price to each commodity so that, for example, 1 metric ton of wheat has the same price, regardless of where it is produced. Coffee and tea are excluded because, although edible, they have no nutritive value. (FAO)

Foreign direct investment, net inflows Net inflows of investment to acquire a lasting interest in or a management control over (10 percent or more of voting stock) in an enterprise operating in an economy other than that of the investor. It is the sum of equity capital, reinvestment of earnings, other long-term capital, and short-term capital as shown in the balance of payments. (IMF)

Forest area Land under natural or planted stands of trees of at least 5 meters in height in situ, whether productive or not, and excludes tree stands in agriculture production systems (for example, in fruit plantations and agroforestry systems) and trees in urban parks and gardens. (FAO)

Freshwater resources, internal renewable resources The average annual flows of river and groundwater from rainfall. (FAO)

Freshwater withdrawals, annual Total water withdrawals, not counting evaporation losses from storage basins but including water from desalination plants in countries where they are a significant source. Withdrawals also include water from desalination sources. Withdrawals for agriculture and industry are total withdrawals for irrigation and livestock production and for direct industrial use (including for cooling thermoelectric plants). Withdrawals for domestic uses include drinking water; municipal use or supply; and use for public services, commercial establishments, and home. (FAO)

Gross capital formation (commonly called *investment*) Outlays on additions to the fixed assets of the economy, net of changes in the level of inventories, and net acquisitions of valuables. Fixed assets include land improvements (such as fences, ditches, and drains); plant, machinery, and equipment purchases; and the construction of roads, railways, and dwellings. (World Bank, OECD, UN)

Gross domestic product (GDP) The sum of gross value added by all resident producers in the economy plus any product taxes (less subsidies) not included in the value of the products. It is calculated using purchaser prices and without deductions for the depreciation of fabricated assets or for the depletion and degradation of natural resources. (World Bank)

Gross domestic product (GDP) per capita Gross domestic product divided by midyear population. (World Bank)

Gross national income (GNI) Gross domestic product plus net receipts of primary income (compensation of employees and property income) from abroad. Data are converted to dollars using the World Bank Atlas method. (World Bank)

Gross national income (GNI) per capita Gross national income divided by midyear population. (World Bank)

Gross national income (GNI), PPP Gross national income converted to international dollars using purchasing power parity rates. An international dollar has the same purchasing power over GNI as a U.S. dollar has in the United States. (World Bank)

Heavily Indebted Poor Countries (HIPC) Initiative A program of official creditors designed to relieve the poorest, most heavily indebted countries of their debt to certain multilateral creditors, including the World Bank and International Monetary Fund. (World Bank)

High-income economies Those with a gross national income (GNI) per capita of $12,196 or more in 2009.

HIV, adult prevalence of The proportion of people ages 15–49 who are infected with HIV. (UNAIDS)

Households reporting adult women and men as the usual person collecting water Proportion of households reporting adult women and men as the usual person collecting water. (Nishta Sinha, 2010, "Infrastructure, Gender Differences, and Impacts: The Evidence")

Immunization rate, measles, child Percentage of children aged 12–23 months who received a vaccination for measles before 12 months of age or at any time before the survey. A child is considered adequately immunized against measles after receiving one dose of vaccine. (WHO and UNICEF)

Industry The output of the industrial sector corresponding to International Standard Industrial

Classification (ISIC) divisions 2–5 (ISIC revision 2) or tabulation categories C–F (ISIC revision 3). (ILO)

Interest payments Payments of interest on government debt—including long-term bonds, long-term loans, and other debt instruments—to both domestic and foreign residents. (World Bank)

International migrant, stock The number of people born in a country other than that in which they live; this includes refugees. (UNPD)

Internet users Proportion of people with access to the World Wide Web. (ITU)

Irrigated land Refers to areas purposely provided with water, including land irrigated by controlled flooding. (FAO)

Labor force participation rate The proportion of the population ages 15 and older that is economically active: all people who supply labor for the production of goods and services during a specified period. (ILO)

Life expectancy at birth The number of years a newborn infant would live if prevailing patterns of mortality at the time of its birth were to stay the same throughout its life. (World Bank)

Lifetime risk of maternal death The probability that a 15-year-old female will die eventually from a maternal cause assuming that current levels of fertility and mortality (including maternal mortality) do not change in the future, taking into account competing causes of death. (WHO; UNICEF; UNFPA; World Bank)

Low-income economies Those with a gross national income (GNI) per capita of $995 or less in 2009. (World Bank)

Malnutrition, underweight children, prevalence of The percentage of children under-5 whose weight for age is more than two standard deviations below the median for the international reference population aged 0–59 months. The data are based on the new international child growth standards for infants and young children, called the Child Growth Standards, released in 2006 by the World Health Organization. (WHO)

Manufacturing The output of industries corresponding to International Standard Industrial Classification (ISIC) divisions 15–37.

Manufactured products Commodities classified in SITC revision 2, sections 5–8, excluding division 68.

Merchandise trade The sum of merchandise exports and imports measured in current U.S. dollars. Also referred to as trade in goods. (WTO)

Middle-income economies Those with a gross national income (GNI) per capita of more than $995 but less than $12,196 in 2009. (World Bank)

Mobile cellular telephone subscriptions Subscriptions to a public mobile telephone service using cellular technology, which provide access to the public switched telephone network. Postpaid and prepaid subscriptions are included. (ITU)

Mortality rate, infant The number of infants dying before reaching one year of age, per 1,000 live births in a given year. (Harmonized estimates of WHO, UNICEF, and World Bank)

Mortality rate, under-5 The probability that a newborn baby will die before reaching age 5, if subject to current age-specific mortality rates. The probability is expressed as a rate per 1,000. (Harmonized estimates by WHO, UNICEF, UNFPA, UNPD, and World Bank)

Mortality ratio, maternal The number of women who die from pregnancy-related causes during pregnancy and childbirth, per 100,000 live births. (Modeled estimates by WHO, UNICEF, UNFPA, World Bank)

Multilateral Debt Relief Initiative (MDRI) Further reduces the debt of heavily indebted poor countries and provides resources for meeting the Millennium Development Goals. Under the MDRI the International Development Association, International Monetary Fund, African Development Fund, and Inter-American Development Bank provide 100 percent debt relief on eligible debts due to them from countries that completed the HIPC Initiative process. (World Bank)

Nationally protected areas Totally or partially protected areas of at least 1,000 hectares that are designated as national parks, natural monuments, nature reserves or wildlife sanctuaries, protected landscapes or seascapes, or scientific reserves with limited public access. The terrestrial protected areas exclude marine areas, unclassified areas, littoral (intertidal) areas, and sites protected under local or provincial law. (UNEP; WCMC)

Net migration The total number of immigrants less the total number of emigrants, including both citizens and noncitizens. Data are five-year estimates. (UNDP)

Number of people receiving antiretroviral therapy The number of people who received antiretroviral drugs to suppress the HIV virus and stop the progression of HIV disease. (WHO)

Official development assistance (ODA) Disbursement of loans made on concessional terms (net of repayments) and grants by official agencies of the members of the Development Assistance Committee (DAC), by multilateral institutions, and by non-DAC countries to promote economic development and welfare in countries and territories in the DAC list of ODA recipients. (OECD DAC)

Overqualification rate The share of people working in jobs or occupations for which their skills are too high. Education and job qualification levels are grouped into three categories: low, intermediate, and high. An overqualified individual is one who holds a job that requires lesser qualifications than one that would theoretically be available at his or her education level. Overqualification rates are calculated for individuals with an intermediate or higher education. (OECD)

People receiving antiretroviral therapy People living with HIV who are receiving antiretroviral therapy treatment. (UNSD)

Particulate matter concentration Fine suspended particulates less than 10 microns in diameter (PM10) that are capable of penetrating deep into the respiratory tract and causing significant health damage. Data are urban-population-weighted PM10 levels in residential areas of cities with more than 100,000 residents. The estimates represent the average annual exposure level of the average urban resident to outdoor particulate matter. (World Bank)

Percent of repeaters, primary The number of students enrolled in the same grade as in the previous year as a percentage of all students enrolled in primary school. (UIS)

Population ages 0–14 The percentage of total population between ages 0 and 14. (United Nations, *World Population Prospects, 2008 Revision*)

Population ages 15–64 The percentage of total population between ages 15 and 64. (United Nations, *World Population Prospects, 2008 Revision*)

Population ages 65+ The percentage of total population aged 65 and older. (United Nations, *World Population Prospects, 2008 Revision*)

Population, average annual growth rate The exponential rate of change in population for the period indicated. (World Bank)

Population, total Midyear population that includes all residents regardless of legal status or citizenship— except for refugees not permanently settled in the country of asylum, who are generally considered part of the population of their country of origin. (World Bank)

Population below $1 a day The proportion of the population living on less than $1.25 a day at 2005 purchasing power parity prices. (World Bank)

Population below $2 a day The proportion of the population living on less than $2 a day at 2005 purchasing power parity prices. (World Bank)

Population density Midyear population divided by land area in square kilometers. (World Bank)

Population, rural Calculated as the difference between the total population and the urban population. (World Bank)

Population, urban The midyear population of areas defined as urban in each country and reported to the United Nations. (UN *World Urbanization Prospects, 2007 Revision*; World Bank estimates)

Portfolio equity flow Net inflows from equity securities other than those recorded as direct investment, including shares, stocks, depository receipts, and direct purchases of shares in local stock markets by foreign investors. (World Bank)

Pregnant women receiving prenatal care The proportion of women attended at least once during pregnancy by skilled health personnel for reasons related to pregnancy. (Household surveys)

Primary completion rate The proportion of students completing the last year of primary school, calculated by taking the total number of students in the last grade of primary school, minus the number of repeaters in that grade, divided by the total number of children of official graduation age. (UIS)

Private participation in infrastructure Investment commitments in infrastructure projects in telecommunications, energy, transport, and water and sanitation with private participation that have reached financial closure and directly or indirectly serve the public. All investment (public and private) in projects in which a private company assumes the operating risk is included. (World Bank)

Public sector management and institutions A proxy measure of governance that includes assessments of property rights and rule-based governance; quality of budgetary and financial management; efficiency of revenue mobilization; quality of public administration; and transparency, accountability, and corruption in the public sector. (World Bank)

Purchasing power parity (PPP) conversion factor The number of units of a country's currency required to buy the same amount of goods and services in the domestic market as a U.S. dollar would buy in the United States. (World Bank)

Ratio of female-to-male hourly wage The ratio of the female hourly wage to male hourly wage. (Household surveys)

Refugees People recognized as refugees under the 1951 Convention Relating to the Status of Refugees or its 1967 Protocol; the 1969 Organization of African Unity Convention Governing the Specific Aspects of Refugee Problems in Africa; people recognized as refugees in accordance with the UNHCR statute; people granted a refugee-like humanitarian status; and people provided with temporary protection. Palestinian refugees are people (and their descendants) whose residence was Palestine between June 1946 and May 1948 and who lost their homes and means of livelihood as a result of the 1948 Arab-Israeli conflict. (UNHCR; UNRWA)

Sanitation, access to an improved facility The share of the urban population with access to at least adequate excreta disposal facilities (private or shared but not public) that can effectively prevent human, animal, and insect contact with excreta. Improved facilities range from simple but protected pit latrines to flush toilets with a sewage connection. (WHO; UNICEF)

Services Corresponds to International Standard Industrial Classification (ISIC) divisions 6–9 (ISIC revision 2) or tabulation categories G–P (ISIC revision 3). (ILO)

Slum dwellers People living in areas lacking one or more of the following conditions: durable housing of a permanent nature, sufficient living space, easy access to safe water, access to adequate sanitation, and security of tenure that prevents forced evictions. (UN Habitat)

Tariff, simple mean The unweighted average of the effectively applied rates for all products subject to tariffs. (World Bank; UNCTAD; WTO)

Teenage mothers The percentage of women ages 15–19 who already have children or are currently pregnant. (Household surveys)

Textiles Commodities classified in SITC revision 2, divisions 26, 65, and 84.

Time spent fetching water Minutes per day that people spent fetching water. (Nishta Sinha, 2010, "Infrastructure, Gender Differences, and Impacts: The Evidence")

Trade The two-way flow of exports and imports of goods (merchandise trade) and services (service trade).

Trade in services The sum of services exports and imports. (IMF)

Treated bednets, use of The proportion of children ages 0–59 months who slept under an insecticide-treated bednet the night before the survey. (UNICEF)

Tuberculosis, death rate The number of deaths due to tuberculosis per 100,000 people. Deaths from all forms of tuberculosis, including HIV-positive people with tuberculosis, are included. (WHO)

Undernourishment, prevalence of The percentage of the population that is undernourished—whose dietary energy consumption is continuously below a minimum dietary energy requirement for maintaining a healthy life and carrying out light physical activity. (FAO)

Unofficial payments to public officials The percentage of firms expected to make unofficial or informal payments to public officials to "get things done" with regard to customs, taxes, licenses, regulations, and services. (World Bank)

Value added The net output of an industry after adding up all outputs and subtracting intermediate inputs. The industrial origin of value added is determined by the International Standard Industrial Classification (ISIC) revision 3.

Water source, access to an improved The share of the population with reasonable access to an adequate amount of water from an improved source, such as a household connection, public standpipe, borehole, protected well or spring, or rainwater collection. Unimproved sources include vendors, tanker trucks, and unprotected wells and springs. Reasonable access is defined as the availability of at least 20 liters per person per day from a source within 1 kilometer of the dwelling. (WHO; UNICEF)

Women in parliament The percentage of parliamentary seats in a single or lower chamber occupied by women. (IPU)

Women who said distance to health facility is a problem when accessing healthcare Percentage of women who reported having big problems with the distance to a health facility in accessing healthcare for themselves when they are sick. (Household surveys)

Workers' remittances and compensation of employees, received and paid Current transfers by migrant workers and wages and salaries earned by nonresident workers. (World Bank; IMF)

World Bank Atlas method A conversion factor to convert national currency units to U.S. dollars at prevailing exchange rates, adjusted for inflation and averaged over three years. The purpose is to reduce the effect of exchange rate fluctuations in the cross-country comparison of national incomes. (World Bank)

Data sources

The indicators presented in this *Atlas* are compiled by international agencies and by public and private organizations, usually on the basis of survey data or administrative statistics obtained from national governments. The principal source of each indicator is given in parentheses following the definition.

The World Bank publishes these and many other statistical series in the *World Development Indicators*, available in print, as a CD-ROM, and online. Excerpts from this *Atlas*; additional information about sources, definitions, and statistical methods; and suggestions for further reading are available at data.worldbank.org.

Data notes and symbols

The data in this book are for the most recent year, unless otherwise noted.
• Growth rates are proportional changes from the previous year.
• Regional aggregates include data for low- and middle-income economies only.
• Figures in *italics* indicate data for years or periods other than those specified.

Data are shown for economies with populations greater than 30,000, or less if they are members of the World Bank. The term *country* (used interchangeably with *economy*) does not imply political independence or official recognition by the World Bank, but refers to any economy for which the authorities report separate social or economic statistics.

The regional groupings of countries include only low- and middle-income economies. For the income groups, every economy is classified as low income, middle income, or high income.
• *Low-income economies* are those with a gross national income (GNI) per capita of $995 or less in 2009.
• *Middle-income economies* are those with a GNI per capita of $996 or more but less than $12,195.
• *Lower-middle-income economies* and *upper-middle-income economies* are separated at a GNI per capita of $3,945.
• *High-income economies* are those with a GNI per capita of $12,196 or more.

Symbols used in the data tables

.. means that data are not available or that aggregates cannot be calculated because of missing data.
0 or 0.0 means zero or less than half the unit shown.
$ stands for current U.S. dollars.
The methods used to calculate regional and income group aggregates are denoted by:
s (simple total), t (total including estimates for missing data), u (unweighted average), and w (weighted average).

Abbreviations

CDIAC	Carbon Dioxide Information Analysis Center	PPP	Purchasing Power Parity
CPIA	Country Policy and Institutional Assessment	SAR	Special Administrative Region
DAC	Development Assistance Committee of the Organisation for Economic Co-operation and Development	UCW	Understanding Children's Work
		UIS	UNESCO Institute for Statistics
		UN	United Nations
DHS	Demographic and Health Surveys	UNAIDS	Joint United Nations Programme on HIV/AIDS
FAO	Food and Agriculture Organization of the United Nations	UNDP	United Nations Development Programme
		UNEP	United Nations Environment Programme
FDI	Foreign Direct Investment	UNESCO	United Nations Educational, Scientific and Cultural Organization
GDP	Gross Domestic Product		
GNI	Gross National Income	UNFPA	United Nations Population Fund
HIPC	Heavily Indebted Poor Countries	UN Habitat	United Nations Human Settlements Program
ICT	Information and Communications Technology	UNHCR	The Office of the United Nations High Commissioner for Refugees
IDA	International Development Association		
IEA	International Energy Agency	UNICEF	United Nations Children's Fund
ILO	International Labour Organization	UNIFEM	United Nations Development Fund for Women
IMF	International Monetary Fund	UNPD	United Nations Population Division
IPU	Inter-Parliamentary Union	UNSD	United Nations Statistics Division
ITU	International Telecommunication Union	UNRWA	United Nations Relief and Works Agency for Palestine Refugees in the Near East
MDGs	Millennium Development Goals		
MDRI	Multilateral Debt Relief Initiative	WCMC	World Conservation Monitoring Centre
MRY	Most recent year	WDI	World Development Indicators
ODA	Official Development Assistance	WHO	World Health Organization
OECD	Organisation for Economic Co-operation and Development	WRI	World Resources Institute
		WTO	World Trade Organization
PPI	Private Participation in Infrastructure		

For more information

• *World Development Indicators (WDI)* and the WDI database are the World Bank's premier compilation of data about development. This *Atlas* complements the *World Development Indicators* by providing a geographical view of pertinent data. *World Development Indicators* and the WDI database are available at: data.worldbank.org/data-catalog/world-development-indicators
• *Global Development Finance* and the GDF database are the World Bank's comprehensive compilation of data on external debt and financial flows. They are available at: data.worldbank.org/data-catalog/global-development-finance
• *Africa Development Indicators*, the World Bank's most detailed collection of data on Africa, is available in one volume at: www.worldbank.org/adi
• **The Millennium Development Goals (MDG)** and the data and indicators required to track progress toward them are available at: www.developmentgoals.org
• **The PARIS21 Consortium** and information about how it promotes evidence-based policy making and monitoring are available at: www.paris21.org
• **The Statistical Capacity Building Program**, which offers tools and advice for statistical capacity building in developing countries, can be accessed at: www.worldbank.org/data/bbsc
• **The International Comparison Program (ICP)** and information about the ICP and the final results from the 2005 round can be found at: www.worldbank.org/data/icp

Index

Note: Page numbers in **bold** refer to maps; page numbers in *italics* refer to information presented in graphs and tables.

abortion 55, 57
accountability 66, 69
adjusted net saving (ANS) 124–5, *124–5*, **126–7**, *127*
African Development Fund 97
agriculture 62, 63, *63–5*, **64–5**
    and child labor 34, *34*, 37
    and deforestation 113
    and environmental degradation 104–5
    intensive methods 104–5
    and international trade 81, *81*
    productivity 104
    sustainability 105
    and trade barriers *81*
    and water supplies *108*, 109, *111*
aid 13, *13*, 92–5, *92–5*, **94–5**
    debt relief 92–3, *96*, 97
    humanitarian 93
    net 92, *92*, *94*
AIDS 12, *12*, 51, 58, **60–1**
    see also HIV
ANS *see* adjusted net saving
antenatal care 12, *12*, 42, 54, 55, 57
antiretroviral therapy 58, *58*
assets 124

bednets, insecticide-impregnated 48, 59, *59*
biodiversity 112–13
brain drain 87, *87*
breastfeeding 48, 49
business
    reform 75
    start-ups 78–9, **78–9**, *129*, *131*, *133*
Business Fighting Corruption Through Collective Action Initiative 66

capital
    human 124, 125
    natural 124–5, *124*, *126–7*
    physical 124
carbon dioxide emissions 118–19, *118*, *122–3*, **122–3**, *129*, *131*, *133*
carbon sinks 112
cereals 104, *105*
child labor 34–7, *34–7*, **36–7**, 38
    agricultural 34, *34*, 37
    and education 34–5, *35*
    girls 25, 43
    unpaid 34, *34*
child mortality 11, *11*, 19, 48–51, *48–51*, **50–1**, *128*, *130*, *132*
childbirth 12, 42, *42*, 54, *54*
childcare practices 48, 49
children
    health care for 48–9
    and HIV 58, 61
    rights of 25
    underweight 25, *53*
cities 29, 100–3, *100–3*, **102–3**
climate change 105, 108, 118–23, *118–19*, *122–3*, **122–3**
coal 119, *119*, *121*
communicable diseases 58–61, *58–61*, **60–1**
Construction Sector Transparency Initiative (CoST) 66
contraception 55, *55*, 56
corruption 66, *66–9*, 67, **68–9**

debt, external 96–9, *96–9*, **98–9**
debt relief 92–3, *96*, 97

debt service *129*, *131*, *133*
    ratios 96–7, *96*, *99*
deforestation 112–13, **114–15**, *115*
developing (low/middle income) economies 8–9, **8–9**, 14
diarrhea 48, *51*, 101
disease
    chronic/non-communicable 29, 59, *61*
    combating 12, *12*
    communicable 58–61, *58–61*, **60–1**
    deaths from 12
domestic labor 25, 42–3, *43*
donor countries 92–3, *93*, *95*

Earth Summit 1992 13
eAtlas 6–7
economic growth 18–23, *18–21*, **20–1**
    investment for 74–7, *74–7*, **76–7**
economic integration, global 80–5, *80–5*, **82–5**
economic wellbeing 124
economies
    classification 8–9, **8–9**
    global structure 62–5, *62–5*, **64–5**
    gross national income ranking *128*, *130*, *132*
ecosystems 109, 113
education 38–41, *38–41*, **40–1**
    attendance 39, **39**
    and child labor 34–5
    and employment 34–5, *35*
    enrollment in 15, *15*, 39, **39**, *41*, 45
    female 11, *41*, 43, 44–5, **44–5**, 55
    non-attendance 38
    primary 10, *10*, 38–9, *38–41*, 44–5, **44–5**
    primary completion rates 38, *38*, 40, **40–1**
    and remittances 87
    secondary 15, *15*, 39, **39**, 44–5, **44–5**
    tertiary 39, *39*
    universal primary 10, *10*, 38
EITI *see* Extractive Industries Transparency Initiative
electricity supplies 70, *121*
employment
    paid 35
    vulnerable *47*
    see also child labor; labor
energy
    renewable sources *121*
    security 118–23, *119*, *120–1*, **120–1**
environment
    deforestation 112–13, **114–15**, *115*
    degradation 104–5, 109
    exploitation 113
    protection 112–17, *112–17*, **114–17**
    sustainability issues 13, *13*
    and urbanization 100, 101
exchange rates 14, 15
exports 80–1, *82–3*, **82–3**
external debt 96–9, *96–9*, **98–9**
Extractive Industries Transparency Initiative (EITI) 66

fertility rate 28, 29, 56–7, **56–7**
    adolescent 55, *55*
fetilizers 104, 105
financial crisis 2007-9 18–19, *21*
    and external debt 96, *99*
    and international trade 80–1, *80*, 83
food prices 104

food production 104–7, *104–7*, **106–7**
foreign direct investment (FDI) 81, *81*, 84–5, **84–5**, *129*, *131*, *133*
forests 112, 117, 119
    loss 112–13, **114–15**, *115*
    tropical 113, *113*
fossil fuels 118, 119, *119*, *121*
fragile lands 105
freshwater supplies 108–9, *108*, *111*

gas 119, *119*, *121*
GDP *see* gross domestic product
gender 42–7
    and education 11, *41*, 43, 44–5, **44–5**, 55
    and employment 46–7, **46–7**
    equity 11, *11*, 44–5, **44–5**, 55
    see also women
Gini coefficient 19, *19*
global economic structure 62–5, *62–5*, **64–5**
global integration 80–5, *80–5*, **82–5**
global partnership for development 13, *13*
global warming 119
goods 80–1
governance 66–9, *66–9*, **68–9**, 75
government policy, and investment 74
greenhouse gas emissions *103*, 112, 118–19, *118*, *122–3*, **122–3**, *129*, *131*, *133*
gross capital formation 74–7, *74–7*, **76–7**
gross domestic product (GDP) 18, 19, *20*, **20–1**, 62–3
gross national income (GNI) 14, *128*, *130*, *132*
    per capita 8, 14–15, *15–17*, **16–17**, *128*, *130*, *132*, *134*
Group of Eight (G8) summit 2005 92

hazards, workplace 34, *35*
health, and urbanization 101
health care
    budgets 59
    child 48–9
    HIV 58, *58*
    maternal 42, *42*, 54, *54*, 55, 57
health facilities 42, *42*
Heavily Indebted Poor Countries (HIPC) 97
high-income (developed) economies 8, **8–9**, 14
HIV
    antiretroviral therapy 58, *58*
    and children 58, 61
    and the Millennium Development Goals 12, *12*
    mother-to-child transmission 48, 58
    prevalence 58, *58*, 60–1, **60–1**
    and women 12, *12*, 48, 58, 61
    see also AIDS
hunger, eradication 10
hydropower *121*

IBRD *see* International Bank for Reconstruction and Development
IFC *see* International Financial Corporation
illiteracy 45
IMF *see* International Monetary Fund
immigration 28, 86, 87
immunizations 11, *11*
imports 82–3, **82–3**
income
    and eating habits 104
    gap 18
    inequality 19, *19*, 22–3, **22–3**
    measures 14–17, *14–15*, **16–17**
    of the poor 24–5, 25

and remittances 87
see also high-income economies;
  low-income economies; middle-income
  economies
indicators of development, key *128–33*
industry 62, *65*
inequality
  gender 11, *11*, 44–5, **44–5**, 55
  income 19, *19*, 22–3, **22–3**
  of opportunity 19
inequality ratio *22*
information and communication technology
  70, 71, *71–3*, **72–3**
  see also Internet
infrastructure 42, 70–3, *70–3*, **72–3**
institutions 66–7
integration, global 80–5, *80–5*, **82–5**
Inter-American Development Bank 97
Intergovernmental Panel on Climate Change
  (IPCC) 119
International Bank for Reconstruction and
  Development (IBRD) 97
International Comparison Program 25
International Financial Corporation (IFC) 97
International Monetary Fund (IMF) 97
international poverty line 24–7, 25, **26–7**
international trade 80–1, *80–1*
Internet 71, *71–3*, **72–3**, *129*, *131*, *133*
investment 80
  foreign direct 81, *81*, 84–5, **84–5**, *129*,
    131, *133*
  for growth 74–9, *74–7*, **76–7**
  in infrastructure 70–1, *70*
  physical (gross capital formation) 74–7,
    74–7, **76–7**
IPCC *see* Intergovernmental Panel on
  Climate Change
irrigation 104, 105, *108*, 109
isolation 70

labor
  domestic 25, 42–3, *43*
  see also child labor; employment
land
  degradation 104–5
  fragile 105
  protected *112*, 113, *115–16*, **115–16**
life expectancy at birth 28, 32–3, **32–3**
  by country *128*, *130*, *132*
  and GNI per capita 15, *15*
living standards 14, 15
low-income economies 8–9, **8–9**, 14

malaria 12, 48, 51, 58–9, *61*
malnutrition 49, 52–3, **52–3**, 105, *107*
manufacturing 81
market exchange rates 14, 15
maternal health 12, *12*, 42, *42*, 54–7
maternal health care 42, *42*, 54, *54*, 55, *57*
maternal mortality rates 12, 42, 54–5, *54*, 57
MDRI *see* Multilateral Debt Relief Initiative
measles 11, *11*, 49
merchandise trade 82–3, **82–3**, *129*, *131*, *133*
middle-income economies 8–9, **8–9**, 14
MIGA *see* Multilateral Investment Guarantee
  Agency
migration 28, 86–91, *86–9*, **88–9**
Millennium Development Goals 10–13, *10–13*,
  67, 108
  child mortality reduction 11, *11*
  combating disease 12, *12*
  environmental sustainability 13, *13*
  eradication of extreme poverty and
    hunger 10, *10*, 25
  gender equality and female empowerment
    11, *11*
  global partnership for development 13, *13*

improving maternal health 12, *12*
  universal primary education 10, *10*
mobile phones 71, *71*
mortality
  child 11, *11*, 19, 48–51, *48–51*, **50–1**, *128*,
    130, *132*
  and disease 12
  maternal 12, 42, 54–5, *54*, 57
Multilateral Debt Relief Initiative (MDRI) 97
Multilateral Investment Guarantee Agency
  (MIGA) 97

nationally protected areas *112*, 113, *115–16*,
  115–16
natural resources 124–5, *126–7*
  rents *124*, *125*, *127*
nutrition 54
  child 49, *52–3*, **52–3**
  food prices *104*
  food production 104–7, *104–7*, **106–7**
  malnutrition 49, 52–3, **52–3**, 105, *107*
  undernourishment 24, 104, 105, *106–7*,
    106–7
  underweight **25**, *52–3*, **52–3**

official development assistance (ODA) 92,
  92, *94*
online atlas 6–7
opportunity 19
Organisation for Economic Co-operation
  and Development (OECD), Development
  Assistance Committee (DAC) 92, *93*, *95*
overgrazing 105
overqualification rate 87, *87*

pandemics 12
particulate matter concentration *100*, 101
pesticides 104
pneumonia 51
political participation *45*, *69*
pollution
  air 100, 101
  and urbanization 100, *100*, 101, *103*
  water *100*, 101, 109
  see also greenhouse gas emissions
population
  aging 28–9, *29*, 59, 86
  figures by country *128*, *130*, *132*
population growth
  and energy use 118
  and food production 104
  and transition 28–33, *28–31*, **30–1**
  and water supplies 109, *111*
poverty 24–7, *24–7*, **26–7**
  and child mortality 48, *49*
  and communicable disease 58
  and economic growth 19
  eradication 10, *10*
  extreme 10, *10*, 19, 24–5, 27
  and global recession 19
  and infrastructure 70
  and maternal health care 54, *55*
  and pollution 101
poverty line, international 24–7, 25, **26–7**
pregnancy 12, *12*, 54–5, *55*, 57
  antenatal care 12, *12*, 42, 54, *55*, 57
  complications 54, *57*
  teenage 55, *55*
prenatal care 12, *12*
protected areas *112*, 113, *115–16*, **115–16**
purchasing power parities (PPPs) 14, *14*, 15, 25

rainforests 113, *113*
ratios, external debt 96–7
recession 71
  global 2009 18–19, *18*, 71
reforestation 113, **114–15**, *115*

refugees *89*
regional groupings 8–9
remittances 86–7, *86–7*, 90–1, **90–1**, 93
renewable energy *121*
reproductive health 12, *12*, 42, *42*, 54–7
roads 42, 70
rural areas
  and child mortality 49
  and infrastructure 70
  and maternal health care 42, *42*
  and underweight children 53
  and water supplies 109

sanitation 13, 70–1, *70*, 101, *101*
savings 74
  see also adjusted net saving
service sector 62–3, *62*, *65*, 80–1, *83*
slum dwellings 29, 100–1, *101*
Stolen Asset Recovery (StAR) Initiative 66
sustainability 13, *13*, 105

tariffs 81, *81*, 83
teenage mothers 55, *55*
textiles 81
timber industry 113
trade
  barriers to 81, *81*, 83
  international 80–1, *80–1*
  merchandise 82–3, **82–3**, *129*, *131*, *133*
transport infrastructure 42, 70
tuberculosis 12, 58, *59*, 61
tying arrangements *95*

undernourishment 24, 104, 105, *106–7*, **106–7**
underweight **25**, *52–3*, **52–3**
United Nations International Conference on
  Financing for Development 2002 92
urban environment 42, *42*, 100–3, *100–3*,
  102–3
urbanization 29, *31*, 100–3, *100–3*, **102–3**, 108

violence, organized 67

water pollution *100*, 101, 109
water supplies 108–11, *108–11*, **110–11**
  by country *128*, *130*, *132*
  infrastructure 42–3, 70–1, *70*
  Millennium Development Goals
    regarding 13, *13*
  women and 42, 43, *43*
wealth 124–7, *124–7*, **124–7**
women 42–7, *42–7*
  and education 11, *41*, 43, 44–5, **44–5**, 55
  in employment 46–7, **46–7**
  empowerment 11, *11*, 42
  and HIV/AIDS 12, *12*, 48, 58, *61*
  maternal health 12, *12*, 42, *42*, 54–7
  water collection duties 42, 43, *43*
  see also pregnancy
workplace hazards 34, *35*
World Bank 99
  classification of economies 8–9, **8–9**
  Country Policy and Institutional
    Assessment 67
  and debt relief 97
  International Development Association
    67, 97
  and poverty 19
  web site 9
World Bank Group 96, 97
World Health Organization (WHO) 12, 13